Gender and Morality in Anglo-American Culture, 1650-1800

Ruth H. Bloch

UNIVERSITY OF CALIFORNIA PRESS
Berkeley · *Los Angeles* · *London*

University of California Press
Berkeley and Los Angeles, California

University of California Press, Ltd.
London, England

© 2003 by the Regents of the University of California

Library of Congress Cataloging-in-Publication Data

Bloch, Ruth H., 1949–
   Gender and morality in Anglo-American culture,
1650–1800 / Ruth H. Bloch.
      p.   cm.
   Includes bibliographical references and index.
   ISBN 0–520–23405–7 (cloth : alk. paper) —
ISBN 0–520–23406–5 (pbk. : alk. paper)
   1. Women — United States—History.   2. Women
colonists — United States — History.   3. United
States — History — Colonial period, ca. 1600–1775.
4. Sex role — United States—History.   5. Ethics —
United States — History.   I. Title.

HQ1416 .B53 2003
305.4'0973 — dc21   2002003987

Manufactured in the United States of America

12   11   10   09   08   07   06   05   04   03
10   9   8   7   6   5   4   3   2   1

The paper used in this publication is both acid-free and
totally chlorine-free (TCF). It meets the minimum
requirements of ANSI/NISO Z39.48–1992 (R 1997)
(*Permanence of Paper*) ⊗

For Ben and Aaron

Contents

Acknowledgments

This book represents much of my creative career as a women's historian, and my debts are large and multiple. Specific acknowledgments for the pre-published papers appear at the opening of each of their respective endnotes, but I have many more thanks to give. At different points in its development, my research has benefited from grants from the American Council for Learned Societies, the National Endowment of the Humanities, the Center for the Study of Women at the University of California at Los Angeles, and the University of California Academic Senate. My editor, Monica McCormick, generously welcomed the opportunity to edit this collection and skillfully ushered the manuscript through the publication process. Over the years leading up to this book, numerous colleagues at UCLA and around the nation have given my work steadfast support and cogent criticism, especially Joyce Appleby, Robert Abzug, Edward Berenson, Charles Capper, Ellen DuBois, Daniel Howe, Naomi Lamoreaux, Temma Kaplan, Carol Karlsen, Nikki Keddie, Jan Lewis, Kathryn Norberg, Debora Silverman, Joan Waugh, and Mary Yeager. Graduate research assistants Holly Brewer, Rachelle Friedman, Ellie Hickerson, Anne Lombard, and Jonathan Sassi were always helpful. Professional panels of historians, referee reports, and discussion groups too numerous to enumerate have continuously helped me to think through my ideas. Personal friends have also been essential to the life context of my scholarship, including Jeff Alexander, Wendy and Jeff Bricmont, Joan Chodorow, Nancy Chodorow, Franny Cohen, Judy

Fiskin, Jackie Greenberg, Rich McCoy, Felice Perlman, and Marsha Wagner. Special thanks to Maria Lymberis. I am most deeply grateful to Daniel Freudenberger. My sons, Ben and Aaron Alexander-Bloch, to whom this volume is lovingly dedicated, have at once provided endless distraction and a practical education on gender and morality both.

Introduction

At the beginning of the twenty-first century we are nearing the collapse of a system of gender relations that has dominated American culture for two hundred years. When politicians, journalists, and social commentators bemoan the contemporary "crisis of the family," they point to divorce, single motherhood, institutional childcare, latchkey children, youth violence, and other departures from supposedly traditional family life. To them the past represents a contrasting ideal, one of enduring marriages, parental authority, youthful obedience, paternal financial responsibility, and maternal childcare. Whether or not such practices actually prevailed in families of the past, the nostalgia for them reflects longstanding and widespread assumptions about what families ought to be — assumptions that are still often taken for granted across the political spectrum. That romantic love should lead to lasting marriage is still widely believed, as are the notions that nurturing is the essence of good mothering and that stable marriages produce successful children. The ideological intensity of this discourse inheres in the overwhelming symbolic significance of gender and family as sites of both individual identity formation and collective socialization. Public debate about child rearing and the position of women is never just about the family per se; it is also about larger issues of human happiness and social morality.

Many stereotypes today associated with "traditional" American values can be traced back to the colonial and revolutionary periods of our national history. It was then that women's roles as wives and mothers became redefined within a newfound idealization of domesticity. The very capacity to be selfless became viewed as an essentially feminine trait, altering long-held assumptions about the foundations of human virtue. A shift in the understanding of sexual nature produced the widespread perception of women as less sexual than men, and of sexual relationships as an arena of moral growth.

Aspects of this transformation have been subject to historical analysis for decades. The genesis and character of what is typically called Victorianism has been the focus of much of this scholarly inquiry. Particular attention has been given to the topics of sexual repression and the ideal of "true womanhood." Documenting the dissemination of such ideas about women and sex among the middle and upper classes in Europe and America is by now fairly complete. Literary evidence alone from the nineteenth century abundantly makes this case, and while there will always be room for refinement, historians generally accept that dominant nineteenth-century ideas about gender relations were different than eighteenth-century ones. The scholarly disagreements that persist mostly involve questions about social effects. Some historians contend that the ideas did not correspond to personal behavior, even among those upper- and middle-class groups most concerned with perpetuating elite notions of respectability; others argue that they did not penetrate deeply into working-class and minority racial and ethnic groups. That a change in ideas about gender occurred and was historically important to widely propagated cultural values, however, few would deny.[1]

In the face of this consensus, it is quite remarkable how little attention has been paid to the process of transformation itself and to possible explanations for it. This volume of essays explores the eighteenth-century genesis of what has by now become the traditional ideal of gender and family relations. By historicizing this ideal within the context of older and alternative "traditions," I question the claim that it represents a monolithic past. I also aim to illuminate its causal origins in colonial and revolutionary America by tracing its development through the religious, literary, political, and intellectual history of the period. Above all, I seek to locate thoughts and images associated with the personal domain of gender and family within several broader constellations of early modern Anglo-American ideas about the moral good.

THE ARGUMENT AND ORGANIZATION

By situating notions of domesticity and gender difference inside this broader cultural context, I point especially to the ideational (as opposed to the material) sources of change. All eight of the essays in this book concern the relationship between notions of masculinity and femininity and wider cultural systems of value, and all of them emphasize the role of symbols and ideas in shaping definitions of gender. They are organized into three parts according to context and theme, proceeding from the most general (Part 1) to the more historically specific (Parts 2 and 3) and, chronologically, from an emphasis on the colonial period (Part 2) to a concentration on the American Revolution (Part 3). Readers especially sensitive to developments in the writing of women's history will notice slight shifts in my perspective over the last twenty years, and the short prefaces appearing at the beginnings of the essays in the body of this volume are meant to provide this historiographical orientation. However, none of the developments in my own approach are important or remarkable enough, in my view, to justify arranging the essays according to their dates of publication. Rather, what binds the pieces together is a generally consistent line of theoretical and historical interpretation.

Part 1: Overviews

The book opens with two synthetic essays, one theoretical and one comparative, that lay out the interpretive logic behind the more focused investigations of American history that follow.

Chapter 1, "A Culturalist Critique of Trends in Feminist Theory," sets the theoretical stage for the historical essays that comprise the bulk of this volume. The essay begins by defining what I mean by culture as "myths, symbols, rituals, and other structures of collective meaning." The purpose of this essay is partly polemical, arguing against Marxism, essentialism, and some varieties of postmodernism. In advocating what I call a "culturalist" approach, in which gender intersects with other systems of meaning, such as theology, aesthetics, and political ideology, I suggest an alternative to the materialist explanations of gender that have come to pervade so much of modern feminist thought. Those who reduce gender to a metaphor of power or wealth miss the manifold ways that gender also symbolizes human interconnection and emotional bonds. In the course of this argument, I attempt to distinguish between types of human motivations by drawing an imaginary line between what people do in order to achieve coercive power and material gain and what they do in order to achieve an intangible sense of meaning. The more historical essays on gender relations that follow upon this theoretical one all draw upon this analytical distinction between interests and meaning.

Taken together, they point to the possibilities of such a "culturalist" approach to women's history.

Chapter 2, "Untangling the Roots of Modern Sex Roles," stems from a much earlier encounter with similar theoretical issues. The conceptual framework of the argument — the distinction between "symbols" and "roles" — addresses the same concerns about the relationship between material and ideational factors that run through other essays in this volume. An interpretive synthesis of much of the scholarship that was available in the mid 1970s on England and America between the sixteenth and the nineteenth-centuries, the essay takes a transatlantic perspective in identifying successive periods of change in the status of women. Repudiating one-directional models of either improvement or decline, the interpretation distinguishes between definitions of gender that emphasize male-female similarities and those that underscore differences. In its unusually broad overview of several nations over a long period of time, the essay serves as a general historical introduction to the more distinctly American and eighteenth-century pieces that follow in Parts 2 and 3.

Part 2: Colonial Transitions

The essays in this middle section of the book are united by their common concern with the eighteenth century as a pivotal moment in the Anglo-American construction of gender. Each depicts a fundamental shift in the way colonial Americans understood the relationship of women to the larger social and moral order, and each describes the process as a gradual one. The section is entitled "Colonial" in order to underscore changes that began quite independently of, and prior to, the American Revolution.

Chapter 3, "American Feminine Ideals in Transition: The Rise of the Moral Mother, 1785–1815," illustrates fundamental changes in the religious, literary, and medical images of mothers between the seventeenth and late-eighteenth centuries. Much like Chapter 2, "Untangling the Roots of Modern Sex Roles," it offers an interpretation that balances the influence of religious and Enlightenment ideas against the effects of early commercial capitalism and industrialism. It sets these general historical developments of the eighteenth century against the backdrop of earlier familial roles and feminine ideals, especially those of seventeenth-century New England Puritanism. Over the course of the eighteenth century, it argues, the feminine ideals of practical helpmeet and aristocratic refinement both gave way to the idealization of moral motherhood.[2] While giving attention to the immediate post-Revolutionary period, the essay minimizes the role of the Revolution and instead stresses the impact of more gradual developments, like Enlightenment rationalism, evangelical Protestantism, and realignments in the familial division of labor.

Chapter 4, "Women and the Law of Courtship in Eighteenth-Century America," similarly stresses underlying changes in assumptions about gender by describing how the legal regulation of marriage shifted from seventeenth-century legislative action to an increased reliance upon civil suits in the eighteenth century. The long-term shift to the civil litigation of disputes over courtship, it argues, enabled early American courts rapidly to apply to decisions about cases increasingly sympathetic popular attitudes toward innocent women wronged by deceitful men. This shift in jurisdiction gave female plaintiffs in seduction and breach-of-promise cases considerable leverage by the end of the eighteenth century. More institutional than the other essays included in this collection, its legal focus highlights two mutually reinforcing developments — the rise of the common law and the rise of sentimental conceptions of women — suggesting ways that changing notions of private life in eighteenth-century culture affected the public power of government.

Chapter 5, "Women, Love, and Virtue in the Thought of Edwards and Franklin," turns to the intellectual underpinnings of the emerging sentimental ideas about women. The essay compares the ideas of two men generally recognized as the dominant intellectual figures of colonial British America: the religious revivalist Jonathan Edwards and the scientific moralizer Benjamin Franklin. Interpreting their individual relationships to women as embodiments of the emerging tensions between evangelical and utilitarian conceptions of gender, this analysis connects their personal experiences and perceptions of love and marriage to larger systems of eighteenth-century moral thought. Edwards and Franklin both lived in the midst of the transition from Puritanism to the Enlightenment, and it is well known that each in a different way addressed fundamental questions about human autonomy, the foundations of virtue, and the limits of rationality. This essay suggests ways to connect their theological and philosophical ideas with shifting popular conceptions of women in the mid eighteenth century.

Part 3: Revolutionary Syntheses

The three essays grouped together in this concluding part of the book all examine how pre-Revolutionary ideas of women and gender played off against the evolving classical republican and liberal political ideologies of the American Revolution. If the Revolution did not initiate the revised constructions of gender that emerged in the eighteenth century, it at least accelerated their development and imbued them with lasting ideological significance.

Chapter 6, "Religion, Literary Sentimentalism, and Popular Revolutionary Ideology," opens this part with a general argument about the relationship between Anglo-American popular culture and revolutionary consciousness. Concentrating upon American evangelical religion and the early novel of the middle of the eighteenth century, it demonstrates important thematic continuities between these cultural forms and the political radicalism that emerged in the 1760s and 1770s. The essay challenges the tendency of historians to divide revolutionary ideology into dichotomous "liberal" and "republican" parts by showing that overlapping anti-authoritarian and familial images imbedded both liberal and classical republican political traditions in a wider context. Instead of standing as polar opposites, the individualism associated with liberalism and the collectivism associated with republicanism came together, it argues, in fictional narratives of romance and religious exhortations to righteousness. Only by expanding our understanding of Revolutionary discourse beyond directly political writings can we appreciate this convergence of values. Underlying issues of gender and their relationship to both sexual and social morality surface most clearly in the familial themes that pervaded both the political and the popular culture of the period. Stories about courtship and seduction carried what became revolutionary themes of anti-authoritarianism, purity, and self-sacrifice. By simultaneously evoking both personal freedom and domestic harmony, the gender dynamics portrayed in this popular literature helped to reconcile otherwise competing commitments to individual autonomy and the larger social good.

Chapter 7, "The Gendered Meanings of Virtue in Revolutionary America," takes on a more specific and fundamental question about American revolutionary ideology: how political understandings of "virtue" became in the late eighteenth century increasingly private and feminized. Virtue, at once a religious and civic concept, was repeatedly invoked by patriots seeking to inspire allegiance to the colonists' cause. In its first phase of development, the Revolution gave rise to an intensely masculine ethos of resistance and war, drawing from the stoic republican value of heroic self-sacrifice as essential to the public good. Later on, as the new nation turned to the task of settling internal institutional problems, a more liberal politics, founded upon the principle of self-interest, began to hold sway. The value of self-sacrificial virtue then became increasingly apolitical and was associated instead with religion and family. Always linked to notions of gender, virtue took on a distinctively feminine cast as an essentially emotional and intuitive quality, a perspective bolstered by recent trends in transatlantic psychological theory and religious belief. Appeals to virtue thus resonated with multiple meanings during the revolutionary period, drawing variously from sentimental literature, evangelical Protestantism, moral philosophy, and both classical republican and liberal political thought. In a relatively short period of time, the Revolution compressed many features of a transformation in gender definitions that had begun long before. The growing glorification of female domestic morality that stemmed from earlier eighteenth-century roots gained greater shape and stimulation from the ideological shifts of the American Revolution.

Chapter 8, "Gender and the Public/Private Dichotomy in Revolutionary Thought," similarly presents the post-Revolutionary idealization of female domesticity as the product of trends that predate the Revolution but which were filtered through its political ideologies. Whereas the first chapter in this part of the book, "Religion, Literary Sentimentalism, and Popular Revolutionary Ideology," suggests that tensions within revolutionary ideology were partially resolved within popular culture, this chapter distinguishes among several intellectual orientations within revolutionary ideology itself. Its unifying theme is essentially political: the distinction between public and private. Like previous chapters, it traces different late-eighteenth-century Anglo-American assumptions about gender to a combination of cultural sources: classical political theory, dissenting Protestantism, Enlightenment liberalism, and Scottish moral philosophy. Taking a new look at post-Revolutionary formulations of male-female "separate spheres," it argues that the underlying definitions of public and private changed during the Revolutionary period. Following the work of a new generation of economic historians, this chapter also considers the impact of the so-called "consumer revolution" that preceded the industrial one. It reveals striking parallels between liberal theories of economic exchange and notions of romantic heterosexual love and argues that together they structured the ways that late-eighteenth-century Americans conceived of the relationship between the family and the wider society. In a fitting conclusion to this volume, this chapter questions the extent to which this period was characterized by an ideology of separate spheres that delineated sharp contrasts between masculine and feminine traits. Rather, it points to the emergence of two conflicting conceptions of gender relations in late-eighteenth-century American culture, one based upon the assumption of difference, the other on a less dichotomous ideal of mutual identification.

UNIFYING THEMES

Each of these chapters approaches this history in a different way and may be read separately, but my interpretation gains full force only when they are read together. The entire volume revolves around this basic question: why did the constellation of attitudes toward gender relations that we normally associate with the nineteenth-century white middle class emerge when it did? My answer, essentially a cultural one, stresses long-term developments in religious, intellectual, and literary history that gave rise to a sentimental yet respectful view of female moral authority by the end of the eighteenth century. While, individually, each of my essays focuses on a distinctive aspect of this process, they repeatedly point to theological and psychological premises about the relative moral value of reason on the one hand and of emotion on the other. I explore from various angles the interrelationship of the ascendancy of the sentimental novel, religious revivalism, and tensions within Enlightenment thought.

The convergence of these various religious, fictional, and philosophical currents in eighteenth-century Anglo-American culture led not only to their mutual reinforcement, but to equally significant clashes between them. Such conflicts among intellectual positions receive particular attention in Chapters 5 and 8 ("Women, Love, and Virtue in the Thought of Edwards and Franklin" and "Gender and the Public/Private Distinction in Revolutionary Thought"), where I delineate basic tensions between spiritual and utilitarian approaches to human psychology and between individualistic and collectivist orientations to society. Stressing the creative interplay of conflict and convergence within Anglo-American thought, I underscore the complexity of the transformation in eighteenth-century gender definitions at the same time as I seek to identify the particular cultural influences behind that transformation.

By locating changes so broadly in the eighteenth century, my work inevitably addresses the perennial problem of American distinctiveness. In particular, my approach calls into question the implied "American exceptionalism" of interpretations that concentrate on the American Revolution. In my view, changes in American understandings of gender relations were one variation on a much larger, transatlantic theme. The essays contained in this volume repeatedly invoke the context of evolving

British and European thought and the increased transmission of British and European ideas. The broad historical overview presented in Chapter 2 ("Untangling the Roots of Modern Sex Roles") makes this point especially strongly by attributing changes to broad religious and economic developments, like the Protestant and Catholic Reformations and early capitalism, rather than by highlighting the particularities of national histories. Its synthesis of four centuries goes so far as to depict America, England, and France as proceeding along the same winding path. While the essays contained in Parts 2 and 3 introduce more distinctively American variables, I have in large part retained this transnational perspective on early Anglo-American culture. People on both sides of the Atlantic, I often suggest, were affected by similar, international intellectual and economic developments. Neither the emotionalism that was characteristic of romanticism and pietism nor the increased affluence and competitiveness of the enlarging commercial market stayed within national boundaries. In my work I have attended especially to Scottish moral philosophy and English sentimental fiction as they reverberated in America.

My emphasis upon transatlantic developments certainly makes the United States appear less distinctive. But I still think there *was* something exceptional about the American case. The differences between Britain and America surfaced well before the Revolution, and I believe they largely reflected religious differences, as well as the relative autonomy from regulatory institutions of male heads of households.[3] The unusual strength of the dissenting Protestant tradition in colonial America from the seventeenth century on, reinforced by revivalism in the colonies in the mid eighteenth century, made Americans particularly receptive to sentimentalist understandings of women. Gender-neutral Protestant understandings of the priesthood of all believers, combined with an evangelical emphasis upon inner faith and feeling, together laid the groundwork for what became a feminized moral psychology.

The seeds of many of the new ideas about gender and morality came from abroad, but America proved especially fertile soil for their germination, growth, and even mutation in line with local conditions. As I suggest in Chapter 4 ("Women and the Law of Courtship"), the initial efforts of the American colonies to legislate domestic morality, combined with the early growth of civil litigation, prepared the way for changes in attitudes toward women during the eighteenth century to be assimilated into legal judgments by the time of the American Revolution. The early American regulation of courtship and marriage foreshadowed, rather than followed, English law. Intellectual as well as legal differences between the two sides of the Atlantic also manifested themselves early on. While late-eighteenth-century attitudes toward women themselves derived in part from English and Scottish sentimentalist writings imported into the colonies, as I emphasize in Chapter 7 ("The Gendered Meanings of Virtue"), their meanings were altered in the course of transmission. What most distinguished the American evolution of these ideas, I argue throughout this volume, was their broad social reach, the near merger of evangelical and Enlightenment points of view, and the way they modulated with revolutionary ideology from the 1770s through the 1790s.

These elements of American cultural distinctiveness in the eighteenth century have had, in my view, continuing influence. Many widespread and characteristically American assumptions about gender relations stem from the colonial and revolutionary period. America's infatuation with romantic courtship, joined to the conviction that it should lead to life-long monogamy, can be traced back to this earlier era, as can the related high expectations of marital happiness and the attending deep disappointments, which have contributed over time to widespread divorce.[4] Americans still have a distinctive view of the family and sexual relations as a quintessentially "private" domain, a perspective shaped by the liberal ideology of the Revolution. Somewhat in contradiction to this insistence upon private rights, Americans also persist in drawing connections between sexual and public morality, especially when assessing political leadership. These traits of modern America, so often contrasted with other countries, have a long history. The essays presented in this collection are meant to shed light on their origins.

I title this volume *Gender and Morality* because I view conceptions of masculinity and femininity through the prism of changing cultural understandings of good and evil, or right and wrong. Such fundamental value judgments encompass emotion as well as intellect, particularly feelings toward others that are expressed in values, symbols, and narratives that have shared, as well as individual, resonance. Even such intimate symbols as "mother" and "lover" possess cultural significance that can change over time, a theme of several chapters, including "Feminine Ideals in Transition," "Religion, Literary Sentimentalism, and Popular Revolutionary Ideology," and "The Public/Private Dichotomy." One reason I have taken such interest in ideas about familial relationships is precisely their combined moral and emotional quality. Like my analytical focus on cultural and intellectual history, this approach distinguishes these essays from the vast majority of works in early American women's history. While others have generally concentrated either on women's status before the law or on women's labor and the household economy, my central concern has been to relate representations of gender to broader systems of Anglo-American moral thought, specifically Puritanism, evangelicalism, utilitarianism, and classical republicanism. These intellectual traditions all addressed fundamental ethical questions about the responsibilities of the individual to the collectivity, the psychological origins of motivations to be good, and the dominant norms guiding social behavior.

This collection of essays is particularly concerned to undercover the gender dimension of such thinking — the ways in which changing notions of morality in America between 1650 and 1800 played off changing ideas of women and, to a lesser extent, men. Changes in the rules of colonial American courtship and in the premises of British moral philosophy reveal how morality — both in the narrow sense of sexual norms and in the largest sense of obligations to others — was significantly defined along gender lines. The growing confidence in the social utility of rational self-interest and the increasingly sentimental view of benevolence altered American understandings of femininity and masculinity both.

ALTERNATIVE INTERPRETATIONS

In seeking to make sense of shifting constructions of gender in eighteenth-century America by relating them to understandings of morality, this book falls squarely within the domain of intellectual history. The interconnections I stress are mostly among sets of ideas, even though by "ideas" I mean a wide range of historically documented thoughts — including expressions of emotion and symbolic references, as well as the abstract and elaborated theories commonly associated with intellectuals. I take this ideational focus not because I believe that material circumstances play no part in the construction of gender, but because many historians and feminists have been too quick to settle for a direct causal link. By concentrating instead on the realm of ideas, these essays aim to correct the tendency to see gender as determined by concrete structures of power and wealth.

A generation ago, historians and historical sociologists pointed to the advent of the industrial revolution to explain prevailing nineteenth-century views of women as highly idealized wives and mothers and paragons of religious morality. According to this widespread interpretation, factory labor pulled men outside the home and left middle-class women to the exclusive care of house and children. A physical division of roles was thus seen to underlie the widening gap between ideals of masculinity and femininity. As men were forced by economic necessity into the increasingly competitive and rationalist world of work outside the home, women performed the obverse functionalist imperative of maintaining altruistic values and emotional nurturance inside the home.[5]

Most of this older scholarship refers to economic developments of the early nineteenth century, when men increasingly labored at more specialized sites of employment than they had on family farms or craft shops, which were traditionally situated adjacent to domestic dwellings. Since the late 1970s, however, scholarship has made it increasingly clear that the elevation of female domesticity occurred earlier. Within the field of early American history, Linda Kerber and Mary Beth Norton published particularly influential books in 1980 indicating that the American Revolution was an important catalyst for these new attitudes by and about women.[6] In England, where factory production began earlier and where historians have lately seen a "commercial revolution" occurring in the eighteenth century, residues of the standard economic interpretation have been easier to sustain. The growth of wealth through expanded manufacturing and trade, and the attendant pursuit of leisure by newly middle-class women no longer needed in the old-fashioned household economy, certainly helps to explain the rise of an idealized female domesticity, at least among the affluent.[7]

To an extent, the recent emphasis on "commerce" rather than "industry" works for the eighteenth-century American colonies as well, where commercial agriculture rose rapidly, and overseas merchants increasingly dominated the still small but growing urban elite.[8] The historian Elaine Crane vividly documents the impact of commercial growth upon the social position of women in early New England. In her view it is a story of declining economic power leading to declining status.[9] That the valorization of female domesticity, modesty, and self-sacrifice occurred at the same time only confirms such a negative assessment. According to this economically-driven account, the growth of an idealized view of women as the guardians of domestic morality calls for little historical explanation in itself. Rather it drew upon longstanding, implicitly pejorative stereotypes of women in order to justify their loss of social standing. In this context, the American Revolution offered nothing remarkably new.[10]

Those scholars of American women's history who have argued instead for the importance of the Revolution place more emphasis upon political than upon economic change. By participating in the early patriot movement and providing support during the war for independence, women gained a newfound political consciousness. Linda Kerber and Mary Beth Norton have most persuasively advanced this argument.[11] In different ways each demonstrates that the revolutionary experience of American women opened up possibilities for the future expansion of women's rights — although, in Kerber's formulation, the ideal of the "republican mother" curbed the more radical implications of Revolutionary ideology and kept the politicization of women within restrictive domestic bounds. Since the publication of these important books in 1980, several other American historians have further elaborated, often brilliantly, the relationship between revolutionary ideals of equality and virtue and the changing status of women.[12]

As the essays in Part 3 of this volume illustrate, I have also contributed to this development, but with a difference: my essays all situate the Revolution within a much longer transformation of gender definitions, beginning decades before. To date the beginnings of this transformation before both industrialization and the American Revolution is not to suggest that the process was over by 1776, but to maintain that it took a much longer time to emerge and that it cannot be tied closely to a particular economic system or political event. The Revolution accelerated a shift in the meanings of gender relations that was long in the making, a shift that had less to do with the exigencies of power and politics than with cultural understandings of the emotions and affective relationships.

As much as economic and political currents run through my own analysis, my primary focus in this book remains on the flow of expression. I take this view not because I doubt the influence of material conditions or state power, but because the connections between them and notions of gender and morality are always mediated by intervening systems of ideas, symbols, and values, albeit at times economic and political ones. For this reason, my contribution to the debate over women and the American Revolution highlights the many points of intersection between gender and revolutionary ideology. Rarely do wealth and power apply themselves directly to changing gender definitions, for conceptions of masculinity and femininity are too deeply embedded in cultural tradition to respond to external manipulation alone. Thus, the common claim that the status of women stems from economic relations or allocations of power states the obvious and illuminates too little. More telling in my view is the way people *think* about and *express* economic, political, and other social relationships in gender terms. These patterns of thought largely structure the reception of material change, and in dynamic periods like the eighteenth century ideas often interact in striking new ways.

Cultural explanations, no less than materialist ones, can fall into determinism, a problem that this book also seeks to address. Just as material forces can seem beyond human control, so culture too can appear as monolithic and self-perpetuating. The work presented here, however, is largely about cultural change. In Parts 2 and 3, several essays describe the dynamic repercussions of intellectual innovation. The eighteenth-century philosophical idea of virtue as being rooted in the affections, for example, plays a major part both in Chapter 5 ("Women, Love, and Virtue in the Thought of Edwards and Franklin") and in Chapter 7 ("The Gendered Meanings of Virtue"). In several essays I also underscore widespread cultural instability and the creative possibilities inherent in intellectual conflict. The widening division between evangelicalism and the Enlightenment in late colonial America appears in different manifestations in Chapters 3 and 5 ("Feminist Ideals in Transition" and "Women, Love and Virtue in the Thought of Edwards and Franklin"). In Part 3, on the American Revolution, the related competition between what historians have described as the "liberal" and "classical republican" components of American political ideology come under scrutiny in Chapters 6 and 8 ("Religion, Literary Sentimentalism and Popular Revolutionary Ideology" and "The Public/Private Dichotomy in American Revolutionary Thought").[13] Within eighteenth-century American culture, notions of gender were caught up in these cultural oppositions and, as a consequence, were themselves highly unstable and prone to transformation.

FEMINIST IMPLICATIONS

At the heart of today's thinking about gender are conflicting views of what is arguably the core value of the modern world: equality. Within the contemporary feminist movement there is little consensus about the details of ideally egalitarian relationships between women and men. Rather, a creative tension exists between an idea of male-female equality as sameness and an idea of male-female equality as equivalent worth.[14] As several of the chapters here seek to demonstrate, this conflict between ideals of male-female equality has also been played out historically at various junctures, similarly without resolution. Chapter 2 ("Untangling the Roots of Modern Sex Roles") delineates a dialectical pattern of development, in which sixteenth- and seventeenth-century assumptions about gender similarities were largely supplanted in the eighteenth and nineteenth centuries by more polarized conceptions of male-female difference. Neither perception, I argue, ever eradicated the other, even though the balance between them shifted. Until the late eighteenth century this dialectic between gender similarity and gender difference left the still highly hierarchical premise of male superiority largely undisturbed. Even as egalitarian ideas have gained ground, however, the dual conceptions of similarity and difference have remained embedded in our thinking about gender.

These underlying tensions in our views of equality reverberate through feminist attitudes about yet another central American value: individualism. Here, too, contemporary ambivalences have a long history, dating back at least to the eighteenth century. Virtually all the essays represented in this collection explore ways in which competing commitments to individual self-interest and communal welfare bear on definitions of masculinity and femininity. Chapter 1 ("A Culturalist Critique of Feminist Theory") makes a case for the value of interdependency in opposition to interest-driven feminist theories. Chapter 2 ("Untangling the Roots of Modern Sex Roles") takes a broader historical view of the problem, pointing out how earlier ideals of male-female reciprocity gave way to the idea of mutually dependent but separate male and female spheres. Chapters 5, 6, and 8 ("Women, Love, and Virtue in the Thought of Edwards and Franklin," "Religion, Literary Sentimentalism, and Popular Revolutionary Ideology," and "The Public/Private Dichotomy in American Revolutionary Thought") all show how disagreements about the individual's relationship to society interplayed with changing assumptions about femininity. In an era of increasing autonomy for American men, women (as lovers, wives, and mothers) increasingly symbolized contrary ideals of interconnectedness.

Just as notions of gender similarity and difference continue to intermix, this dichotomy between male individualism and female interconnectedness has continued to be fluid. A number of my essays, most notably Chapter 6 ("Religion, Literary Sentimentalism, and Popular Revolutionary Ideology") and Chapter 8 ("The Public/Private Dichotomy in American Revolutionary Thought"), show how the coexistence of conflicting communitarian and individualistic attitudes toward the sexes persisted through the late eighteenth century. Not surprisingly, feminists, along with other Americans, are still contending with this cultural conundrum today.

The standard argument for abortion, for example, features an appeal to the right of privacy, while other feminist causes claim women's distinctive identification with family and community. That these very different kinds of arguments can be made simultaneously, both of them with considerable effect, attests to the endurance of eighteenth-century ambivalences about gender.

Historians of American women frequently debate whether the changes I trace to the eighteenth century have proved good or bad for women. To a degree, their views hinge on broader assessments of the trajectory of women's history: where some see progress through the colonial period, others see decline.[15] Historians, like other people, also vary in their attitudes toward what this Introduction began with: the contemporary view of the "traditional" family. Some have taken a favorable view of what is somewhat nostalgically portrayed as the nineteenth-century middle-class norm, emphasizing such developments as love-based marriage, low rates of divorce, and improvements in the education and care of children. Value judgments about the eighteenth century also turn on perspectives on the gains made in women's rights in the nineteenth and twentieth centuries, and whether the women's movement seems continuous with eighteenth-century developments or a reaction against them.[16] As several historians, including myself, have argued, one of great ironies of nineteenth century is that the very limitation in the parameters of acceptable femininity propelled women into public life. The question of whether the position of women has improved or declined over time is thorny for another reason as well. The changes that occurred were never cut and dried. In the late eighteenth century, vital issues like female education were subject to intense debate. As I repeatedly contend in these essays, the period was characterized by conflicts within Anglo-American culture, and many of the basic tensions evident then are still with us today.

With hindsight one can see different possibilities arising from the eighteenth century. From Enlightenment theories about human rationality and universal rights, for example, it seems a logical step to the greater opportunities in the nineteenth century for women to attend school, to divorce, and to hold separate property. On the other hand, the late-eighteenth-century glorification of domesticity, the decline of the household economy, and the developing sex trade can all be seen as harbingers of the worst aspects of the modern oppression of women. Yet each of these claims can also be turned upside down. The glorification of domesticity, for example, can be viewed as indispensable to the long-range upgrading of the status of women, just as the opening of the sex trade can be regarded as a step toward greater freedom for some men and women both. Similarly, the Enlightenment emphasis on rationality and individual rights quite arguably had negative as well as positive implications for women, relegating their common domestic responsibilities to the margins of social and political life. For all of these reasons, I have always been struck by the inadequacies of unilinear models of women's history. Instead of documenting either progress or decline, the essays in this volume present a story of creative contradiction and paradoxical change.

What has been remarkably constant within this history of contradiction and change, however, is the refraction of definitions of gender through conceptions of morality. Just as notions of gender are fraught with moral implications today, so they were in the eighteenth century. Differences between men and women, both in degree and in kind, have always been largely understood within frameworks of good and evil, virtue and vice, right and wrong. Perhaps we should deplore this connection and wish that gender would become morally a more neutral category, similar to, say, eye color. But as long as sexuality, reproduction, and the rearing of children remain central to human interactive experience it is difficult to see gender losing its moral charge. It is, indeed, virtually impossible to separate assumptions about gender from basic social values, like equality, mutual responsibility, compassion, and individual freedom. There is opportunity as well as limitation in this bond between gender and morality. For notions of morality vary among groups and change over time. It is this dual set of concerns — the links between gender and morality and the historical interactions between them — that frame the major themes of this book.

PART ONE

Overviews

CHAPTER I

A Culturalist Critique
of Trends in Feminist Theory

PREFACE   "A Culturalist Critique of Feminist Theory," written in the early 1990s during the height of the debate over postmodernism, takes issue with essentialist, Marxist, and Foucauldian approaches to the construction of gender and argues instead for a "culturalist" interpretation. I maintain that changes in gender relations need to be understood in relation to the historical evolution of larger cultural constellations of symbols, values, and ideas (including religion, literature, moral philosophy, and politics). The core of the argument is that gender is far more than a metaphor for power or wealth, that it derives as importantly from intangible definitions of meaning. My understanding of the word "culture" derives partly from the arts but more importantly from anthropology, dating back to Franz Boaz and Emile Durkheim at the turn of the twentieth century and more recently represented by such figures as Ruth Benedict, Victor Turner, Mary Douglas, and Clifford Geertz. More contemporary words like "discourse," "language," "construction," and "representation" (like the old-fashioned "idea," "thought," and "belief") imply greater abstraction but usually refer to the same ideational level of social experience that designates "culture." I make such a pointed defense of cultural explanations largely because feminist scholars — like most intellectuals with a desire for fundamental social change — too often resort to a reflexive materialism. My contrary emphasis resists this flattening of interpretation and, with it, the latent determinism of both Marxist and postmodern notions of causality. When this essay first appeared in the journal *Contention*, it provoked pointed criticisms by Sandra Harding and Barbara Laslett, who objected to my dichotomous distinction between the cultural and the material. I agree that no such separation actually exists in real life, or in history, but in my view the scholarly interpretation of human experience depends on using such conceptual categories. If I were writing this essay today, however, I would counterbalance my emphasis upon gender as a positive symbol of interdependency with a stronger acknowledgment of the negative sides of attachment, including the possibilities of sadistic and exclusionary notions of gender. The argument for the autonomy of culture does not preclude patterns of meaning that reinforce, rather than mitigate, hierarchies of power and wealth, as many of the historical essays presented later in this volume show.

. . .

Perhaps the most fundamental claim of modern feminism is that anatomy is not destiny. With few exceptions, feminists blame society, not the body, for producing women's subordination. Yet in rejecting biological arguments, feminists have faced a formidable theoretical problem: what is it about society that explains the position of women?[1] This essay explores some of the most common answers that have been given to this question, arguing that one of the very strengths of feminist theory — its refusal to accord the anatomical difference of sex the ability to determine social life — has itself encouraged what may in fact be an equally fallacious intellectual tendency. The rejection of biology as the source of gender relations has fostered contrary, but similarly reductive explanations, based instead on wealth and power.

Most recent feminist theorists have faced a formidable theoretical problem of their own: how can women's distinctive social position be explained if not biologically? In the following pages, I will attempt to clarify what I mean by the term "culture," itself one of the most widely appropriated and misunderstood concepts in social science. Indeed, a striking feature of feminist theory, like most social thought, is precisely its extensive invocation of the term. The view that gender relations are "cultural" has been a standard cliché of the anti-biological argument. The very term "gender" — as distinguished from "sex" — has derived its widespread appeal from its supposedly cultural definition. As a cultural rather than purely physical fact, "gender" is meant to refer not merely to the male and the female but to the contingent and variable symbols that define masculinity and femininity within a particular social group. In my view, however, this cultural perspective has not gone far enough. Within some feminist theory it even threatens to subvert itself. For, while gender is often *defined* as cultural, it is not itself typically *understood* culturally. Feminist theorists too often reduce culture, and with it the cultural symbolism of gender, to the material relations of class or some other self-interested assertion of power by one group over another. The subjective meaning that men and women attribute to gender identity becomes in this view essentially the result of false consciousness or (in a non-Marxist variation) instrumental manipulation. Lost from such an understanding is the way that gender becomes socially meaningful and articulates with other common structures of meaning. Nor is this limited conceptualization of culture and gender merely a narrowly academic problem. It is an important theoretical flaw that diminishes our appreciation of how feminism might work to change the world.

Feminist practice has been, in this respect, far ahead of feminist theory. The new wave feminists of the late 1960s and 1970s started with the subversive cry "the personal is political" and sought to transform the subjective meanings of being female or male. At the beginning, feminist activism consisted largely of participation in consciousness-raising groups and emotionally wrought confrontations with men in political organizations, families, and intimate relationships. While ritual bra-burning was a sensationalist media fabrication, women affected by the movement often altered their public appearance — rejecting skirts, bras, and cosmetics and usually no longer shaving their armpits and legs. To be sure, most participants may have only superficially understood their actions as a struggle against confining stereotypes and the behaviors of specific men. What was to them simply being "open" and "natural," however, amounted to defining a cultural code of their own. The underlying significance of the practice of the women's liberation movement was to identify and transform that aspect of culture that we have since come to call "gender." New wave feminists of the 1960s and 1970s perceived themselves as enmeshed in a variable system of meanings, both internalized and imposed from outside, that defined sex roles, images of men and women, and sexuality.

The concept of culture, while not explicitly invoked by feminist activists in the 1960s, was simultaneously being refined by symbolic anthropologists. Clifford Geertz, Mary Douglas, Victor Turner, Claude Lévi-Strauss, and others drew on older traditions of social theory to describe many of the symbolic structures and ritual behaviors that define

collective life. A basic feature of this developing perspective was its insistence on the causal autonomy of culture. It consequently objected to
Marxist and other attempts to reduce an ideological "superstructure" to
an underlying "base" of material relations. Myths, symbols, rituals, and
other structures of collective meaning emerge, according to this view of
culture, from the creative interaction of older cultural traditions, contemporary conditions, and human practice. Culture, in other words,
both constrains and enables social actors, just as it is experienced simultaneously as internal and external to the individual.

   This basic definition and theory of culture, while familiar enough to
"culturally-oriented" social scientists, has been in my view too much
overlooked by feminists theorizing on the subject of gender. With some
qualifications and revisions, the understanding of culture developed
within symbolic anthropology in the 1960s still has potential for feminism. It can help, for example, to illuminate the way popular definitions
of femininity — such as the idea of women as nonviolent and responsive
to others — have been both experienced as oppressive and refashioned as
a basis of feminist solidarity. From this perspective, much of the work of
the women's movement can be seen as specifically cultural, involving at
once iconoclastic challenges to conventional definitions of femininity and
the creative construction of new ones. Even the open expression of non-
monogamous and lesbian sexuality and the common restructuring of
domestic obligations of women and men are not merely efforts to express
natural impulses or to equalize work. They are, as significantly, cultural
acts reformulating gender definitions of sexuality and labor. Despite significant differences among feminists, such practices have forged a new
common meaning — a new, feminist variation of American culture has
come into being. This cultural work of feminism continues, of course,
even today. Although stripped of much of the effervescence and utopi-
anism of the sixties and early seventies, it still takes place within women's
studies programs, in public demonstrations of pro-choice activists, in the
work of women artists and theologians, and in innumerable encounters
of everyday life. The myriad ways that individual women seek to live up
to shared ideals of independence, equality, and social responsibility are
themselves testimony to the continuing cultural impact of the women's
movement.

   Yet for reasons largely idiosyncratic to left-wing academic thought,
feminist theory has rarely reflected on this cultural dimension of feminist
practice.[2] Scholars, like other feminists, have been engaged in this process
of cultural transformation, but they have rarely deemed culture some-

thing to theorize about. In the 1970s a few feminist academics, most notably anthropologists and historians, applied a culturalist perspective to their own research on other times and places. [3] During the same period feminist literary critics concerned to expose patriarchal views of women or to underscore the "unifying voice in women's literature" also took an essentially culturalist approach in their explorations of intellectual context. [4] Generally, however, these studies stopped short of generating a broader theory of gender as culture. [5] The tendency of anthropological theories of culture to overlook conflict and change provides one explanation for this neglect. A second reason is the residual Marxism of much feminist social science, which favors material over cultural analysis. A third is the tendency of many feminist scholars in the humanities to focus on the specific cultural productions of writers and artists without investigating the concept of culture itself or drawing a clear connection between the meanings of texts and the processes of social change. Yet a fourth reason why feminist theorists have tended not to concentrate on gender as culture stems from the practical exigencies of the feminist movement itself. Its "cultural work" notwithstanding, the main legal and reform agenda of the movement has been, of course, to end discrimination against women. Feminist intellectuals have therefore been inclined to conceive of women not as cultural agents or symbols but as the victims of social institutions representing tangible power and wealth.

With the infusion of French poststructural theories into the American academic left, the concept of culture has seemingly taken on a new life. The center of gravity within the world of social theory has in the past decade shifted from political economy and sociology to literary criticism and philosophy. Among contemporary feminist intellectuals it is the poststructuralist literary critics and philosophers who have come the closest to insisting on the importance of gender as a cultural construction. In contrast to the relatively static and consensual theories of earlier cultural anthropologists, poststructuralists describe culture as unstable and contradictory, a perspective that is more amenable to radical interpretation, as shown by the influential example of Michel Foucault. But, for all the sophistication and insight of this now popular kind of cultural criticism, its advocates tend either to lack a theory of social change or else to resort to a materialist one. While they insist on the centrality of culture to human experience, they deny its causal autonomy in relation to other oppressive structures like class and race. Of course, radical poststructuralists would in general resist this distinction — claiming that race and class are themselves cultural constructions — but when it comes to

explaining historical variation and change (a task few attempt) they do
not practice what they preach. [6] Indeed, whereas Marxist critics of poststructuralism find fault with what they take to be its abstract idealism, I
would question its often implicit materialism and interest-driven view of
humanity. As I will elaborate below, the influence of poststructuralism
has merely reinforced a tendency among feminist theories to reduce gender to inequalities of wealth and power.

For all these intellectual and political reasons, feminists have for the
most part overlooked the benefits of a nonreductive theory of culture.
While feminism was launched with the self-empowering slogan "the personal is political," it has too often produced theories in which the personal itself is no more than a shallow reflection of impersonal structures
of power. The net effect of such theorizing is to divest "gender" of both
intrinsic meaning — subjectivity — and explanatory value. Definitions of
masculinity and femininity become epiphenomena, the extension of
structures of domination and oppression that typically come down to
class and, more recently, race. If we understand culture as the system of
meaning that expresses collective needs and ideals that go beyond the
utilitarian pursuit of power, then culture has only a precarious place
within feminist theory, especially outside the humanities. The result is
that such human motives as curiosity about the natural world, the appreciation of beauty, the desire for intimacy, or the quest for spiritual experience have been in effect eliminated from feminist analysis of society.
The basic fact that men tend to dominate women seems to justify a pre-
occupation with the dimension of domination alone. Even when connections are drawn between definitions of gender and other aspects of
culture, like science, religion, and art, the common denominator between
them typically is power. Drawing from Marxism and poststructuralism
alike, feminists tend to conceive of culture as the reflection of dominant
interests. Gender occupies a subservient position in an analytic hierarchy
that situates power, not meaning, on top.

By presenting a brief survey of the main developments in feminist theory in the last twenty-five years, I aim to give substance to these general
criticisms. During this period there has been a continuous interaction
between neo-Marxist materialism in various forms and a series of sexual,
psychoanalytic, and linguistic theories, none of which has gained clear
ascendancy. What fundamentally unites writers of varying persuasions is
their common enlistment in the feminist project of defining gender as a
nonbiological social fact. Even though many feminists concede that biology is a partial source of gender distinctions, others insist that our under-

standing of biology is itself constructed by gender difference. [7] Virtually all agree that the task of feminism is to look at society, not nature, for it is only as social actors that we can hope to transform gender relations.

How feminists analyze the social conditions of womanhood has varied greatly. Some conceptualize the distinctive position of women in terms of the social inequality of the sexes, others in terms of the attitudinal and psychological differences between them. Some stress the negative effects of oppression, others the positive attributes of female identity or "sisterhood." The non-Marxists have generally countered (or at least supplemented) an emphasis on capitalism and class relations with arguments for the importance of male sexual domination, the process of identity formation in early childhood, and the social imperatives of language. Neither Marxism nor its major theoretical alternatives has, however, advanced a social theory of gender that gives primacy to culture as more than an instrument of oppression (or, conversely, as resistance to oppression). While feminist theorists have gone to great lengths to explore the positive and negative valences of equality and difference, the central proposition that gender is both an aspect and a product of a wider cultural system has been largely ignored. A look at the evolution of feminist social theory since the late 1960s reveals the cost of this neglect.

EARLY FEMINIST SOCIAL THEORY:
CAPITALISM VS. PATRIARCHY

In the first decade of feminist debate, the main contending theories of society were socialist feminism and the theory of patriarchy, both of which focused on the problem of inequality. Although some early works of feminist protest, such as Betty Friedan's *The Feminine Mystique* and Kate Millett's *Sexual Politics,* exposed the cultural manifestations of female oppression, those theorists who sought instead to unravel the social causes of gender inequality typically failed to consider gender as culture. Rather, the argument between the contesting patriarchy and socialist schools turned on the extent to which female subordination was caused by men, as a sex, and the extent to which it stemmed from the more impersonal dynamics of the capitalist system. [8] The oldest debate within contemporary feminist theory, this discussion has gone through many subtle permutations and continues to resonate today. Catherine MacKinnon's recent treatment of pornography and rape develops the earlier perspective of patriarchal theory by advancing the view that violence and domination are inherent in male heterosexuality. In her memorable words, "Sexuality is to feminism what work is to marxism: that which is most one's own, yet most taken away. . . . [As] the organized expropriation of the work of some for the benefit of others defines a class, workers, the organized appropriation of the sexuality of some for the use of others defines the sex, woman." [9] If theorists of patriarchy like MacKinnon would underscore the contrast between feminism and Marxism, a neo-Marxist perspective dating back to the late 1960s has also retained its vitality through years of debate. The socialist feminist assertion that female oppression flows from capitalist class relations still can be heard in such diverse and important works of the 1980s as Nancy Hartsock's *Money, Sex, and Power,* Alison Jaggar's *Feminist Politics and Human Nature,* and Christine Stansell's *City of Women.* [10] For all the differences between patriarchy and Marxist theories, they come together in asserting the primacy of material categories — respectively, the biological fact of sex and the economic one of capitalism. [11] Both neglect the importance of gender symbolism in its own terms.

WOMEN'S "CULTURE" AND WOMEN'S PSYCHE

In the mid-1970s, these two competing theories of women's oppression were joined by a new set of arguments that emphasized the particularities of "women's culture." The word culture here refers not to broad patterns of meaning that construct notions of femininity but to a loose mixture of moral, psychological, and ideological characteristics that bind women together as a social group. Inasmuch as myths and symbols were the focus of analysis, as was frequently the case in literary and religious studies, such examinations of culture were typically confined to descriptions of notions of femininity itself. Aside from the view that cultural definitions of women could be either oppressive or emancipatory, thus serving the interests of either dominant patriarchal or subordinate feminist groups, little effort was made to explain the causal origins of myths and symbols of femininity. That these myths and symbols could be explained with reference to other myths and symbols (which may not have been specifically about women) went against what was a more socially reductionist grain. For this literature tended to uphold what came to be called "women's culture," understood as a set of beliefs that reflected the distinctive and concrete experience of women as women. Attention shifted from inequality to difference, and with this change in perspective came a closer look at the common features of womanhood.

Many different kinds of writers involved in this redefiniton of feminist scholarship turned to the study of the special characteristics of women's social and familial relationships. In American history these concerns gave rise to groundbreaking studies of nineteenth-century female friendship, women's education, and voluntary associations by scholars like Nancy Cott, Carroll Smith-Rosenberg, and Kathryn Kish Sklar. [12] In the field of literary criticism, the work of Patricia Meyer Spacks, Elaine Showalter, Sandra Gilbert, and Susan Gubar uncovered the literary history of neglected women writers and revealed ways that their texts challenged the prevailing gender ideology. [13] The view that women have distinctive forms of expression found substantiation in the more explicitly theoretical works of feminist psychoanalysis, most notably that of Nancy Chodorow's description of mother-daughter relationships, followed by Carol Gilligan's survey of female moral values. [14] Taken together, all these disparate works powerfully reinforced a sense of the common experience and values of women. Their accounts of this common "women's culture," however, were not themselves cultural but rather descriptive and psychoanalytic. What, if anything, produced the distinctive qualities of femininity, other than the apparently near-universal dynamics of family life and the division of public and private spheres, remained unexplored.

The emerging interest in women's subjectivity and community in the English-speaking world received reinforcement from an infusion of French feminist theory in the late 1970s and early 1980s. Asserting the existence of an intrinsic femininity in polar opposition to male-dominated social life, French feminists pushed the notion of a "women's *écriture*" in a more radical direction. Similarly grounded in psychoanalytic ideas about the primacy of mother-infant bonds, these writers advanced a powerful, at times utopian and primitivist, vision of women set in contrast to the destructive force of phallogocentric language and civilization. The widely read novel *Les Guerillères* by Monique Wittig perhaps best exemplifies this tendency within French feminism in its vivid portrayal of an ideal society of revolutionary and erotic women. [15] In America this visionary quality, if not all the theoretical underpinnings, also found expression in the radical female-separatist works of Mary Daly and Andrea Dworkin. [16] For all the often acute and inspiring insights into the difference between women and men, however, in this work the sources of the difference usually remain decidedly vague. Only a few of the proponents of "women's culture," most notably Mary Daly in her early theological writings, have sought to analyze femininity and masculinity in specifically cultural terms.

Because of their tendency to take gender difference for granted, many feminists who have insisted on women's distinctive identity and culture have proven vulnerable to the charge of implicit biological determinism, or what is commonly disparaged as "essentialism." [17] For, their critics object, if women's subjectivity is distinctive, what is the ultimate source of this difference from men if not women's bodies? And if it is women's bodies, what is our hope for feminist social transformation? Although some theorists like Chodorow at least partly answer such objections by pointing to interactive processes of identity formation rather than to bodily essences, the nagging question of social causality remains. Those most inclined to celebrate distinctive female attributes have tended to avoid the issue of causality altogether. Instead of analyzing "women's culture" as a cultural formation with its own internal structure and history, the advocates of "women's culture" tend to accept it as a given, as generated by the chronic facts of biology, female mothering, or oppression. Even though most of them would strenuously reject the "essentialist" label, they have little in the way of an alternative social theory to offer. The closest a few of them get is a sophisticated reworking of psychoanalytic theory. Yet, however powerful these insights into individuals and families may be, psychoanalysis in and of itself can say very little about broader social patterns, historical changes, or variations among different groups.

Politically, moreover, the implication of some of the work emphasizing gender difference is that women's particular values and roles are socially beneficial in relation to the patriarchal order and that, for this reason, they need not be fundamentally reformed. Instead of pursuing what one recent polemicist has called "the equality trap," these writers suggest that women need instead to receive more appreciation and reward for what they have traditionally been and done. Nicky Hart's case in *Contention* (nos. 1–2) for state compensation to mothers is but one variation of this argument. For all of her disagreements with Hart, Elizabeth Fox-Genovese's own *Feminism Without Illusions* advances a similar polemic against individualistic feminism by linking justice for women to the revitalization of traditional social structures like the family and local community organizations. Although Fox-Genovese specifically denounces "the siren calls of nostalgic and utopian communitarianism" and calls for a "new vision" of communities, the conservative implications of her desire to "protect" sex and gender "asymmetry" have not been lost on liberal, egalitarian feminists who are still pressing for the full inclusion of women into male bastions of wealth and power. [18] In perhaps the most publicized egalitarian attack on "difference" theory, the journalist Susan Faludi goes so far as to categorize prominent feminist writers like Carol Gilligan and Betty Friedan as part of a backlash against feminism, in the company of men like Ronald Reagan and George Bush.[19]

Feminist theorists stressing the social, moral, and psychological differences between women and men have also proven vulnerable to accusations that they have falsely generalized from their own culture to others. Following on the heels of African-American literary critics like Hortense Spillers and Barbara Smith, for example, Elizabeth Spelman, in her recent book *Inessential Woman,* forcefully argues that the effort to define a distinctive women's culture or voice falsely universalizes from the experience of privileged white women.[20] This case against elite white essentialism and its universalizing implications has been further reinforced by post-Kuhnian developments in studies of sexuality which point to the culturally specific and historically variable understanding of the body itself.[21]

POSTSTRUCTURALISM AND THE PROBLEM OF "OTHERNESS"

The critique of essentialism has gained increased strength with the rise of poststructuralist theory since the early 1980s. A key text in this transition was Gayle Rubin's 1975 article "Traffic in Women" in *Toward an Anthropology of Women.* By distinguishing between the economy and the sex/gender system as separate elements of social organization, Rubin turned a feminist revision of both Freud and Lévi-Strauss against biological determinism and Marxist feminism.[22] Rubin made a strong case for the autonomy and causal role of the sex/gender system in the genesis of women's oppression, stressing its origins in culturally variable kinship systems rather than in nature itself. Separating herself clearly from both the Marxist emphasis on capitalism and the patriarchy theorists' emphasis on male aggression, Rubin drew inspiration from the structuralist psychoanalyst Jacques Lacan to cast a clear light on the artificial role of the incest taboo in shaping sexuality and gender. Unlike more recent poststructuralists who have similarly drawn on Lacan to emphasize the conventionality of gender, however, Rubin, while calling for a "revolution in kinship" and the end of the Oedipus complex, largely ignored the role of culture in producing and sustaining gender.[23] For Rubin the sex/gender system was historically rooted in the reproductive needs of the species and the social need for human reciprocity and exchange — needs that, in her view, modern society no longer requires antiquated kinship systems to fill. Since the appearance of Rubin's essay, poststructuralists rallying behind the phrase "the social construction of gender" have concentrated more on the cultural system of language and symbols that continue to shape and perpetuate gender distinctions even in the modern world.

As part of a feminist variation on the broader intellectual phenomenon of "the linguistic turn," these writers have increasingly shifted away from categorizing woman as a sex to concentrating on the cultural representations of sexual difference and attitudes toward femininity and masculinity. [24] The recent outpouring of poststructuralist feminist theorizing has been marked by the influence of Foucauldian and deconstructionist literary theory, concentrating its attention on symbols and ideologies. French feminist theorists such as Luce Irigaray and Hélène Cixous, who through Jacques Lacan formed a bridge between poststructural linguistics and psychoanalysis, have contributed greatly to this phase of theoretical development.

The shift in focus from women as a social group to gender as a symbolic construction also highlights the importance of cultural diversity. According to the postmodern perception that our knowledge is structured by language, it is no longer possible to think of the category of "woman" as fixed or given. The appeal of this insight from a feminist point of view is that it opens the door to the possibility of limitless change. It also makes room for the contributions of Third World women and American women of color whom earlier feminist scholars had largely ignored. The detaching of gender from anatomy has opened to view multiple variations on the themes of women and men. "Woman" itself became a positional term, in the words of the poststructuralist feminist Luce Irigaray, "the possibility, the place, the sign of relations among men." [25] Defined not in relation to female biological difference but in relation to its oppositional term, "man," "woman" (much like "black" or "lower class") constitutes a marker of "otherness."

While poststructuralism has pointed to the cultural variability of gender, an unintended effect of emphasizing "difference" has been to undermine the analytical significance of "gender" itself. In such accounts of social life, gender ceases to be a determining variable. Conceptually and politically, the solidarity of women across class and racial lines has become increasingly problematic. If women no longer have something in common by virtue of being women — if, instead we are broken into distinct groups by virtue of the multiplicity of the positions of "otherness," especially in relation to class, ethnic, or racial identities — why bother theorizing about sex or gender at all? Instead, increasing attention is given to the task of describing variations and differences among women and exposing conflicts between them. [26] To young feminist intellectuals of the late sixties and seventies the very perception of sexual inequality seemed tremendously illuminating. Now, however, the tendency is to shy away from generalizations. Sensitivity to difference leads to an endless fragmentation of social groups, to a focus on groups defined only partly by gender, and to an understanding that gender itself is variously constructed by other social characteristics. Every woman's situation is virtually unique, defined by particularities of economic organization, political structure, and national or minority groups.

To a degree, the logic of this approach runs against the very effort to explain the condition(s) of women. Indeed, in keeping with postmodernist skepticism about theories of causality, feminist scholars have increasingly denied any intention of providing systematic explanations. As the postmodernist psychoanalyst Jane Flax surveys the fragmented field of knowledge: "The very search for a cause or 'root' of gender relationships or, more narrowly, male domination may partially reflect a mode of thinking that is itself grounded in particular forms of gender or other relations in which domination is present. Perhaps 'reality' can have 'a' structure only from the falsely universalizing structure of the dominant group." [27] A recent feminist literary anthology similarly begins with the disclaimer, "One never arrives at a point where one can fix — or has a fix on — the questions and answers; far from arriving at definitive solutions, the cumulative effect of reading and writing here is of resistance to certainty and stasis." [28] A major thrust of feminist accounts of the Enlightenment and modern science has been to challenge the premises of Western rationalism on the grounds of its inherently masculinist bias. [29] Within the academic disciplines it is, not surprisingly, historians and literary critics who are the most comfortable with this reaction against traditional social science methodology. Historical and literary scholarship both characteristically avoid generating abstract or general laws. Historians, trained to concentrate on particularities, customarily insist on the specificity of time and place. Literary critics likewise traditionally focus on the details of individual texts. The recent movement in literature toward historical analysis known as the "new historicism" combines the particularities of text with the particularities of context. Understandably, highly publicized attacks on feminist scholarship in *The New York Review of Books* have come from within the same fields of social history and literary criticism in which feminists have gained the most strength. [30]

Despite all the feminist critiques of western rationalism, however, the impulse toward explanation and generalization remains strong. It typically lurks beneath the surface of the word "social" in the standard incantation "the social construction of gender." Although "social" is by one definition an umbrella term that encompasses all nonbiological features of human life, by another, originally Marxist, definition it refers essentially to class relationships. In left-wing discourse generally, phrases like "social structure," "social relations," and "social conflict" usually still signify the organization and dynamics of class. Today, in the post-Marxist world of Michel Foucault and Pierre Bourdieu, culture is rarely explained by class alone, but by the more sweeping invocation of a context of domination and oppression. Such a perspective remains tied, however, to a critique of capitalism and liberal democracy.

For Foucault this oppressive social context of culture is subsumed under the rubric of power. Despite the centrality of discourse in his theory, discourse is not understood as an independent cultural formation but as the means to gain, justify, and preserve power. The concept of power itself, while in ordinary language an elusive one with multiple resonances, for Foucault finally boils down to the exercise of force: "Nothing is more material, physical, corporeal." [31] Similarly, Lacanian psychoanalytic theory, by connecting language and civilization with the domination of the phallus in the Oedipus conflict, links culture to power. In contemporary feminist theory we see clear resonances of such ideas. Scholars with a radical poststructuralist orientation typically interpret ideology, and with it the symbolic representations of gender, as both a symptom and an agent of domination. Stressing what she calls the legitimizing function of gender, for example, Joan Scott asserts that "gender is a primary field within which or by means of which power is articulated." [32] Judith Butler, who indicts Lacan, Foucault, Wittig, and other icons of poststructuralist feminism for their implicitly naturalist assumptions about the body, follows them in her view of culture as constructed by power — in this case the power of dominant heterosexuality. Gender is, as she puts it, "an illusion . . . maintained for the purposes of the regulation of sexuality within the obligatory frame of reproductive heterosexuality." [33] The metaphorical language in which such interpretations of gender symbolism are enmeshed — "regulation," "contestation," "deployment," "site," "field," "territory" — suggests an analogy between cultural formations and the actions of a police state. [34]

To a surprising degree, given Foucault's own antipathy towards Marxism, the hierarchical relations that many poststructuralist feminists see gender as expressing are still class relations and the oppressive imperatives of a capitalist economy. Gayatri Chakravorty Spivak, a leading proponent of Third World feminist deconstructionism, insists "that the practice of capitalism is intimately linked with the practice of masculinism." [35] The residual materialism of feminist poststructuralism is similarly exemplified in the work of Mary Poovey, an English literary critic who acknowledges her simultaneous debt to both Marx and Foucault. As she sums up her social theory of literary production, "The conditions that produce both texts and . . . individual subjects are material in the ever elusive last instance." [36] Far from implying a fundamentally different historical analysis, the Foucauldian element of her criticism differs from traditional Marxism only in its insistence on the "elusiveness" of this material last instance.

GENDER AND THE RACE/CLASS ANALOGY

The view that gender is a symbolic screen for material power relations helps to explain why feminist intellectuals in America so readily draw an implicit analogy between gender, class, and race. Implied in this trilogy of terms, of course, is the comparability of these categories. Although the specific litany "race, class, and gender" has been increasingly invoked in the context of recent debates over multiculturalism, this equation is hardly new. Marxist and socialist feminists in the 1970s pointed to the similarities between the condition of women and that of the proletariat, stressing the parallel features of wage slavery and unpaid housework, of alienation and sexual objectification, of production and reproduction. Nancy Hartsock's idea of a "feminist standpoint," which rested on the analogy with Marx's proletariat, further extended this perspective. [37] There is, in addition, the old tradition within American feminism, going back to the abolitionist influence within the first women's rights movement in the nineteenth century, of drawing parallels between the oppression of women and blacks. Despite the fact that black feminists have at times objected to this equation, arguing that it obscures the unique position of black women, to this day the analogy remains a common rhetorical feature of feminist thought. [38] Academic feminists who argue for the three-factor analysis of race, class, and gender often stress the similarity of the status of racial minorities, workers, and women. In the words of historian Gerda Lerner, "Race, class, and gender oppression are inseparable; they construct, reinforce, and support one another." [39] For some writing within a neo-Marxist framework this similarity consists of overlapping material inequalities. [40] For others, however, for whom gender has come to mean a set of symbolic constructions that vary by class and racial group, gender is not only presented as analogous to class and race but as virtually reducible to them.

In both neo-Marxist and poststructuralist work, then, gender is retreating into the dependent position it assumed in earlier discussions of the female body: it is becoming an empty vessel, which is then filled with the residues of other kinds of domination. The feminist Foucauldian perspective that analyzes gender symbolism as a tool of oppression suffers from the same weaknesses as the older theories of Marxism or patriarchy. So do the still more recent efforts to draw from the work of Jürgen Habermas in order to root modern gender definition in the rise of a "bourgeois public sphere." The literary critic Rita Felski, for example, in her argument against the radical claims of *l'écriture feminine,* advances a model of a "feminist counter-public sphere" explained by the context of "late capitalism" and its "bourgeois" character. [41] Felski rightly insists upon the "relative autonomy" of art within society. But while "art" is for her essentially genre, narrative, and other formal literary conventions, "society" — which in her view unavoidably conditions art — seems driven by the dynamics of class and oppression alone.

Are social conceptions of gender no more than reflections of more "objective," that is, presumably material, structures of political and economic inequality? For all the greater sophistication implied in the "linguistic turn," the cultural analysis of gender too frequently echoes early feminist ideas of woman-as-victim. Only now, instead of woman being the victim of patriarchy or of capitalism, the victim is the very concept of gender-as-culture. Even where gender is still defended as a primary factor in social life, it typically refers to the social conditions of being male and female, not to symbolic life. In their recent synthesis of the history of European women, for example, Bonnie Anderson and Judith Zinsser assert that "gender has been the most important factor" shaping women's lives, overriding all other differences such as class, region, or epoch. [42] Yet, after a preliminary chapter describing ancient intellectual traditions that justify the subordination or, less frequently, the empowerment of women, the remainder of their lengthy narrative disregards cultural definitions of gender in preference for social history. Cultural views of women, they argue, "changed remarkably little over time," an assertion hinging on a definition of culture that is concerned with the issues of subordination and empowerment alone. [43]

This impasse can be overcome only by developing a broader and specifically culturalist perspective. Feminist critiques of poststructural-ism, however, have actually argued the exact opposite. Rather than sug-gesting other ways of analyzing culture, they have objected to the very emphasis on the ideological components of gender, calling for renewed attention to the "social" lives of women instead. This critique originates from a materialist position that insists on the primacy of concrete expe-rience as against the purportedly abstract and merely ideational notions of gender. Related to this objection are the complaints of many social sci-entists and social historians that to study gender symbolism instead of "real women" is to privilege an elite. Yet the cultural understanding of gender, with its rejection of the view that women comprise an easily definable social group, neither inherently discounts the subjective experi-ence of actual women nor necessarily values one class over another. These problems, as difficult as they may be, are methodological and empirical rather than theoretical. The real issue at stake is how one ana-lyzes the experience of any social group. Beneath the argument that the study of "real" women is more valuable than the study of gender there lies the claim that women's experience is fundamentally constructed by material relations of wealth and power, not by symbolic systems.

Ironically, feminist poststructuralists often concur with their chief crit-ics on this very point. Far from truly privileging the cultural over the material, they typically derive gender from the dynamics of class and racial domination. In a revealing recent debate between Linda Gordon and Joan Scott, Gordon accuses postmodernist scholarship of being too remote from the social realities of women's oppression to be truly politi-cal; Scott defends the recent scholarship by pointing out the singular pre-occupation of feminist poststructuralism with matters of power. [44] Regardless of who had the better of this argument, neither writer ques-tioned the postmodernist premise that culture essentially embodies power relations. The construction of gendered meaning in response to demands for spiritual fulfillment, aesthetic pleasure, or the anxieties of human existence are either ignored or treated as epiphenomena of a "more real" driving force that is Nietzschean in character: it is a reflec-tion of the quest of theologians, artists, and philosophers for increasing their prestige and the domination of their race or class.

To challenge this reductive perspective on culture raises immediate questions about the study of gender. Is gender more than a metaphor for power? If so, what does it signify? The claim that gender is not solely the product of unequal relations of subjection and domination rekindles some of the issues in the literature on women's culture and subjectivity that first arose in the mid-1970s. That literature had taken issue with feminist Marxist and patriarchal theories for denying agency to women. It advanced the view that distinctive features of women's roles and values are produced not simply by male or capitalist oppression but by women themselves and that, as such, these values are often commendable. The strident objection to such work as romanticized, universalizing, and essentialist put this initial response to dominational theory on the defensive. Recent efforts to particularize and relativize have further eclipsed a vision of "women's culture" and, along with it, the notion that the symbolism of women and femininity involves something other than the dynamics of oppression.

Feminist theorizing has, in other words, come close to throwing out the baby with the bath water. To recognize the centrality of culture, with all its changes and variations, need not imply that culture is primarily reflective of power. The more voluntaristic insights of "women's culture" need to be incorporated into the more recent discursive analyses of gender. Without making claims about women's inherent nature, we can see ways in which conceptions of gender have coded broader cultural perspectives on human interconnectedness. This is particularly obvious in conceptions of pregnancy and birth, nursing and childcare, and erotic relations. Cultural constructions of these activities, such as the sentimental image of motherhood and the belief in romantic love, are, to be sure, partly about unequal power. But they are also about the permeability of boundaries between human beings and the pleasures and satisfactions, as well as the sufferings and disappointments, of intimacy. This is perhaps especially evident in the speech and writings of women, although not exclusively so. The meanings associated with maternal nurturance and sexual attachment are by no means universal. As symbolic structures, motherhood and love obviously vary a great deal in their content and associations. Inasmuch as such symbols represent the human capacity for relational identification with another, however, they encode a dimension of social life as universal as the dynamics of power. Even gender symbols that signify destruction or self-contained isolation — e.g., the witch, the monk, the cowboy — speak to the same set of underlying relational issues.

To emphasize relations and boundaries as reference points for the cultural construction of gender dovetails with the insights of feminist psychoanalytic theorists who have been influenced by object relations theory. In their discussions of human development, they, too, stress the importance of relationality as opposed to the power dynamics associated with the castration complex. As Nancy Chodorow makes clear in her essay "Psychoanalytic Feminism," this is where feminist Lacanian and object relations theories diverge. Whereas for Lacanians such as Juliet Mitchell, "there can be no experiences not generated by male dominance nor can there be a femininity defined in itself," Chodorow and other object relations feminists "see women's relational qualities as desirable and more fully human than masculine autonomy." [45] Yet even among object relations feminists there has recently been a notable shift towards defining gender in terms of power. The most conspicuous example is Jessica Benjamin's *The Bonds of Love,* in which intimate human relations are defined by the dynamics of domination. Jane Flax similarly suggests that the power of men over women is virtually the only universal feature of gender definition: "The actual content of being a man or woman and the rigidity of the categories themselves are highly variable across cultures and time. Nevertheless, gender relations so far as we have been able to understand them have been (more or less) relations of domination." [46] If even non-Lacanian psychoanalytic theorists have become increasingly taken with the postmodern view of human relations as structured by power, it is partly because psychoanalysis can provide no alternative theory of culture. Even those psychoanalytic theorists who, like Chodorow, insist on the importance of relationality see gender as a product of individual, psychological relationships rather than the patterned interrelationships of culture. An idea of culture as providing symbols and values that impinge upon, rather than reflect, the formation of gender identity within families is foreign (if not necessarily antagonistic) to psychoanalytic thought. The question of how individual identity articulates with collective systems of meaning is one that feminist psychoanalysts have yet to explore.

The analysis of gender as the cultural representation of human interdependency and relationality does not preclude the analysis of it as the representation of power. Both sets of perceptions are true. They are even in a sense connected to each other: to be interdependent is still to be in part dependent, and therefore to be vulnerable to the exercise of power. To argue that feminist theorists need a stronger theory of culture is not to imply that cultural analysis would necessarily concentrate on interrelationality instead of inequality. Oppressive exercises of wealth and power are rendered socially meaningful by an independently structured cultural system; as such, they need to be better understood as cultural acts rather than taken for granted as a function of human nature, male nature, or capitalism. A cultural analysis of the meanings of gender would address the social problem of gender inequality without reducing it to either individual psychodynamics, political struggle, or class relations.

A recognition of the cultural embeddedness of gender need not imply a static view of history that divests women and men of agency. Cultures change at least as much as material structures of wealth and power, and it has always been an implicit goal of feminism to effect cultural as well as political and economic change. This is, indeed, a case where theory needs to catch up with praxis. Instead of advancing theories that render this cultural work at best epiphenomenal, at worst irrelevant, feminist intellectuals should be theorizing its importance to social change. [47]

TOWARD A CULTURALIST FEMINIST THEORY

This essay has attempted to offer constructive criticism of major recent trends in feminist theory. Like many feminist poststructuralists, I am advocating a theoretical perspective on society that emphasizes the symbolic analysis of gender. I take issue, however, with the materialist theory of causality of radical poststructuralists who define gender symbolism as a product of race, class, or power. There are, I have argued, at least two key elements to an alternative, more culturalist, theoretical undertaking.

The first is the recognition that gender symbolism tends to be at least as much about interconnectedness as about power. Integral to this assertion is a view of human beings as driven not merely by utilitarian interests but also by existential questions of meaning. The social purpose of gender definitions within various cultures is to interpret such human qualities as mutual dependency and the mysteries of procreation at least as much as to justify structures of domination. Precisely how gender is defined varies by time, place, and social group; such cultural variations in gender meaning at once transcend and inform the life experience of individuals.

The second element of a culturalist feminist theory is the insistence that gender is embedded in wider systems of meaning. The interpretation of gender difference is not an isolated and independent component of a given culture, but one that intersects with many other ways that people address fundamental questions about human experience. The definition of gender is a part of a larger cultural whole and is therefore fundamentally structured by broader religious, aesthetic, and scientific concerns.

Many empirical demonstrations of these two elements of a culturalist feminist theory exist in the scholarly literature, although they rarely receive theoretical elaboration. To choose an illustration from my own area of study, changing gender definitions in the early modern west in the sixteenth and seventeenth centuries were closely tied to the Reformation of Christianity. To understand the historical emergence of the widespread view of women as morally superior to men (a critical development of the eighteenth century that still reverberates today), one must appreciate how popular ideas about human salvation increasingly elevated the role of emotions in religious experience. Although historians have sought to interpret this development differently — for example, by connecting the ideal of motherhood to the separation of home and work associated with industrialization, or to the political experience of women in the American Revolution — such perspectives inadequately account for the earlier timing, symbolic content, and transatlantic character of the symbolic redefinition. [48]

To save the cultural analysis of gender from being merely a dependent variable of class or race or power, feminist scholars need to look more closely at other kinds of social contexts: at religious beliefs, aesthetic and narrative traditions, scientific and moral thought. Too many academic specialists still view such cultural phenomena as religion, literature, folklore, art, philosophy, and science as either separate from a hypostacized "society" or as a product of it. As feminist scholars of religion and science such as Caroline Bynum, Donna Haraway, and Evelyn Fox-Keller have begun to show us, these are arenas of cultural expression in which the symbolic and gendered meaning of human relationships are most clearly defined by men and women alike. [49] Feminist theory would do well to utilize such empirical building blocks in the construction of a more systematic and self-conscious culturalist analysis of gender.

By interpreting culture as an index to meaning, we can begin to understand gender as no more exclusively a function of race, class, or power than of biology. It is structures of meaning that provide the framework both for debates over anatomical differences and for struggles over sexual power. Most feminist theory to the contrary, materialism is not the only "social" alternative to biologism. A stronger theory of culture, in which gender symbolism receives analysis in its own terms, would help to free us from being caught between the Charybdis of materialism and the Scylla of biology. Only when the cultural dimension of society is taken more seriously will we be able to lend new and deeper meaning to the popular phrase among feminist intellectuals, "the social construction of gender."

CHAPTER 2

Untangling the Roots
of Modern Sex Roles

A Survey of Four Centuries of Change

PREFACE   The 1978 date of the essay "Untangling the Roots" is dis-
closed by the words "sex roles" in its title. Were it written today, "gender"
would surely be routinely substituted for "sex" and "sexual symbolism."
Many of the references in the citations also evoke the bygone scholarly era
of the 1970s, reminding us that so much has been written on the history
of European and American women since then. Compared to my current
perspective, this essay gives more attention to material forces, particularly
to the onset of industrialization. And it tends to assume an overly tidy fit
between normative pronouncements about such matters as female sexuality and woman's sphere and the actual social relations between men and
women. Nonetheless, despite the benefits of almost twenty-five years of
hindsight, the central themes of this essay remain in my view very ger-
mane to current debates. Synthesizing the early modern history of
America and England, it describes a succession of long-term transformations from 1500 to 1900 and offers a periodization that is still useful
today. The argument revolves around a fundamental and enduring causal
theme — the mutual reinforcement of religious and economic change. The
chronological scheme of organization also still usefully breaks down the
four centuries into two periods, the first occurring generally in the sixteenth and seventeenth centuries and the second in the eighteenth and
nineteenth centuries, each with its distinctive religious and economic
underpinnings. Perhaps most importantly, as the phrase "Untangling the
Roots" suggests, the essay highlights the twisted, multidirectionality of

change. By advancing a strong objection to simple, unilinear stories of progress or decline and by demonstrating the historical trade-offs between assumptions of gender similarity and difference, "Untangling the Roots" takes an interpretive stance that remains fundamental to the rest of the essays in this volume.

·   ·   ·

The modern history of sex roles, far from exhibiting one continuous line of development, as many scholars suggest,[1] has proceeded in different, even contradictory, directions.

The history of sex roles and sexual symbolism can be viewed as an interplay between two fundamentally different definitions of the social relations of the sexes, one of which stresses similarity, the other distinctiveness. Each of these definitions has predominated at times in the past, but neither has altogether eclipsed the other. Indeed, despite our increasing commitment to an ideal of sexual equality, the tension between similarity and distinctiveness in men and women remains unresolved in our culture today. This survey of past tensions and shifts may clarify some of our current confusion.

There were, I hope to illustrate, two crucial transitions in the definition of sex roles for the Protestant English and American middle classes from the sixteenth to the nineteenth centuries. My synthesis focuses on the middle class (broadly defined as commercial farmers, independent artisans, merchants, and professionals) because that has been the focus of the historical scholarship on which I rely, and because the middle class in English-speaking capitalist nations seems to have initiated changes eventually affecting most of the Western world.

During the first transition, associated with the rise of Protestantism and commercial capitalism in sixteenth- and seventeenth-century England, traditional horizontal and qualitative sex distinctions, attributing to each sex a separate sphere of activity, were eclipsed by a vertical, hierarchical definition that stressed qualitative similarities. Female inferiority came to be seen more as a matter of degree than of kind. Then, in the eighteenth and nineteenth centuries, with the rise of romantic evangelical Protestantism and industrialism, the cultural definition again shifted, with differences in kind subsuming differences in degree. While sexual hierarchy remained integral to this revised definition, the pervasive opinion was that each sex had its own modes of expression and its own separate sources of authority.

THE SIXTEENTH AND SEVENTEENTH CENTURIES:
HIERARCHY AND SIMILARITY

In the sixteenth and seventeenth centuries, the rise of Protestantism, the centralized state, and early commercial capitalism reinforced the conjugal family unit and patriarchal dominance within family life. The dissolution of feudal economic, political, and ecclesiastical networks made the home the focus of many religious, educational, and commercial activities. At the same time, the primary authority over women and children was increasingly concentrated in their husbands and fathers. This consolidation of male hierarchal control, however, came alongside a simultaneous tendency to blur many distinctions between the sexes. Somewhat paradoxically, women lost some distinctiveness and autonomy but gained greater access to traditionally masculine sources of respect.

The theology of the English Reformation incorporated both sides of this dual process. On one hand, the Protestants' judgmental, Old Testament image of God expressed a high evaluation of the paternal role, and the Reformation also eliminated female figures from the sacred religious symbolism. While Catholics could pray to women saints and the Virgin Mary, Protestants felt the unmediated power of a thundering patriarchal God. And the Protestant attack on Mariolatry became an essential feature of its anti-Catholic propaganda. For example, in 1641 an English pamphleteer strenuously objected to the Catholic portrayal of Christ "as a sucking child in his mother's arms . . . an underling to a woman."[2] In addition, the Protestants' abolition of celibate orders diminished the independent, sacred status women had possessed within pre-Reformation Catholicism. Without convents women no longer had the opportunity to pursue separate religious vocations.

On the other hand, reformed theology vigorously proclaimed the priesthood of all believers.[3] In its early, more rebellious phase the Protestant movement appealed especially to women who wished to prove theological issues and to participate more fully in a collective religious life. Protestant women not only read Scripture and sang psalms alongside men, but for a brief period some actually preached and contested theological points with their pastors in public.[4] Even after leaders like Calvin and Beza firmly rejected the possibility of full sexual equality and the feminist thrust became confined within the radical democratic sects, Protestantism, without a doubt, partially improved the status of women. Perhaps most important, the Protestants insisted that everyone should read the Scriptures, thereby actively encouraging literacy among women as well as lower-class men. In addition, although women still could not become ministers, the Protestant clergy wielded none of the sacred authority of the Catholic priests. The laity, male and female, now established individual relationships with God unmediated by a male ecclesiastical hierarchy. Indeed, the very maleness of the symbol of God could work to encourage the regenerate of both sexes to conceive of themselves as female in relation to him, thereby blurring sexual distinctions among the elect.[5]

Religious norms prescribing marital relationships seem to have undergone a similar shift: Hierarchical sexual order went essentially unchallenged, but males and females came to be thought of in more similar terms. The Protestants, like the Christian humanists before them, sought to consolidate the marriage bond by attacking the most oppressive symptoms of sexual inequality, such as wife beating and the double standard in sexual mores, and by elaborating on the reciprocal duties of love and companionship that attend marriage.[6] Although always secondary to procreation, the fulfillment of sexual desire continued to be regarded as a primary purpose of marriage, as it had been among the Catholics. In fact, by their elimination of the higher celibate religious life, Protestants accorded human sexual nature even more fundamental respect.[7] Moreover, in this period there emerged a tendency to perceive fewer innate sexual distinctions. The traditional view had been that women had more difficulty controlling their irrational impulses and were therefore prone to extreme behavior — extremes of virtue, like Mary, or extremes of vice, like Eve. This notion survived, surfacing, for example, in the witchcraft prosecutions of the sixteenth and seventeenth centuries, but gradually the image of women as especially vulnerable to temptation received less emphasis. The Protestant critique of male celibacy as unfeasible did much to revise the traditional medical theory that men could control their sexual desires better than women could.[8]

At the same time as this upgrading of the value of the conjugal pair, however, church and state took steps to insure parental (meaning primarily paternal) consent to marital unions. Whereas previously the Catholic Church had often relaxed this requirement, even recognizing clandestine marriages sealed by the act of intercourse, by the late sixteenth century both Protestantism and Counter-Reformation Catholicism insisted on parental sanction.[9] Within the relationship the ideal of reciprocal love was similarly limited by hierarchic normative constraints. Although Protestant writings on marriage stressed the importance of love, they also specified that the husband's duty to love his wife was predicated on her duty to obey. Far from offering a critique of the wife's subordinate place in Catholic society, Protestants believed that families should be modeled after the Old Testament patriarchal structures, a position that insisted upon female submission in all worldly matters. Among English and American Puritans the belief in male dominance was generally articulated in terms of the seventeenth-century Ramist system of dichotomies arranged in a vertical order. According to this logic, all human interaction fit into a two-sided pattern of dominant and subordinate roles. Thus within the family husbands properly dominated wives, parents dominated children, and masters dominated servants.[10] A married couple, according to the celebrated divine, William Perkins, was "that whereby two persons standing in mutual relation to each other, are combined together as it were one. And of these two, the one is always higher, and beareth rule, the other is lower, and yieldeth subjections."[11] With leadership came the duty to love and esteem, but all affection was to be channeled by a rigidly hierarchical, patriarchally dominated framework.

Parental roles too appear to have fused together elements of mutuality and paternal control. Fathers, most of whom worked in or near the home, necessarily took a large part in child rearing and occupational training. And their responsibilities grew still larger in the course of the sixteenth and seventeenth centuries. Since Protestant clergy wielded no special sacred authority and the lay family life assumed greater spiritual significance, fathers took over certain priestly functions. They directed family prayer and assumed the main responsibility for providing their dependents with a minimal Christian education and helping their sons in the theologically crucial task of securing appropriate vocations.[12] In seventeenth-century America, Protestantism, combined with wilderness conditions, further accentuated the importance of family life and reinforced the paternal role.[13] Laws were even enacted in New England requiring the placement of all single persons under the authority of a family head, and provisions were made for town selectmen to oversee these patriarchs in order to insure that they were fulfilling their duties. In both England and America, moreover, the growing body of prescriptive literature on child rearing appears to have addressed its advice largely to fathers.[14] Indeed, according to the Puritan divine John Robinson (the founder of Plymouth Colony), fathers would often actually have to undo their wives' less morally responsible early influence: "Children, in their first days, have the greater benefit of good mothers. . . . But afterwards, when they come to riper years, good fathers are more behoveful for their forming in virtue and good manners, by their greater wisdom and authority: and ofttimes also, by correcting the fruits of their mother's indulgence, by their severity."[15]

Mothers were generally accorded the responsibility for small children, but from our vantage point it is nevertheless striking how quickly an infant's world extended to other crucial adult figures. Not only was the father supposed to take over once the child reached what was deemed an educable age, but both parents commonly shared child rearing with a variety of other adults of both sexes. Parents who could afford it frequently employed wet nurses to suckle their infant children.[16] Moreover, even when the infant did remain at home to be nursed by its natural mother, in England and Europe the chances were high that one or both parents would die during its childhood, whereupon often the remaining parent would remarry or orphans would be absorbed into other households.[17] In those unusual cases when the older generation lived long enough, family constellations could temporarily expand to include grandparents.[18] The common practice of hiring servants and putting children out to service also caused great fluctuations in household membership in both Europe and the American colonies. Children often left their parents to work in other households and, conversely, many homes contained at least one resident servant or slave.[19] Thus, while the formal structure of most families remained nuclear,[20] they were not at all "nuclear" in the sense that we usually understand the term today. More important, filial relationships were far less exclusively centered on mothers. Children drew support, and undoubtedly received discipline, from several sources: from the father as well as the mother, and possibly from a wet nurse, older siblings, other adult kin, stepparents, domestic servants, apprentices or journeymen about the household, and guardians or instructors other than their parents.

The boundaries of female roles in the sixteenth and seventeenth centuries can thus be seen as at once horizontally diffuse and hierarchically defined. Women shared exalted status as saintly Christians, loving spouses, and responsible child rearers but did so as more direct subordinates of men. The same basic pattern played itself out in economic as well as family and religious life. In this period women began losing many of their traditionally separate spheres of labor. They continued to engage in production but increasingly fell under the supervision of men. Significantly, Protestant literature stressed the religious value of men's vocations but insisted that the primary vocation of women was to be wives. As one seventeenth-century Puritan described the Creation, "No sooner was she a Woman, but presently a Wife; so that Woman and

Wife are of the same standing."[21] And indeed, while seventeenth-century women actively participated in economic life — performing such tasks as tending farm animals, producing and marketing foodstuffs, harvesting, spinning, and assisting their artisan and tradesmen husbands — their work continued to be generally unrecognized despite the greater emphasis on male work identity. Even though the wives of artisans, tradesmen, and merchants frequently took over their husbands' enterprises when widowed, both formal apprenticeship and equal membership in the guilds were customarily denied to women.[22] This lack of occupational status, combined with a greater tendency for women to shift employment depending on their marriages and the current demands for labor, apparently contributed to a relatively weak work identity. Seventeenth-century female autobiographers, for example, viewed their own lives within the framework of their husbands' occupations or political and religious activities.[23] This self-conception was reinforced by the growing importance of the domestic economy structured around the conjugal pair. Only the midwives and those women employed in such skilled, all-female trades as upholstery, millinery, and mantua making really enjoyed an independent position in the economy. And with the expansion of the commercial market and the development of medical technique in the seventeenth century, males began to displace females at the top of even those occupations.[24]

In the seventeenth-century British-American colonies, the imbalance in the sex ratio and the prevailing shortage of labor somewhat delayed the emergence of this pattern of increased sexual hierarchy and diminished differentiation of roles. For example, the bargaining position of women in the marriage market greatly improved due to the low proportion of women in the population.[25] In addition, more American women — particularly heirs of deceased fathers or husbands — seem to have owned and managed their own property than was possible in the Old World, and they also enjoyed slightly greater opportunities to engage in independent, relatively high-status employment.[26] This was, however, only a temporary phenomenon, offset by subsequent economic growth. Whereas in Europe, for example, midwives were being replaced by male surgeons at the upper levels of society already in the seventeenth century, in America the shift began occurring only with the professionalization of medicine in the late eighteenth century.[27]

In general, then, previously separate feminine spheres of authority in religion, the family, and the economy contracted over the course of the sixteenth and seventeenth centuries, often falling directly under male control. Men and women assumed more immediately hierarchical relationships in various areas of life. Yet at the same time as these changes in religious symbolism and clerical and economic organization divested women of many traditional sources of authority, qualitative sexual distinctions were undermined. Significantly, early seventeenth-century English literature defending women in the lively controversy over female nature that arose in these transitional years tended to emphasize the same qualities in women that were most admired in men. Wisdom, courage, sexual constancy, and piety were the chief virtues of both sexes — only women were, in addition, more modest and submissive to virtuous men.[28] Thus in roles and in imagery, qualitative distinctions tended to be collapsed in favor of quantitative ones: Women were measured against essentially the same standard as men and were judged worthy of a position one rung beneath.

THE EIGHTEENTH AND NINETEENTH CENTURIES: POLARIZATION AND DISTINCTIVENESS

If, during the sixteenth and seventeenth centuries, sex roles and sexual symbolism became less differentiated and differences in degree tended to be stressed more than differences in kind, during the eighteenth and nineteenth centuries sexual definitions diverged widely once again, although along different lines than in the premodern period. Qualitative, horizontal distinctions between the sexes now received more emphasis than the earlier quantitative, vertical ones. Male and female imagery and activities became more distinct and increasingly associated with contrasting "rational" and "affective" styles. This process of sexual differentiation closely corresponded to the progressive divergence of science and art, state and church, work and home. Just as in the sixteenth and seventeenth centuries the realignment of sex roles and symbolism was associated with the sweeping social transformations brought on by the Reformation and commercial capitalism, so, too, major changes during the late eighteenth and nineteenth centuries corresponded to developments in culture and economy — above all, romantic, evangelical Protestantism and industrialism. While men generally dominated the highly fluid and competitive economic and political spheres, women increasingly gained ascendancy in the sacred, moral, and emotional spheres of life: religious benevolence, sentimental fiction, and the family.

Any review of the now familiar evolution of the "woman's sphere" must start with the decline of economic production in the home and the transformation of domestic work into an activity with no commercial value. This trend was first visible in affluent middle-class families, where women supported by their husbands could afford to stay at home and devote themselves to the primary care of their families. In the emerging working class, which included many former artisans and farmers displaced by the industrial revolution, this was less often the case. Women in these families continued to work for pay outside the home, but gradually, as conditions improved, even they withdrew from the paid labor force once they started families. By the middle of the nineteenth century the vast majority of working-class mothers apparently were no longer gainfully employed.[29]

With the economic developments that separated the home from work came somewhat complementary changes in sexual behavior and belief. In the sixteenth and seventeenth centuries, the higher evaluation of family life had led to a greater acceptance of the sexual activity of both sexes within marriage, weakening the earlier belief that women had more ungovernable sexual appetites than men. Beginning in the eighteenth century, the balance shifted in the opposite direction, toward a widespread belief that most women lacked strong libidinal drives. The ideology of romantic love, while in one sense a rebellion against property-based, parentally controlled marriages, ironically also served to bring erotic love and deep affectual commitments under greater rational control: its idealized, asexual view of women erected a barrier between the sexes and greatly inhibited the indulgence of sexual feelings.[30]

By the time of the Victorian period, a dominant medical opinion was that men should moderate the amount of their sexual activity because they possessed only limited amounts of semen and excessive ejaculation led to the depletion of other physical and mental reserves of energy.[31] Such a repressive theory of male sexuality, with its revealing analogy to the economic model of scarcity, undoubtedly spoke to the great need for ambitious young men to control their impulses during this challenging period of rapid industrial and commercial growth.[32] And not only did the rational exigencies of the expanding economy reward men who channeled their energy into profit-making activity, but also the reorganization of roles within the middle-class family itself reinforced this trend toward a more repressive sexuality. The emerging divisions between home and work, between the passive nurturer and the active breadwinner, widened the distance between the sexes. And while men materially benefited from this arrangement by refocusing more attention on the marketplace, women in turn could wield some power by controlling their physical accessibility.[33] In a period of great social mobility, declining parental controls over marriage, and, in England, a great surplus of marriageable women, female sexual repression served in part as a defense against the threat of depersonalized sexual exploitation.[34] Nor were such threats sheer fantasy, for the underside of this rigid sexual restraint within proper, middle-class relationships was a steady growth in pornographic literature and lower-class prostitution.[35]

Just as Victorian sexual mores did not preclude an underworld of illicit sexual activity, so, too, the discipline and self-denial that spurred rapid economic growth also gave rise to cathartic emotional release in the religious revivals, in the movements for benevolence and social reform, and in sentimental literature. In their endeavor to retain some spiritual center, some intimate relationship with nature, some ethos of community, such movements in part represent a revulsion against the calculative and competitive, impersonal requirements of the industrial age. And yet, in addition to their hostility to the alienating aspects of early industrial society, these cultural developments also represent a complementary process, giving shape to the opposite side of the same nineteenth-century coin. Rational and affective styles became increasingly institutionalized in markedly different areas of life during this period. Competitive rationality surely triumphed in economics, but affect simultaneously flowered in the sacred and personal realms of romantic art, evangelical religion, and the family.

Because the less cognitive, rational orientations tended to be increasingly associated with the female sex, religion, benevolence, and sentimental literature offered early nineteenth-century upper- and middle-class women the greatest opportunities for participation in public life. Indeed, in New England the relative number of females belonging to churches climbed dramatically in the eighteenth century, and, while women remained most prominent in the newest and more radical sects, like the Shakers, with the religious revivals women assumed a more important place in the mainstream evangelical faith.[36] Religion appealed more to women not only because men had turned more attention toward the secular world of affairs but also because changes in religion resonated with simultaneous changes in the conception of women.

While Reformation Protestantism had repudiated many of the emotive elements of Catholic religious devotion and preached the containment of interpersonal emotional commitments within the family and direct relationships to God, eighteenth-century revivalism reintroduced more diffuse, highly demonstrative displays of feeling into English and American

Protestantism. An emphasis on the omnipotence and stern judgment of a transcendent God gradually gave way to a Christianity that stressed the humanity of Christ and the intimate love relationship between human beings and God. God had gradually grown more dependable, more forgiving, and more accessible. In a society in which working fathers had grown substantially more remote, it is psychologically significant that divine authority assumed those mild characteristics that the culture deemed essentially feminine.[37] Intricate doctrinal issues gradually lost most of their salience as the faithful turned to direct emotional experience as the standard and source of truth. Moreover, with increased toleration and, in America, the movement toward disestablishment of the churches, organized religion took a less direct role politically. Rather than communicate an articulate political theory comparable with that of Puritanism, nineteenth-century religion concentrated on personal life. Evangelical religion especially encouraged female participation, for although the women of the age may have remained relatively unpracticed in politics and theology, their gifts for emotional expression went unchallenged.

Toward the end of the eighteenth century, fictional and religious literature began attributing to women not only a commendable piety but also the primary power to enforce religious and moral standards.[38] In European Catholic society, particularly after the Counter-Reformation, nuns had engaged in substantial welfare work, and, among the Protestants, Quaker women had already formed charitable organizations. But it was only in the early nineteenth century that large numbers of Protestant upper- and middle-class women devoted themselves to benevolent activity as a major expression of their Christian belief. Sparked by fears of social disorder and sustained by the aggressive piety of the evangelical faith, this burst of religious benevolence consumed enormous proselytizing energy. Organizations like the Bible, Tract, and Missionary societies, Sunday schools, and institutions to provide work for indigent mothers and distressed orphans sprang up everywhere. These benevolent activities initially concentrated on charity and the conversion of souls but rapidly expanded into campaigns for social reform like temperance, anti-prostitution, and anti-slavery. Although influential men like William Wilberforce and Lyman Beecher always constituted the highest level of leadership, women formed their own (often auxiliary) societies, raised money by sewing and by pledging small donations through the "cent societies," often enlisted as missionaries, and performed the bulk of the grassroots labor, visiting the poor and distributing literature.[39]

Women also exercised moral guardianship in the public domain through their vast productions of sentimental literature. For all their domestic platitudes, these writers recommended that men become more graceful, emotive, and gentle — more like women — in order to improve themselves and save the world from commercial decadence. Indeed, there was an aggressive quality to all this participation of English and American middle-class women in literary, benevolent, and reform movements. They were often seeking not only to spread evangelical Christian virtues but also to universalize what they deemed essentially feminine traits.[40]

The participation of women in these various movements inevitably derived ultimate legitimacy from motherhood. Female writers and reformers, even nineteenth-century feminists, typically presented themselves as simply extending their maternal influence into the public domain.[41] For it was as mothers in the home that women most commonly and most safely wielded their relatively newfound religious and moral authority. As economic developments deprived middle-class mothers of their earlier productive functions while simultaneously pulling fathers away from the family, mothers assumed virtually complete responsibility for raising children. Not only did the responsibilities of parents become more sharply divided, but also the number of other adults intimately involved with young children decreased. Wet nurses went out of fashion; stepparents became less common with a general decline in mortality rates; middle-class children ceased entering service or apprenticeship and lived at home longer; apprentices and journeymen left the home along with the father; and fewer domestic servants seem to have been employed.[42] Child rearing became more exclusively the province of the mother.

As in the case of the tightening sexual morality, these structural changes appear at first to have been primarily a middle-class phenomenon. More English working-class mothers and children worked outside the home, and their households evidently contained more lodgers and resident kin.[43] In addition, due to the common practice of fathers employing their own children as machine assistants early in the cotton spinning and other industries, the factories did not immediately eliminate all features of the domestic system of production. For a time, some fathers were able to preserve their traditional socializing role, supervising and training their children in their work. But this arrangement could at best only approximate the domestic system. Wives were generally absent, and few workers could ever have enough children the right age. Slowly, factory organization eroded the family system of production.[44] And, with

the gradual decline of child labor and in the proportion of working
mothers, the working-class family also experienced a growing division in
parental roles.

Earlier treatises on childhood education had been addressed to fathers
and often concerned children other than their own, but by the nineteenth
century almost all of the middle-class child-rearing literature spoke only
to mothers. American middle-class women consumed vast numbers of
instructive volumes written primarily by evangelical women and clergymen, and beginning in the 1810s in New England, groups of devout
mothers even gathered in "maternal associations" to discuss how they
could best infuse their children's souls with Christian virtues.[45] As the
dominant feminine ideal of the nineteenth century, moral motherhood
evolved in sharp contrast to the masculine ideal of individual worldly
success.

The Victorian definition of sex roles maintained its hegemony, especially among the British and American middle classes, until well into the
present century. Although now regarded as "traditional" rather than
"modern," the highly differentiated sex roles characteristic of the late
nineteenth century were products of several centuries of change. In the
sixteenth century, male and female worlds converged, undermining many
earlier sexual barriers but also divesting many formerly feminine spheres
of much of their autonomy. In the nineteenth, sexual distinctions again
sharpened, increasing female authority over several vital, albeit limited,
spheres of life. Neither view has ever eradicated the other, and both continue to affect the status of women. An understanding of the history of
both attitudes might help us to untangle the roots of modern sexual definitions — to sort out our contradictory legacy of equality and inequality,
flexibility and rigidity, commonality and separateness.

PART TWO

Colonial Transitions

CHAPTER 3

American Feminine Ideals in Transition

The Rise of the Moral Mother, 1785–1815

PREFACE   In "American Feminine Ideals in Transition," first published in 1978, I describe the confluence of religious and radical Enlightenment views of motherhood. I zero in on the years 1785–1815 not to highlight the American Revolution but to illustrate how much literary images of mothers had changed since the seventeenth century. In keeping with other interpretations of the 1970s, I still viewed early industrialism as a pivotal factor in producing a newly idealized image of motherhood. My emphasis, however, here as elsewhere, is cultural and intellectual, and the essay for the most part concerns the transition from Puritanism to an uneasy combination of evangelical Protestant and Enlightenment thought at the turn of the nineteenth century. Were this essay written today it would undoubtedly take more explicit issue with historians who have since stressed the emergence of "the republican mother." Rather than stress the influence of the Revolution, it presents the increased value placed upon maternal morality as a longer-term, transnational, and essentially cultural rather than political process. Yet in this essay the history of these religious and intellectual developments from the late seventeenth to the late eighteenth century remains largely unexplored. The two following essays in this section, on the law of courtship and the ideas of Jonathan Edwards and Benjamin Franklin, more directly address this intervening colonial period.

. . .

Motherhood has long held a special place of honor in the symbolism of American life. Still a dominant value today, the ideal of motherhood probably achieved its quintessential expression in the writings of the mid-nineteenth century. Women, according to the prevailing Victorian image, were supremely virtuous, pious, tender, and understanding. Although women were also idealized as virgins, wives, and Christians, it was above all as mothers that women were attributed social influence as the chief transmitters of religious and moral values. Indeed, other respectable female roles — wife, charity worker, teacher, sentimental writer — were in large part culturally defined as extensions of motherhood, all similarly regarded as nurturant, empathic, and morally directive.[1]

The Victorian maternal ideal was first manifest as part of the culture of the most articulate, Anglo-American, Protestant, middle and upper classes. Some of its features, particularly its asexuality, probably never permeated as deeply into the culture of other American groups. However, the high evaluation of maternal influence was destined in time to command a far wider allegiance. By the mid-twentieth century, it would be difficult to identify a more pervasive "all-American" ideal.

Even among the social groups who gained cultural dominance in the Victorian era, however, motherhood had not always been a dominant feminine ideal. Indeed, in seventeenth- and early eighteenth-century literature written and read in America, motherhood was singularly unidealized, usually disregarded as a subject, and even at times actually denigrated. Partially because pre-Victorian writers understated the importance of motherhood, historians of the colonial period have also given the subject far less attention than more overtly economic forms of female labor, women's legal status, and the more common literary depiction of women as wives and Christians. Moreover, the widely acknowledged "transitional" phase between mid-eighteenth and mid-nineteenth century attitudes toward motherhood has received surprisingly little examination. Recently, the valuable work of Linda Kerber and Nancy Cott has begun to fill this scholarly gap, but primarily because they focus on other, broader issues — Kerber on views of women in late eighteenth-century republican ideology and Cott on a wide constellation of changes in New England women's lives between 1780 and 1835 — neither author has given extended attention to changing conceptions of motherhood per se. In particular, no one has yet analyzed the wide range of printed literature circulating in America between the late seventeenth and the early nineteenth centuries, much of it British in origin, that bore on the question of mothering. The relationship between this literature and the consciousness (much less behavior) of even its limited readership is, of course, highly problematic, and many unanswered questions about mothering in this period remain. Yet even when viewed narrowly as the "official" culture of dominant groups, this body of literature reveals a change in attitudes that is of great and continuing significance to the history of American women.[2]

. . .

Prior to the late eighteenth century, two, essentially mutually exclusive, ideal images of women appeared in the literature written and read in America. The first, that of woman as "help-meet," has been the most extensively described by modern historians.[3] It was the earliest and most indigenous American literary ideal, associated above all with New England Puritanism and later, with significant modifications, with a part of the American Enlightenment. In its Puritan version, the help-meet ideal laid great stress on the value of female subordination to men, a position justified both by Old Testament patriarchal models and by general cultural assumptions that women were weaker in reason, more prone to uncontrolled emotional extremes, and in need, therefore, of practical, moral, and intellectual guidance from men. Yet while thus proclaiming female mental inferiority and insisting on the wife's duty to obey her husband (except when he violated divine law), Puritan literature tended to downplay qualitative differences between the sexes and to uphold similar ideal standards for both men and women. Faith, virtue, wisdom, sobriety, industry, mutual love, and fidelity in marriage, and joint obligations to children were typically enjoined on both sexes. Good wives, who were above all defined as pious, frugal, and hardworking, were especially valued for the help they could be to men in furthering both spiritual and worldly concerns.

Some eighteenth-century Enlightenment writings on women published in America also minimized differences between the sexes and emphasized the usefulness of sensible, industrious wives. These writings, however, often revised the earlier help-meet ideal by simultaneously stressing female rational capabilities, advocating more serious education for women, and urging greater equality in marriage. In their defense of women, these authors, even more than the Puritans, tended to place special emphasis on the practical value of diligent housewives.[4]

The second feminine ideal that appeared in the eighteenth-century literature emphasized ornamental refinement.[5] Whereas the help-meet ideal tended to downplay sexual distinctions and to stress the utility of good housewives, this more upper-class ideal instead concentrated on feminine graces and dwelt on the charms of female social companionship in polite company. It came to America primarily by means of imported English literature, especially sentimental romances and didactic pieces on female education and etiquette, many of which were popular enough to be reprinted in America. Eighteenth-century periodicals, largely extracted from contemporary English magazines, were also full of articles conveying an ornamental image of women. According to this vision, often described in highly ornate eighteenth-century prose and verse, women were exquisite beings — beautiful, delicate, pure, and refined. Although modesty and piety constituted key features of this ideal, as they did of the help-meet image, charm and fashionable female "accomplishments" such as musical performance, drawing, and speaking French tended to be incorporated as well. Originally associated with the chivalric tradition of romantic love, this image of ornamental refinement still retained aristocratic overtones and probably strongly appealed to those elements of the eighteenth-century English and American prosperous middle-classes aspiring to gentility.

. . .

Both of these eighteenth-century feminine ideals, the help-meet and the ornament, dwelt primarily on woman's relationships to God and man as Christian, wife, and social companion. Neither placed much emphasis on motherhood. In practically all of the literature on women circulating in America prior to the late eighteenth century, the theme of motherhood tended either to be ignored altogether in favor of such topics as courtship or marriage, or it was subsumed among a variety of other religious and domestic obligations shared with men. This is not to say that women, in reality, had no special maternal relationships to their children; women not only gave birth, they usually nursed and tended small children far more than men. Yet despite this actual behavior, motherhood received less normative emphasis and symbolic appreciation in early American literature than did many other aspects of women's lives.

Throughout most of the colonial period, relationships between mothers and infants rarely drew literary attention. Although we know that mothers generally took care of their babies, their behavior for the most part evidently remained ascriptively controlled, dictated by custom passed down from one generation to the next without any felt need for written scrutiny. Inasmuch as mothering became a matter for literary treatment at all, it was far from idealized. Puritan writers whose works circulated in New England did occasionally turn to the subject, but the main maternal functions that aroused their commentary were regarded as biological givens: childbearing and breastfeeding.

Childbirth, God's special curse on the daughters of Eve, received notice from Puritan writers because, above all, it raised the specter of death. In an age when women often died in delivery, and infants frequently thereafter, ministers viewed pregnancy primarily as an occasion to exhort women to guard their health and, more importantly, to seek their spiritual salvation.[6] Partly in response to this high risk of mortality, fertile women who successfully bore many children also drew some special recognition.[7]

The only other aspect of mothers' relationships with infants to receive much attention in early American literature was breastfeeding. Ministers addressed this issue specifically in order to urge mothers to nurse their own children. During this period, it was still customary for many urban and landed families throughout western Europe to send babies to suckle wet nurses, and, although the evidence on colonial America is sketchy, in the eighteenth century, wet-nursing seems to have made a few inroads on this side of the Atlantic as well.[8] The Puritan clergy strenuously objected to this practice, insisting that mothers who chose not to nurse their babies opposed the clear will of God as revealed in both Scripture and nature. Ministers commonly cited Biblical examples of mothers suckling babies and also pointed out that God obviously designed the breasts on the female body for this use. To defy this divine intention constituted a basic violation of a mother's calling, a clear-cut sign of sinful sloth, vanity, and selfishness. On occasion this religious case against wet-nursing joined with a medical one, that maternal breastfeeding less often endangered the physical health of the child. Only rarely, and evidently only in imported English treatises, was the impact of wet-nursing upon a child's character raised as a noteworthy consideration. American writers who condemned the practice stressed the importance of the child's health and, especially, the mother's duty to God, not the value of an affective relationship between mother and child.[9]

This absence of literary emphasis on emotional bonds between mothers and children is no indication, of course, that such attachments did not actually exist. Even the act of sending a child out to a wet nurse is not evidence that a mother was indifferent to her baby's health and happiness.[10] Indeed, although maternal love was seldom a theme in early

American literature, it seems to have been largely taken for granted. Several Puritan ministers issued warnings against "a Mother's excessive fondness," the tendency for mothers to spoil or "cocker," their children, "to as it were smoother their Children in their Embraces."[11] The observation that mothers were particularly tender toward their children, however, more often gave rise to criticism than to commendation. Cotton Mather's printed funeral sermon for his own mother, which gave almost sentimental homage to maternal comfort, was a rare departure from this tendency to devalue what seemed distinctive about a mother's love. Yet even there, in characteristically Puritan fashion, the overriding theme of Mather's sermon was that God is still a "better comforter." "What," he asked, "is the best of *Mothers* weigh'd in the Ballance with such a *Father?*"[12]

In keeping with this highly patriarchal Puritan God, early American literature on childrearing gave as much or more notice and appreciation to fathers as to mothers. Compared with the paucity of written material on infancy, there was a great deal to be read about childhood education after the nursing stage. During the seventeenth and eighteenth centuries, children were attracting increased attention as objects of artistic, literary, religious, and pedagogical concern throughout the western world.[13] In New England, where Puritans took an especially vital interest in socialization that would maximize chances of religious conversion, sermons and treatises on family life meticulously enumerated parental responsibilities. Practically all these works assumed that parental obligation was either vested primarily in fathers or shared by both parents without sexual distinction.

Puritan writings on the family generally divided into separate sections that defined ideal relationships between husband and wife, parent and child, and master and servant, specifying the mutual obligations of each figure within the complementary pairs. The main tasks incumbent upon the parent, in addition to insuring the child's physical well-being, were to provide baptism, prayer, religious instruction, and assistance in the choice of a calling and a spouse. Because "parent" was itself a genderless term, these works often conveyed the impression that mothers and fathers ideally performed much the same role.[14] Indeed, those few works that dealt separately with specifically maternal responsibilities — usually as one small part of sermons on virtuous women — reiterated many of the same duties that other works on childrearing commonly assigned to fathers as well. Good mothers were described as caring, pious, and wise; they prayed for their children, instructed and catechized them and reproved their sins; and they served as examples of virtue and faith.[15] None of these were distinctively maternal obligations. At the most, writers would point out that because mothers had closer contact with small children, they had special opportunities to make lasting impressions on young minds.[16] At times, however, commentators actually denigrated the value of this early maternal influence, insisting that fathers subsequently undertook the more serious and ultimately most beneficial education of their children. As Cotton Mather once expounded upon the proverb "A wise son maketh a glad father, but a foolish son is the heaviness of his mother," applying it to children of both sexes:

> It may be worth while to Enquire, Why 'tis rather the Gladness of the *Father* than of the *Mother,* that is here mentioned upon the *Wise Child?* Unto this I answer; 'Tis because the *Father* ordinarily has most *Share* in procuring, and most *Sense* in perceiving, the *Wisdom* of his Children. When Children are come to such *Maturity,* that their Wisdom does become Observable, ordinarily the *Mother* has more dismissed them from her Conversation than the *Father* has from *his* . . . . But if you go on to Enquire, Why 'tis rather the Sadness of the *Mother,* than of the *Father,* that is mentioned upon the Foolish Child? Unto this I answer; 'Tis because when Children miscarry the *Mother is* ordinarily most *Blamed* for *It:* People will be most ready to say, and very *Often* say it very *Justly* too, 'Twas her making Fools of them, that betray'd them into the Sinful Folly.[17]

Those works that outlined the more neutral "parent's" obligations were, moreover, often heavily patriarchal in tone, not only employing the pronoun "he," but also drawing from such Biblical models as Abraham, Joshua, and David.[18] At times, specifically paternal duties, such as presiding over family worship, received special emphasis. Other works on the upbringing of children were explicitly addressed to fathers alone, while only one book published in America prior to the late eighteenth century, an edition of *The Mother's Catechism* attributed to the English cleric John Willison, was designed specifically for mothers.[19] Indeed, ministers often felt it necessary to make a special point that mothers were not "exempted" from the duty to participate in the religious education of their children.[20] Others noted a tendency among children to respect their mothers less than their fathers and reminded them of the Fifth Commandment injunction to honor both parents equally. William Gouge, the English Puritan whose treatise on family life was well known in New England, even sympathetically acknowledged that, at least for boys, the duty to honor mothers despite their manifold female deficiencies was "the truest triall of a childes subjection."[21]

This devaluation of motherhood was, on the one hand, an integral part of broader cultural assumptions about the inferiority of women. The traditional view that women were less rational, less capable of controlling emotions than men, helped to explain not only their unfitness for civil and ecclesiastical leadership and their need to be deferential in marriage, but also their subordinate parental status. Certain qualities regarded as essential to good childrearing, such as self-discipline and theological understanding, were deemed more characteristic of men; and the Protestant Reformation even further accentuated the value of these supposedly masculine traits. Moreover, by abandoning certain Catholic and aristocratic traditions that had enhanced the position of women — such as the worship of Mary and the female saints and the extensive education of at least some privileged women — Puritanism in some ways actually lowered the status of women. At a time when the domestic socialization of children was becoming a matter of greater cultural scrutiny than before throughout the western European world, the paternal role, in particular, drew pronounced emphasis and respect.

On the other hand, despite this elevation of fathers over mothers, the standard against which they were measured was essentially the same. Although mothers had more weaknesses to overcome, as "parents" they were supposed to strive toward an identical ideal. No differentiated maternal role received extended definition. Only childbearing, breastfeeding, and the preliminary education of very small children drew notice as uniquely maternal obligations. Partially because Puritans believed that infants were depraved and that the truly decisive process of conversion only began later on, these early years of predominantly maternal care aroused minimal interest relative to the later period of serious religious instruction, which involved fathers as well.

The lack of emphasis on motherhood in seventeenth- and eighteenth-century Puritan literature reflected, in addition, certain social realities of family life. Fathers not only wielded superior intellectual and moral authority as men, but they also worked in sufficient proximity to their children to take an active part in child rearing. Craftsmen and tradesmen typically conducted their businesses at home; even farmers worked close by and often spent long winter months indoors. Furthermore, although the term "parent" referred to mothers and fathers, other adult figures frequently lived with children and undoubtedly shared child-rearing obligations, thereby further diffusing the parental role. Colonial households, for example, often included servants, many of them adolescents sent by their parents to learn practical skills from other adults.[22] Writings on familial obligations typically advised masters to treat servants as they would their own children; servants, in turn, were enjoined to aid in the religious education of the young.[23] Their involvement in the life of a growing child may well have further undermined the uniqueness of the maternal relationship.

Mothers, moreover, much like fathers and servants, typically engaged in other activities in addition to child rearing. Not only were rudimentary household tasks demanding occupations, but women also had to produce many of their own commodities for domestic use in this preindustrial, and still relatively uncommercial, economy. They often helped their husbands with the craft or trade, and on occasion even owned and managed enterprises inherited from deceased husbands or fathers.[24] If parenthood was not regarded as a predominantly maternal responsibility, neither was motherhood the primary occupation of women.

The prevailing image of women as wives, or "help-meets," rather than mothers, then, while partly a result of deprecatory opinions about both women and children, also accurately described major aspects of women's lives. The more fanciful ornamental ideal of female refinement sought, to the contrary, to elevate women above all the banalities of work. Yet even while taking the otherwise nearly opposite perspective on women, this ideal, too, tended to disregard motherhood in preference for other defining characteristics. The rearing of children was evidently considered far too mundane and undistinguished a feature of a woman's married life to warrant idealization from either point of view.

· · ·

The second volume of Samuel Richardson's novel *Pamela* more than any other work first heralded the new, idealized conception of motherhood. Here the now ex-servant girl Pamela settles into her married life with the country squire Mr. B. and takes on the at once serious and pleasurable task of rearing their children. Although the plot actually revolves around other, more suspenseful themes, the novel dwells periodically on Mrs. B.'s maternal virtue: she unsuccessfully pleads with her husband to allow her to breastfeed her baby; she jeopardizes her own health to nurse her son when he contracts smallpox (probably a consequence of using the wet nurse); she studiously engages in a detailed examination of Locke's *Thoughts on Education;* and, in the closing scene of the novel, she recounts moral tales to enraptured children clustered about her in the nursery.

One suspects that the popularity of *Pamela* was due far less to this domestic sequel than to the passionate romance of the first volume. Yet this work, which appeared in its first American edition as early as 1744, offered a preliminary sketch of a feminine ideal that by the turn of the century had become widespread — particularly in more explicitly didactic religious, educational, and medical literature. By transforming the virginal chambermaid Pamela into the wise matron Mrs. B., Richardson merged parts of the older ideals of domestic competence and ornamental purity with the new image of the moral mother.

Although anticipated by Richardson, this new maternal ideal gained ascendancy in America only toward the end of the eighteenth century. It emerged in the context of an expanding literature on various aspects of women's lives, including female education, courtship, and marriage. Children, too, always objects of great concern in Puritan literature, received ever more specialized and detailed attention over the course of the eighteenth century.[25] The difference between these post-Revolutionary commentaries and earlier publications on women and children was not, however, merely a difference in number but a difference in kind. To be sure, in the literature on women, the older help-meet and ornamental ideals were still much in evidence; and in literature on child rearing, the genderless "parent" was still an object of address. However, an altered conception of motherhood developed alongside these traditional views. Between 1785 and 1815, large numbers of reprinted British and indigenously American works began to appear that stressed the unique value of the maternal role. Not only did the still popular Pamela articulate this new theme, but so did many contemporary books and magazines published in America on such subjects as family religion, children's health and morality, and female manners and education. It was taken up, moreover, by late-eighteenth-century Enlightenment rationalists and evangelical Protestants both, groups representing broad Anglo-American intellectual orientations that became increasingly polarized near the end of the century. Although they tended to define it somewhat differently, the value of moral motherhood was one of the few things about which many on both sides agreed.

During the late eighteenth century, writers began to dwell on the critical importance of proper maternal care during infancy. What had earlier been left to custom for the first time became a matter of widespread written analysis and prescriptive advice. Opposition to wet-nursing, for example, although always pronounced in Puritan America, now enlisted the support of many physicians and other secular commentators, who advanced the cause of maternal breastfeeding on far more comprehensive grounds. Mothers who chose not to nurse their own children were still regarded as essentially profane and were now often charged with violating Enlightenment natural law as well as the Protestant will of God. The child's health became an even more salient factor in these discussions than it had been earlier. And, in addition to extending these older arguments, late-eighteenth-century authors introduced a new set of objections to wet-nursing. They began, for example, to stress the detrimental effects upon the child's character. The strict Calvinist doctrine of infant depravity began giving way to the more environmentalist psychology of the Enlightenment, and many writers came to portray the newborn baby's mind as infinitely impressionable, as "a blank sheet of paper," "spotless as new-fallen snow," capable of being "easily moulded into any Form."[26] Earlier European medical theorists had warned that a nurse could convey bad character, or "humour," through the physical medium of milk, an argument that had never caught on in Puritan America.[27] Now several writers contended that those who nursed babies wielded determining psychological influence, not so much through the milk itself (although the metaphor was on occasion employed) but, more significantly, through their personal interaction. Wet nurses, they argued, could not be trusted to implant desirable characters because they felt less affection for babies than natural mothers and because they might be mentally or morally deficient. "What prudent mother," asked the Rhode Island minister Enos Hitchcock, "will trust the commencement of the education of her child in the hands of a mercenary nurse . . . who knows little more than how to yield nourishment to an infant[?]"[28] Borrowing an expression from Rousseau, a New York midwife named Mary Watkins protested that, in addition, wet-nursing violated "the rights of the mother to see her infant love another woman as well or better than herself."[29] Mindful that "even upon the breast infants are susceptible of impressions," authorities encouraged nursing mothers to be "double careful" of their tempers, "to indulge no ideas but what are chearful, and no sentiments but what are kindly."[30] Indeed, several advised that even if a mother proved incapable of breastfeeding, she should never send her baby away from home to nurse. Rather she herself nevertheless should assume primary control over the physical and emotional care of her child, either by feeding it manually or by keeping a wet nurse on hand under her close supervision.[31]

In another major revision of the case against wet-nursing, writers began to recommend maternal breastfeeding not only as a necessary religious duty, but also as a source of physical and psychological fulfillment for the mother as well as the child. Nursing, as well as infant care generally, came to be viewed as an exquisite pleasure, as an invaluable opportunity to delight in the charms of innocent infancy. Far from requiring physical sacrifice, many authors suggested, breastfeeding actually enhanced the mother's health; nursing mothers became more radiant, contented, graceful, and "harmonious."[32] And, contrary to fashionable opinion, men would find these mothers more attractive as well. As the widely read English physician Hugh Smith phrased this often highly sentimental appeal, "a chaste and tender wife, with a little one at her breast is certainly to her husband the most exquisitely enchanting object upon earth."[33]

Not only were mothers strongly advised to feed their own children, but for the first time they were also furnished with extensive written information about how to do it. They were instructed how to overcome physical problems such as sore nipples, how to use manual devices like the "pot" and the "boat," how often to feed, when to wean, and so on. Medical experts also addressed mothers on various other aspects of infant care. Handbooks on child nurture and disease began to become widely available during this period. Most of these were American reprints of slightly earlier works by well-known English and Scotch obstetricians, but in the early nineteenth century, indigenous American publications also began to appear. These works urged mothers to tend closely to their small children — not just to nurse them competently when sick, but to clothe them loosely rather than swaddle them, to keep them meticulously clean, to exercise them regularly outdoors, to keep them on a special diet for years, and (some texts said) to feed them on demand rather than on schedule.[34]

Although we know next to nothing about actual child-rearing practices, most of these admonitions seem aimed toward increasing the amount of attention paid by mothers to small children. Infant care came to be viewed as an exacting occupation, one requiring not only heightened concentration, but also special expertise. Tasks that had earlier been regulated by unwritten custom now began to be matters for extended analysis and deliberate, rational manipulation. A few of the British physicians openly deplored the superstitious ignorance of most mothers and believed themselves to be on a mission of scientific enlightenment.[35] This medical condescension could, however, also backfire as mothers themselves came to take pride in their craft. *The Maternal Physician,* for example, a book of advice written by an American mother of eight, spoke more directly from the voice of experience. Acknowledging her debt to the books by the doctors, she adds: "These gentlemen must pardon me if I think, after all, that a mother is her child's best physician, in all ordinary cases; and that none but a mother can tell how to *nurse* an infant as it ought to be nursed."[36]

Several of these popular medical handbooks on childcare contained sections offering advice on the psychological as well as the physical management of small children. The dominant message was that mothers should establish gentle but firm moral discipline as early as possible. Just as the impressionability of infant minds became grounds for objecting to wet nurses, so prevailing assumptions about the continuing malleability of small children's characters served to heighten the responsibility assigned to mothers throughout these first formative years. Many writers warned against entrusting children to servants, who were commonly characterized as careless, ignorant, and even potentially corrupt. William Buchan, the author of the manual *Advice to Mothers,* described the far-reaching ramifications of this early maternal moral custody:

> Everything great or good in future life, must be the effect of early impressions; and by whom are those impressions to be made but by mothers, who are most interested in the consequences? Their instructions and example will have a lasting influence and of course, will go farther to form the morals, than all the eloquence of the pulpit, the efforts of schoolmasters, or the corrective power of the civil magistrate, who may, indeed, punish crimes, but cannot implant the seeds of virtue.[37]

Not surprisingly, ministers and secular moralists as well as medical experts often took up this theme, exhorting mothers to use their power to "ingraft," "sow," and "root" steadfast principles of virtue in impressionable young minds.[38] "Weighty beyond expression is the charge devolved on the female parent," solemnly observed the New Hampshire minister Jesse Appleton. "It is not within the province of human wisdom to calculate all the happy consequences resulting from the persevering assiduity of mothers."[39]

As writers thus accorded more significance to maternal care during the first years of life, they in effect upgraded the status of what had always been a female role, for mothers traditionally had been entrusted with very small children, particularly in America, where wet-nursing was relatively rare from the outset. The change in conceptions of motherhood involved, however, not simply a higher evaluation of an age-old occupation but also a substantive redefinition of the maternal role. Many responsibilities that had earlier been assigned to fathers or to parents jointly were transferred to mothers alone. Whereas Puritan writers had portrayed fathers as taking an active, even primary role in childhood education once the children became capable of rational thought and moral discrimination, now fathers began to recede into the background in writings about the domestic education of children.

By the turn of the century, Protestant clergymen frequently stressed the religious influence of mothers without reference to any subsequent paternal intervention at all. Whereas past literature on childhood education had been primarily addressed to fathers, now books and magazines catering to women offered advice on the moral upbringing, discipline, and education of growing children.[40] Catechisms, instructive dialogues, and moral stories for children began to feature mothers in the instructive role. One anonymous publication entitled *The Mother's Gift*, for example, a work that went into several American editions in the late eighteenth and early nineteenth centuries, contained both a catechism and several heavily didactic stories about children's lives in which fathers scarcely appear.[41] Mrs. Elizabeth Helme, the English author of another such educational manual for mothers called *Maternal Instruction*, reprinted in New York in 1804, introduced her work by explaining, "As I regard an informed mother [as] the most proper and attractive of all teachers, I have chosen that character as the principal, in the following sheets."[42] A new Quaker catechism similarly cast "mother" as the questioner, as did other, less formal educational dialogues.[43] Even the earlier *Mother's Catechism* by John Willison now enjoyed an impressive revival.[44] Nor were all of these works aimed solely at the religious and moral education of children. Practical information on the use of tools and money, basic skills such as reading and arithmetic, and even more advanced subjects, such as history, biography, geography, science, and art, all fell within the range of what at least some authors regarded as the mother's appropriate educational role.[45] Although this early maternal instruction scarcely substituted for the more formal education that children, especially boys, would receive later on, professional teachers were evidently to take up where mothers left off. "Business, and many cares, call the father abroad," explained a New Hampshire clergyman, "but home is the mother's province — here she reigns sole mistress the greatest part of her life."[46] Fathers, concurred an English author widely read in America, "can afford but little leisure to superintend the education of their children."[47] Indeed, just as a few Puritan commentators had seen fit to remind mothers that they, too, bore some responsibilities for childhood education, now an occasional work made the reverse point that fathers should not simply leave the rearing of children entirely to mothers alone.[48]

The literature that entrusted mothers with such wide-ranging physical, psychological, religious, and intellectual custody over the young in part accurately reflected concrete social changes that greatly expanded and specialized the maternal role. These structural changes occurred first and far more rapidly in England, still the source of much that was read in America even after the Revolution, but the indigenous as well as the imported literature spoke to a long-range social process beginning in America. A real, although very gradual, realignment in the familial division of labor loosely coincided with this cultural redefinition of motherhood; and it occurred first among the same literate, commercial middle-class groups that provided the largest literary market. Whereas earlier mothers had often shared parental responsibilities with servants and fathers, by the late eighteenth century these other figures had begun to withdraw from the domestic scene. Fewer middle-class households contained servants than had earlier. Those who did become servants in the late eighteenth century, moreover, now usually came from much lower social and cultural backgrounds than their employers, a difference that undoubtedly contributed to the frequency of later warnings against their influence on children.[49] The structural change that altered parental roles the most, however, was the gradual physical removal of the father's place of work from the home, a process already under way in eighteenth-century America among tradesmen, craftsmen, manufacturers, and professionals (if not the majority of farmers), and one that in England was rapidly accelerating with the beginnings of industrialization. Fathers and their assistants who worked outside the domestic premises no longer had continuous contact with children. In the absence of these other parental figures, child-rearing responsibilities slowly became less diffused, more exclusively focused on mothers.[50]

Not only did mothers rear children more by themselves, but simultaneously — and for similar reasons — women became more exclusively preoccupied with their maternal roles. Although literature at the turn of the century still stressed the value of wives who were frugal "economisers," women were becoming less vitally engaged in economic production. Those whose husbands worked away from home could less directly assist their labor. And although the textile industry continued to provide work for some, usually unmarried, women in their homes, the decline of the domestic system of production was already under way in both England

and America by the early nineteenth century.[51] Home manufacturing for domestic use, while still a major activity of most women, was becoming a less demanding job in settled regions as more goods became available at affordable prices on the expanding commercial market. As women were relieved of much of their former economic role and at the same time left in primary care of children, motherhood understandably came to be a more salient feature of adult female life. Still another interrelated development, also associated with increased material comfort as well as some expansion of literacy, was the growth of a female, middle-class reading public in England and America.[52] These more leisured women provided a ready market for authors, many of whom themselves were women, who spoke to their special concerns as mothers.

As women came to be seen as the primary child rearers, motherhood often came to be viewed as a powerful vehicle through which women wielded broad social influence. Physicians and other writers delivering advice on childcare often pointed to the socially beneficial effects of good mothering, some even holding out the possibility of a wholesale "revolution" in human manners and morals.[53] As both Nancy Cott and Ann Douglas have recently observed, New England ministers who spoke to an increasingly female constituency in this period were especially taken with this vision of maternal moral influence permeating throughout society.[54] "Mothers do, in a sense, hold the reins of government and sway the ensigns of national prosperity and glory," the Reverend William Lyman typically glorified the role, "yea, they give direction to the moral sentiments of our rising hopes, and contribute to form their moral state."[55] This was, of course, a particularly compelling argument to those seeking to justify the restriction of women to the ever-narrowing domestic sphere. Characterizing the important responsibilities of motherhood, the minister Thomas Barnard, for example, took a direct swipe at Mary Wollstonecraft's feminist polemic, A *Vindication of the Rights of Woman:* "These are not the fancied, but the real 'Rights of Women.' They give them an extensive power over the fortunes of man in every generation."[56] Yet such argumentation, far from being confined to antifeminists, carried weight even with Wollstonecraft herself who, while insisting that women were capable of other achievements as well, also stressed that "the rearing of children — that is, the laying a *[sic]* foundation of sound health both of body and mind in the rising generation . . . [is] the peculiar destination of women."[57]

As motherhood was deemed a more demanding responsibility than it had been earlier, the complementary view arose that women, in particular, were eminently suited to rear children. Not only were they endowed with the physiology to bear and nurse babies, but, an increasing number of writers suggested, they also possessed the requisite mental qualities to take charge of the minds and morals of growing children. Challenging the traditionally vaunted moral, and often even intellectual, superiority of men, authors increasingly celebrated examples of female piety, learning, courage, and benevolence.[58] Women often came to be depicted not only as virtuous in themselves, but as more virtuous than men, indeed, as the main "conservators of morals" in society by means of their beneficial influence on both men and children.[59] Even New England clergymen regarded "the superior sensibility of females," their "better qualities" of tenderness, compassion, patience, and fortitude as inclining them more naturally toward Christianity than men.[60] In part, this exaltation of female piety came as an appreciative response to the ministers' increasingly female congregations, but it also reflected broad intellectual changes extending far beyond the New England churches, for during this period the qualities traditionally associated with women, particularly emotionalism, came to be more highly valued throughout Anglo-American culture. Not only religion, which became more revivalistic and softer in doctrine, but also sentimental and romantic literature, as well as other, less popular artistic and intellectual movements, all registered this shift. No longer grounds for disparagement, the supposedly natural susceptibility of women to "the heart" now became viewed as the foundation of their superior virtue.

In accord with this newly elevated characterization of female emotions, maternal fondness and tenderness toward children — behavior that had often provoked criticism from Puritan writers — now received highly sentimental acclaim. In *Pamela,* for example, when Richardson describes Mrs. B. disagreeing with a few points in Locke's *Thoughts on Education,* her objections arise from her own more gentle and indulgent approach to children. Around the turn of the century many authors presented tenderness as the primary component of good mothering, indeed, as the very quality most essential to the cultivation of morality in children.[61] In sentimental poetry carried by magazines — flowery verses bearing such titles as "A Mother's Address to a Dying Infant," "Sweet Infant," "Mother to Child" — this adulation of maternal love achieved its most maudlin expression.[62]

Although writers still warned against the tendency of mothers to spoil their children, they no longer relied so much on the father's corrective influence as on the mother's own ability to achieve self-control. At times authors even envisioned the tender mother softening the "too rough and severe Passions of the Father."[63] Although paternal tenderness, too, could give rise to sentimental praise, fathers often appeared as excessively harsh and authoritarian — in fiction, for example, frequently cast in the roles of arranging unhappy marriages for their children.[64] An anonymous volume on women published in Philadelphia in 1797 drew the following extravagant contrast between the feelings of fathers and mothers:

> Where are the tender feelings,, the cries, the powerful emotions of nature? Where is the sentiment, at once sublime and pathetic, that carries every feeling to excess? Is it to be found in the frosty indifference and the rigid severity, of so many fathers? No; it is in the warm impassioned bosom of the mother. . . .
>
> These great expressions of nature, these heartrending emotions, which fill us at once with wonder, compassion and terror, always have belonged, and always will belong only to women. They possess . . . an inexpressible something, which carries them beyond themselves. They seem to discover to us new souls, above the standard of humanity.[65]

Significantly, many writers of the period incorporated a sentimental conception of maternal feelings into more overtly feminist arguments for female intellectual equality.[66] Indeed, the conviction that women innately possessed the best physical, emotional, and moral qualifications for rearing children did not preclude a simultaneous commitment to more extensive female education among feminists and nonfeminists alike. With increasing frequency, in fact, motherhood itself was presented as a compelling reason for improved female education. Raised in opposition to "vain" and "frivolous" instruction in the genteel social ornaments, such as music and French, the argument that girls needed to be prepared for future maternal responsibilities carried a distinctively middle-class, anti-aristocratic, and utilitarian ring. As historian Linda Kerber has emphasized, this appeal had a special resonance in the newly republican United States, where motherhood offered an acceptable outlet for female talent and patriotism despite women's exclusion from politics.[67] Far from an essentially indigenous response to the Revolution, however, it was an argument that became popular among middle-class ideologues on both sides of the Atlantic. Moreover, while in the long run it generally supported conservative desires to keep women in the home, in this transitional period the maternal ideal often lent support to contradictory points of view on female education and social roles.

On the one hand, the ideal served to strengthen the Enlightenment feminist case for a more intellectually rigorous education for women.

According to this line of thought, women, too, possessed human reason and with an advanced education would not only better fulfill their human potential and perhaps even make valuable contributions outside the home; but they would, in addition, handle themselves more rationally as mothers and pass valuable knowledge on to their children.[68] On the other hand, however, the responsibilities of motherhood could support the case for a more serious, but also more specialized, domestic education for women. This was an implicit message of much of the accumulating body of medical and educational child-rearing literature addressed to mothers, which deplored women's ignorance about the practical details of rearing children. Most writers proposing systematic programs of female education did not recommend the actual study of childcare, but many did cite the influence of mothers as a primary reason to tailor curricula to domestic utility. Benjamin Rush, for example, in his *Thoughts upon Female Education,* held that knowledge of foreign languages and musical instruments had no real use even for affluent American women, who, unlike their British counterparts, were, as wives and mothers, vitally engaged in managing households and shaping the "manners and character" of the new republic. Their education should instead concentrate on handwriting, bookkeeping, "the more useful branches of literature," and, especially, Christianity.[69] This emphasis on religious instruction as essential preparation for female domestic responsibilities characterized the writings of various Christian apologists, including several English authors widely read in America around the turn of the century. Whereas Enlightenment feminists like Wollstonecraft argued that the development of female intellect best enabled women to become good mothers as well as the equals of men in other respects, these religious figures stressed the cultivation of female piety, as well as instruction in other "basics," to render women most capable as wives and mothers operating within an exclusively domestic context. Compared with more genteel writers, who also viewed female piety as a central component of true feminine refinement, these generally middle-class Protestants laid far greater stress on the practical domestic utility of female Christian virtue. Hannah More, for example, the famous English Evangelical author of cheap religious tracts, described the care of families as "the profession of ladies" comparable to the demanding professions of men. Decrying the idle vanity of female ornamentation and intellectual prowess, she advocated "a predominance of those more sober studies, which, not having display for their object . . . will not bring celebrity, but improve usefulness."[70] She warned adolescent girls that only religious women make desirable wives: "How can a man of any understanding, (whatever his own religious professions may be) trust that woman with the care of his family, and the education of his children, who wants herself the best incentive to a virtuous life?"[71]

It was this evangelical perspective on motherhood, with its stress on women's religiosity rather than reason and its emphasis on the importance of their exclusively domestic role, that reigned supreme in the Victorian period. Emerging out of this earlier time of flux, this view began to achieve predominance after the turn of the century, bolstered by an upsurge of religious revivalism and a conservative reaction, especially in the churches, against the radicalism of the French Revolution. Indeed, insofar as eighteenth-century feminism involved a non-Christian rationalism, it probably always appealed to a limited base.[72] The evangelical maternal ideal drew from a much more popular and indigenous Protestant tradition, one that began a resurgence in the early nineteenth century with the revivals and the organization of many voluntary "benevolent" associations. Even nonrevivalist "liberal" Protestants were infected with much of this evangelical spirit and similarly promoted this new maternal ideal.[73] The evangelical image of the moral mother triumphed in part because it presented a compelling synthesis of the old and the new. In certain respects it constituted an updated version of the older feminine ideal of help-meet, with its downplaying of female intellect and its emphasis on domestic usefulness and Christian virtue. It also incorporated key features of the ideal of ornamental refinement, particularly its sentimental conception of feminine purity. In other respects, however, the evangelical ideal of the moral mother sharply diverged from these earlier predecessors and conformed more closely to Enlightenment feminist conceptions of women. This is, of course, particularly true of their common elevation of the maternal role. Indeed, it is ironic that influential evangelical polemicists sought to discredit feminism by characterizing it not only as anti-Christian, promiscuous, and vain, but as anti-motherhood as well.[74] For although Enlightenment feminists and evangelical Protestants might disagree about how mothering stood in relation to other female intellectual, economic, domestic, and religious pursuits, they generally agreed about the imperative natural calling, the serious educational requirements, and the extensive social utility of motherhood.

In the long run, the rise of the moral mother, even in its more conservative evangelical version, had ambiguous effects on the status of women. On the one hand, it provided both ideological justification and incentive for the contraction of female activity into the preoccupations of motherhood. The newfound emphasis on the maternal role became an integral part of the rigid sexual differentiation that became so characteristic of nineteenth-century, middle-class Protestant culture. Women came to be perceived as, essentially, "moral mothers," not only in relation to their children, but also in their other major supportive and didactic roles as teachers, charity workers, and sentimental writers. Moreover, the personality traits stereotypically associated with these nineteeenth-century women — the emotionalism, selflessness, and empathy that characteristically contrasted with male rationalism, competitiveness, and individualism — may well have been reinforced by the psychological repercussions of such intensively maternal nurture. For, as psychoanalytic sociologists have suggested, when mothers rear children virtually alone, the psychological responses of the sexes widely diverge: girls become more interdependent and expressive, and boys tend to become more independent and emotionally self-contained.[75] Through this cycle of mutual reinforcement, then, the social, cultural, and psychological impact of the elevation of the maternal role limited the range of acceptable female pursuits and helped to generate highly distinctive and restrictive feminine and masculine styles.

On the other hand, however, the rise of the moral mother also played its part in the long-range upgrading of the social status of women. The abortive rationalist feminism of the late eighteenth century may be more to the taste of contemporary women, but the evangelical ideal of motherhood also broke with tradition by attributing to women strong moral authority and granting them an important field of special expertise. It entitled them to considerable autonomy within what came to be defined as the "woman's sphere," and it even helped to create both the legitimacy and the solidarity necessary for later, more successful, feminist agitation.[76]

CHAPTER 4

Women and the Law of Courtship in Eighteenth-Century America

PREFACE This previously unpublished essay underscores the power of the law in early Anglo-America by turning to the history of legislative and judicial actions. While less rooted in intellectual history than the other pieces contained in this collection, it nonetheless similarly focuses on cultural preconceptions of family and gender relations to account for a transformation in the legal regulation of courtship. The essay traces these changes from the late seventeenth through the eighteenth centuries, concentrating on distinctive attributes of American colonial law as compared to the law of England. In its institutional orientation toward legislatures and courts, it serves as a counterweight to the more abstract and individual concerns of the next essay, on Jonathan Edwards and Benjamin Franklin. Taken together, however, these two essays constitute complementary studies of the same underlying historical process: the gradual and uneven ascendancy of sentimental conceptions of women and of marital love in eighteenth-century Anglo-American culture.

. . .

Developing in the interstices between the history of the family and the history of government, changes in the legal regulation of courtship in colonial British America shifted the relationship between public and private life. Most strikingly, mid-seventeenth-century procedures that were required to legitimate marriages gave way in the eighteenth to simpler declarations of mutual consent between man and wife. A decline in the efforts of colonial legislatures to pass laws designed to control marriage thus enabled individuals, at least on a superficial level, to exercise more choice in marriage. On another, less clearly visible level, changes in the law of courtship took place within legal institutions themselves, marking an important shift from criminal to civil law and from legislative to judicial policy-making. While partly encouraging the privatization of marriage and contributing to the scope of individual freedoms, this increasing reliance on the common law also propelled another branch of government to step into the breach of regulating courtship. What changed, then, was not the involvement of the law in defining sexual morality so much as the shape of such law. The shift towards the common law needs to be seen as a new type of government intervention, one that largely replaced the legislative with the judicial. These changes in jurisdiction lifted the heavy hand of statutory regulation but at the same time tightened the grip of the courts. On yet a third, still deeper level, this movement from statutory to judicial rulings on matters of courtship reflected an underlying transformation of cultural values, one associated with a widespread redefinition of the meanings of gender and marriage. What from one perspective may look like the rise of personal freedom looks from another like the reinstitutionalization of moral codes. Changes in accepted sexual morality and assumptions about gender differences found expression in the new formations of American laws of courtship in the eighteenth century.

In the seventeenth century, many of the American colonies imposed strict laws regulating marriage, which went beyond English tradition. Ecclesiastical courts run by the Church of England were never instituted in the New World, whether by design (as in Puritan New England and Quaker Pennsylvania) or more by neglect (as in officially Anglican Virginia). In their absence, the secular colonial assemblies and courts took on the task of defining laws to govern marriage and extramarital sexual morality. Passing a series of restrictive measures, American colonial legislatures sought to devise a clearer and more enforceable system than that of England, where a confusing mix of medieval religious precedent and recent civil rulings divided responsibilities and impeded enforcement.[1]

The thrust of these early colonial laws was to bolster the authority of parents, particularly fathers, in lieu of the traditional ecclesiastical governance of domestic life.[2] In early New England, Puritans refused to accord marriage a sacramental status, and weddings were performed by magistrates. As is well known, matters of sexual behavior and family life were of intense concern to civil authorities from the earliest years of colonial settlement. In the seventeenth century all the early New England colonies enacted legislation specifying the conditions and procedures of marriage.[3] What is less widely recognized is that even outside New England, most early American colonies implemented similarly restrictive laws about courtship and marriage in the first decades of settlement. New York, New Jersey, and Pennsylvania acted shortly after their founding. Prior to New York falling to British rule, New Netherlands had transported legal customs from Holland, which required the father's consent not only for first marriages of both sons and daughters (or the mother's if the father were dead), but even for second marriages of daughters if they were still under age.[4] New Jersey passed laws requiring the consent of parents or guardians in 1668 and 1682; Pennsylvania enacted a series of laws against clandestine marriage beginning in 1676.[5] Virginia passed a similar law in 1632, but it was only gradually — in subsequent revisions of 1646 and 1661–1662, and then, finally, in a 1696 "act for the prevention of clandestine marriages" — that significant penalties were imposed.[6] By the end of the century almost all of the early colonies had passed statutes that at once prohibited fornication, adultery, sodomy, and other instances of illicit sex and defined legal marriage in ways that insisted upon the parents' or master's consent, the posting of banns, and a public ceremony.

In England, by comparison, despite brief efforts during the Interregnum, it was only in 1753 that Lord Hardwicke's Marriage Act brought greater clarity and discipline to English marriage law. The principles underlying this legal reform were debated for decades, and similar bills aiming to prohibit clandestine marriages had been proposed to Parliament in 1718 and 1735. According to the act's basic provisions, the English state now required church weddings, parental consent for those under twenty-one, and the registration of marriage. The sacramental status of church weddings was ended, for if a marriage performed by a clergyman failed to conform to these additional procedures it would nonetheless be nullified and the children deemed illegitimate. Interestingly, most of the provisions of the Hardwicke Act of 1753 had in the seventeenth century already been written into colonial statute law. Further illustrating a gap between the colonies and mother country, the English act was clearly designed to protect noble families and to discipline profiteering clergymen, targeted groups that were never of particular concern to the early colonial legislatures.[7]

Several early New England laws went still farther, requiring a male suitor to secure the consent of the father or master even prior to initiating a courtship. According to the reasoning explained in these laws, this preemptive intervention was necessary in order that men not "enveagle" or "draw away the affections of young maidens, under pretense of purpose of marriage."[8] In New Haven, the law specified the various strategies a wily illicit suitor could employ, including "speech, writing, message, company-keeping, unnecessary familiarity, disorderly night meetings, sinful dalliance, gifts, or any other way, directly or indirectly."[9] This language is strikingly similar to that of the English Abduction Law of 1558, which imposed stiff penalties on persons who "by Flattery, trifling Gifts and fair Promises" secretly induced the agreement of would-be heiresses to marry without securing proper permission of parents or guardians.[10] While building upon this precedent of English civil law, however, New Englanders vastly expanded its purpose. The English law had been formulated to deny the abductor's claims to property as a result of the unapproved marriage of a minor; it was meant essentially to curb mercenary marriages to young heirs and heiresses. The only American colony that closely followed this precedent was Virginia, where in 1696 a law prohibiting clandestine marriage exacted a penalty similar to the one in England, depriving a woman who secretly married between the ages of twelve and sixteen of her inheritance during the lifetime of her husband.[11] The earlier New England laws, to the contrary, remained mute on the questions of property and age. Instead, they stressed the undoubtedly more widely experienced conflict between unregulated attraction and parental control.[12] What in England, and later Virginia, was designed to protect inherited property was, in effect, transformed in New England into the protection of parental rights to channel the emotional attachments of children.

Early colonial American laws of courtship sanctioned parental control in still another way that extended beyond the provisions of the later Hardwicke Act. Whereas the 1753 English law explicitly defined the age of twenty-one as the time when parental jurisdiction ended, thereby following the precedent of ecclesiastical law going back to 1603, the colonial American laws rarely specified any such age limit and thereby opened the way to a further expansion of parental supervision.[13] The only significant seventeenth-century exception was Virginia, where, apparently in keeping with the guidelines of the canon law, twenty-one was designated as the age limit already in 1632.[14] New Jersey followed suit in 1719.[15] Later, in the middle and late eighteenth century, Pennsylvania and Massachusetts also added specific age limits to their earlier laws on parental consent.[16] Virtually all of the seventeenth-century laws, however, ignored the question of age. This absence was consistent with English and American civil law of this period, in which no single "age of consent" to contracts had yet been defined.[17] Instead, it appears that most of the early colonial laws requiring parental consent were meant to apply to children regardless of age, as long as they were living with or dependent upon their parents or masters. Rather than specifying a precise age of consent, some of the early New England statutes referred to children as "under the covert of parents" or as under parental "care and government."[18] A later Pennsylvania law of 1730 similarly stated that consent was necessary for those either under twenty-one, "under the tuition of their parents, or be indented [sic] servants," insisting that dependent children or servants older than twenty-one needed permission in the same way as minors.[19] As late as 1784 a Connecticut law required a magistrate or minister to have a certificate of consent to the marriage "of such parties that are under the control of parents or guardians," again with no mention of age.[20] To be sure, by the middle of the eighteenth century this wording implied greater freedom for independent children under twenty-one, just as it did greater constraints for dependent ones who were older. In the early years of settlement, however, the majority of unmarried young people, particularly women, were living in the household of a parent or master, and the average age of marriage was well over twenty-one. The legal language specifying the condition of dependency rather than a set age, therefore, broadened the authority of colonial parents over children whom we would today consider adults.

Although the seventeenth-century colonies took these various steps to increase parental control over courtship, only rarely did they go so far as to invalidate irregular marriages. Punishments more commonly ran the gamut from fines to public humiliation, physical punishment, and imprisonment. On the one hand, these American sanctions exceeded those commonly applied by contemporary English ecclesiastical courts (penance and excommunication), but on the other hand they usually fell short of the 1754 English Marriage Act, which later nullified informal marriages and rendered the offspring illegitimate. Those few seventeenth-century colonies that passed these more extreme measures included Rhode Island, which passed a 1647 statute holding that the children of marriages formed contrary to the specified procedure would not be regarded as a "legitimate or lawfullie begotten."[21] The Dutch in New Amsterdam similarly declared that children of clandestine marriage would be illegitimate, and later, the Duke of York's Code during the

Restoration briefly extended this rule of illegitimacy from New York into Delaware, Pennsylvania, and New Jersey between 1676 and 1684.[22] A Virginia law of 1661–1662, which remained on the books until 1696, likewise specified that any "pretended" marriage made by someone other than a clergyman would be null and void and the children illegitimate.[23]

Yet, even in these few colonies, as in England after the later Marriage Act, it is not clear that the technical invalidation of clandestine marriage proved a more effective deterrent than the more moderate punishments used by the other colonies.[24] Instances of "common law" marriage appear in numerous legal cases as well as in descriptive accounts of colonial life. Under the pressure of continuous violations, the colonies that had passed nullification laws uniformly backed down. Rhode Island in 1665 granted amnesty to couples who were "reputed to live together as man and wife by the common observation or account of there [sic] neighbors before this act [of 1647] was passed," declaring their children to be legitimate.[25] Another Rhode Island law in 1698 compromised still further, waiving its prior invalidation of unregistered marriages, judging illegitimacy as too harsh a penalty as long as other normal procedures of marriage besides registration had been followed.[26] Similarly watering down its earlier tough stance, the Virginia assembly in 1696 stiffened the financial penalties upon irregular marriages but in essence admitted defeat by recognizing their validity.[27] In the middle colonies, there is no evidence that the short-lived Duke of York's laws were ever enforced.[28] American colonists quite quickly realized that the supposedly ultimate punishment of nullification was not in itself sufficient to eradicate informal marriage. This was a lesson that the English later learned as well, when the similar failure of the Hardwicke Act led to the more flexible provisions of the 1834 Marriage Bill.[29] What is especially striking about the American case is that most of the colonies never even made the attempt to nullify irregular marriages despite the relative strictness of their other marriage laws.

Perhaps they hesitated for practical reasons, perceiving from the outset that nullification would never work to prevent future illegitimate unions. More likely, the notion of lawmakers creating by statute a new category of lawless families, even temporarily, undercut the more pressing need to instill colonial social order. Instead of opening themselves to the risk of common illegitimacy by raising the bar too high, they declared the illegality of certain marriage procedures, punishing them when possible with fines and, at times, physical punishments, without invalidating the marriages themselves. Irregular marriages existed whatever the rules of courtship, and while enforcement varied considerably in the American colonies, couples living together with children usually gained acceptance as legitimately married and therefore subject to family law.

The fundamental legitimacy of informal marriage in America echoed pre-1754 English ecclesiastical law, but the seventeenth-century colonies otherwise imposed legal restrictions that exceeded those of the mother country. Sanctions against violations of procedural rules were administered by civil authorities rather than by ecclesiastical courts, the punishments targeted the offending couples more than officiating clergymen, and the concrete penalties tended to wield greater clout than the threat of excommunication in England. The early Massachusetts and Connecticut laws that called for parental intervention at the earliest stage of courtship reflect this distinctively American legal context. Compared to their English counterparts, New England parents wielded augmented power over their unmarried children. This concentration upon courtship undoubtedly stemmed from the fact that once a young couple married without parental approval, however illegally, it was impossible for the parents to invalidate the marriage.

Unfortunately, it is impossible to calculate with any precision either the rate of irregular marriage or even, as yet, the rate at which such cases appeared in colonial courts. Available legal records and descriptive accounts do, however, strongly suggest a historical pattern. The early colonies, especially in New England, enforced the marriage laws more rigorously than later on, and the more established and densely populated regions did so more than the weakly administered areas closer to the frontier. Since the geographical expansion of settlement grew more rapidly in the eighteenth than the seventeenth century, variations by time and space reinforce one another. New England in the mid-seventeenth century occupies one end of the spectrum, the southwestern region of the colonies in the mid-eighteenth century the other.

While usually stopping short of invalidation, early New England authorities went to considerable lengths to reduce irregular marriage. Legal records disclose numerous examples of seventeenth-century couples in Massachusetts being fined between five and twenty pounds for the crime of "disorderly marriage."[30] The most notorious case was that of Richard Bellingham, the Governor of Massachusetts Bay, who in 1641, at age forty-nine and only recently widowed, scandalized public opinion by secretly marrying twenty-two-year-old Penelope Pelham, who was herself already "forming a contract with another." It was apparently her prior engagement that prevented Bellingham from securing the necessary permission. Although he was brought to trial before the General Court, his position on the bench as Governor gave him immunity from prosecution, much to the consternation of his moralistic rival, John Winthrop. Benefiting from a legal technicality due to his exalted status, Bellingham is the exception that proves the rule. The financial penalties periodically imposed on ordinary couples who violated the law did not undo their irregular marriages, but such cases reveal the determination of the New England authorities to set a negative example for others. Even the unsuccessful prosecution of Bellingham had the same purpose. Indeed, Winthrop's very objection to his behavior underscores the apparently widespread acceptance of the restrictive marriage law among the mid-seventeenth century Massachusetts Bay population: "He married himself contrary to the constant practice of the country."[31] Most of the cases that came to court in New England did not involve irregular marriages but unapproved courtships and proposals. These relationships were still at an early enough stage for the civil authorities to prohibit them. Punishments levied upon the suitor for persevering with the illegal courtship ranged from fines to imprisonment.[32] Occasionally, early New England authorities also intervened on behalf of couples to question parents or masters about their possibly unreasonable opposition to a courtship.[33]

In addition to enforcing laws about legal marriage, seventeenth-century New England colonies also punished fornication more consistently and severely than their English counterparts. These two types of infractions were closely related, often involving the same offenders, since irregular courtship and marriage almost always included sexual relations. At times the line separating these various types of cases blurred. In 1642, for example, a couple in New Haven was allowed to marry without furnishing legal proof of their parents' consent, both because they credibly claimed to have previously received it and because they had already "sinfully and wickedly made themselves unfit for any other."[34] Indeed, as Roger Thompson noted in his study of sexual relations in Middlesex, Massachusetts, it is likely that premarital sexual behavior usually occurred within a context of at least nominal intentions to wed.[35] Sexual relations were not supposed to occur during courtship, but the many instances of premarital pregnancies point to a different reality. With the possibility of pregnancy always looming large, sexual intercourse on the part of single women always risked exposure to public view and the application of intense pressure to marry from families, churches, and communities. For errant couples unwilling or unable to conform to the normal betrothal procedures, the law could even impose a kind of double jeopardy. Courts that indicted couples for clandestine marriage could add additional penalties for fornication. In 1665 the Rhode Island General Assembly supplemented its 1647 law invalidating clandestine marriages with the additional provision that such unions would also be punished as fornication, repeatedly, until the couple separated or married legally.[36]

Historians have paid more attention to the prosecution of fornication than to actions against irregular marriage — probably both because of the larger number of cases and because fornication more directly involves illicit sexuality, a topic of lively historical interest.[37] When compared to the evidence on marriage regulation, studies of fornication reveal, not surprisingly, that the histories of these two different types of moral transgression were closely intertwined. In England, where fornication fell under the jurisdiction of ecclesiastical courts and where sexual intercourse during the period of betrothal before marriage was largely condoned, prosecution had long since been limited.[38] In seventeenth-century New England, to the contrary, there are numerous instances of both married and unmarried couples being humiliated, whipped, and fined. As Cornelia Dayton highlights in the case of Connecticut, seventeenth-century Puritans tended to charge men, as well as women bearing illegitimate children, with the crime of fornication. As with the passage of legislation prohibiting irregular courtship and marriage, the relatively vigilant prosecution of fornication and bastardy in the seventeenth century reveals the significant efforts of early colonial leaders to tighten control over sexual relations.[39]

The close link between the colonies' attempts to curb fornication and their efforts to regulate marriage is best seen in instances where courts forced fornicating couples to marry. In America the ability to compel marriage fell under the jurisdiction of secular government, which possessed far greater coercive powers than English ecclesiastical courts. Laws against fornication in mid-seventeenth-century Massachusetts, Connecticut, and New York specifically provided for the punishment of "enjoining" marriage in addition to fines and corporal punishment.[40] The evidence from colonial court records suggests that such laws were enforced for several decades; even in Maryland, where no such statute was passed, courts in the 1650s used strong sanctions to encourage couples having sexual relations to marry.[41] This radical intervention by the law to impose matrimony upon fornicators reveals the seriousness with which governments in several colonies took their responsibility to regulate sexuality and marriage.

How well the enforcement of rules against fornication worked in practice is, of course, another issue, just as it is for the prohibition against common law marriage. If the goal was to eliminate extramarital sexuality, the effort clearly failed.[42] Yet seventeenth-century New Englanders almost certainly adhered to a stricter standard of sexual morality than either English men and women of the time or their own eighteenth-century descendants.[43] Seventeenth-century colonies to the south of New England surely enforced laws against irregular marriage and fornication less rigorously than the Puritans. The Dutch in New Netherlands punished several offenders in the 1650s, but after the English colonized New York apparently no more cases came to court.[44] Although an occasional effort to prosecute can be found in Pennsylvania and New Jersey, the enforcement of the marriage law there also seems to have been comparatively weak.[45] In Pennsylvania in 1730, the tightening of the law requiring the consent of a "parent, guardian, master, or mistress" seems to have been aimed largely at the growing numbers of indentured servants.[46] In one such case in Chester County, a servant named Barry McQuaid, who married without his master's permission, was required to serve an additional two years.[47]

In the Chesapeake area, the requirement of a church wedding proved especially burdensome, since there was a chronic shortage of ministers. In the early decades of colonization, the constant influx of young, single immigrants made the rules about parental consent nearly meaningless. Laws regulating courtship and premarital sex principally targeted servants, who were supposed to remain single and abstinent during the period of their indenture. The early legal records of Virginia are liberally sprinkled with cases combining fornication and bastardy, for the most part involving couples in servitude.[48] A sampling of cases in the Maryland archives of the 1650s similarly reveals several cases of irregular marriage, indicating that it must have been frequent.[49] Despite all these efforts to uphold the law, the early Chesapeake colonies were clearly beset with problems of bastardy and secret marriage.[50] Compared to Virginia, Maryland was known for its more relaxed rules about marriage already in the seventeenth century. Only in the rare instances when parents survived and property was at stake did parental consent appear to be necessary.[51] In 1705 the Virginia House of Burgesses even saw fit to impose a special fine on clergymen who crossed the border to marry couples who could not satisfy the requirements of Virginia law.[52] Somewhat later in North Carolina, consensual unions also seem to have been common despite laws empowering civil magistrates to perform marriages in parishes without clergymen. In several cases at the turn of the century, prior to the passage of a 1715 statute imposing separate penalties for fornication, the North Carolina General Court imposed fines upon "disorderly cohabiting" couples if they did not legally marry.[53]

Bastardy rates surely went down throughout the South after the shift from a white to a black slave labor force — if only because the category of bastard could not be applied to slaves, for whom there was no legal marriage. Anti-miscegenation laws also gave slave marriage an increasingly racial definition. Among whites, however, cases of irregular marriage seem to have become even more common in the eighteenth century. In Maryland, the Rev. Henry Addison estimated in 1786 that nine-tenths of the children in his parish were the products of irregular marriages.[54] Among the Scotch-Irish in the Shenandoah Valley to the west, irregular marriages appear to have been still more prevalent. The horrified Anglican minister Charles Woodmason reported that scarcely any unions had been sanctified.[55] Farther south, in the Carolinas, the situation was no better. Commenting in 1728 on the paucity of clergy in North Carolina, William Byrd wryly observed that magistrates and justices of the peace were available only to marry "those who will not take one another's Word."[56]

In the eighteenth century, however, despite indications that the problem had grown, it becomes more difficult to find examples of common-law marriages being challenged anywhere in the colonies.[57] Although there is little positive evidence of colonial courts explicitly upholding informal consensual unions, the movement of legal opinion seems to have gone in the direction of greater permissiveness. In 1739 a Maryland court recognized a common-law marriage as valid so long as both partners were white.[58] Similarly, the Massachusetts Superior Court ruled in two separate cases in 1765 that undocumented marriage was legitimate. In one opinion by Chief Justice and later Loyalist Thomas Hutchinson, the court explicitly cited English ecclesiastical law in defense of marriage "by Cohabitation of the Parties; by publick Fame and Report; by Confession of the married Persons themselves."[59] Significantly, the citation of precedents by Hutchinson altogether ignored the recent change in England under the Hardwicke Act that nullified clandestine marriages.

Indeed, by the time Hutchinson wrote, marriage law in England looked more like the restrictive colonial American law of the seventeenth century. The colonies had forged a different path, one leading towards greater, not lesser, acceptance of irregular marriages. In an essay written in 1773 on the theme of religious liberty, a New York Presbyterian minister reported that marriages were considered valid in America whether or not they were officiated by clergymen or otherwise conformed to the law. Objecting to various expansionist efforts of the Church of England, he noted with satisfaction that "English statutes" on marriage did not apply to the colony and that attempts by the Episcopalians in the 1740s to "monopolize this business [of marriage]" had failed. A husband and wife's "contract in words," verified by witnesses and sealed by cohabitation, sufficed.[60] An interesting, if idiosyncratic, post-revolutionary effort of Thomas Jefferson and other prominent Virginians to prohibit marriages without parental consent for those under age 21 went as far as a "second reading" in the new state legislature in 1785 but never was passed.[61] In 1789 Virginia did, however, extend its 1696 abduction statute, punishing men who took women under the age of 16 without their father's consent and those who abducted older women without the consent of the women themselves.[62] By the time Justice Kent of New York wrote his definitive opinion of 1809 recognizing the validity of common-law marriages, they had been receiving de facto legitimation for generations.[63]

Other changes in the substance and application of the law in the eighteenth century also point to significantly decreased restrictions upon marriage. The requirement of gaining parental consent seems, in particular, to have been taken progressively less seriously. In Pennsylvania, for example, where the marriage law underwent numerous revisions in the late seventeenth century, the wording of legislative acts became less and less insistent. Whereas before 1693 parental consent was an absolute requirement, afterward it was called for only if it was "possible" or "convenient" to get it.[64] Increasingly, in New England and elsewhere, cases of irregularity merely involved weddings performed by clergymen in the absence of a license or other requirement. Whereas in the seventeenth century couples who married without consent were punished directly, by the early eighteenth century the fines were typically levied only against the ministers who married them.[65] In an unusual case in New Jersey in 1700 the widow Elizabeth Basnett lost her tavern license and was fined 20 pounds for "permitting and countenancing in her house an illegal and clandestine marriage" and for providing the bed. Once again, there is no record of the couple itself suffering punishment.[66] Much of the evidence of the widespread violation of marriage laws in the colonial South comes from frustrated Anglican clergymen seeking to shock their English superiors into supplying more ministers.[67] Regardless of whether they were unwilling or unable to conform to the letter of the law, couples who failed to satisfy the requirements of parental consent, church weddings, or licenses were increasing free to marry in the eighteenth century.

It is similarly well known that the prosecution of fornication declined between the late seventeenth and mid eighteenth centuries. Modern studies of New England concur that the accusations of men fell to almost nothing between the early and middle eighteenth century and of women as well by about 1780.[68] Beginning already in the late seventeenth century, New England laws stopped mandating court-ordered marriage in cases of fornication.[69] Instead of the father of an illegitimate child being prosecuted for fornication and charged with a crime, he would be sued by the mother or by her father for the baby's support.

In the face of this evidence that irregular marriage and fornication were less prosecuted over time in colonial America, it is tempting to conclude that rules governing courtship and marriage formation simply grew progressively lax. Some regulatory statutes passed by seventeenth-century legislatures indeed withered. Other laws, however, that were derived instead from the English common law, gained significant new life. Americans appear, in particular, to have made early and continuous use of common-law suits for seduction and breach of promise.[70] These actions were designed not to limit the grounds of marriage — the major thrust of the early colonial statutes — but to redress damages inflicted during false or unsuccessful courtships.

Under the complex English legal system, the enactment of statutory laws never precluded the simultaneous use of the common law for other purposes. Because virtually all historians studying colonial laws on sexuality have focused on criminal actions, especially fornication and rape, no one has given civil suits for seduction and breach of promise the attention they deserve.[71] This is despite the fact that colonial courts themselves often failed to make clear distinctions between types of cases, and charges of seduction and breach of promise were often folded inside actions against fornication, bastardy, slander, or rape. Notwithstanding the efforts of English courts to provide technical guidelines for such suits, in America they took significantly different forms.[72]

To begin with, courts heard complaints about breach of promise and seduction without insisting that they be based on claims of property loss or loss of services.[73] Whereas in seventeenth-century England such actions at common law seem to have been the narrow preserve of an elite claiming significant financial damages, in the colonies quite ordinary people brought such suits when they felt the circumstances warranted them. Issues of personal respect and reputation, not property, predominated. Moreover, complaints about breach of promise did not need to be backed by written evidence, the condition stipulated by Blackstone.[74] Colonial courts appear to have been open to hearing these kinds of complaints about failed and fraudulent courtships even when they were based on relatively inconclusive evidence.

Examples include the following cases from New England, Pennsylvania, and Maryland. In 1661 Mary Linfield of Cambridge, Massachusetts brought John Whitticus to court for having "promised mariage [sic] before sundry witness & afterwards refused the same."[75] The court ruled that there was "just reason" for John to pay Mary recompense from his estate in the order of 50 to 100 pounds, for John had behaved with "much unfaythfullness & fraud" in gaining "her affections towards him." There is no indication in the record that Mary was pregnant, or even that the pair had engaged in sexual intercourse; the breach of promise was sufficient cause for action. The case of John Ball against Michael Bacon tried in Cambridge in 1671 more closely approximated a seduction suit. According to the contrite testimony of John's daughter Mary, Bacon had abused his authority as her master and led her by "temptation" into "abominable sin."[76] Compounding his guilt, Bacon had taken the pregnant Mary out of town on a ferry and then to seclusion in Rhode Island. John Ball pressed charges against Bacon partly to secure payment for costs that Mary had incurred for room and board, and partly to compensate him "for carrying Mary his daughter out of the jurisdiction without his order." The father did not, however, sue for the loss of his daughter's labor, the technical basis of formal suits for seduction. Instead Ball's complaint mixed together features of seduction and abduction, both of which were actions within English common law. A similar Massachusetts case brought by the father of Martha Beale in Charlestown likewise fits into no clear legal category, simultaneously involving accusations of rape, seduction, and breach of promise. Like Mary Ball, Martha was a servant, and she claimed to have been raped and then promised marriage by John Row, the son of her master. No pregnancy had occurred. John claimed he had promised marriage only upon the condition of pregnancy, and only under the compulsion of his father, Martha's master, to whom she had directly confided. The court in response ordered Row either to marry Beale or to pay her father a penalty. After negotiating a compromise over the amount of money owed, he paid.[77]

In 1685, the same year as Beale's complaint against Row, a Pennsylvania case, also combining several actions, was similarly decided in the woman's favor. Apparently Bridgett Cock had extracted a promise of marriage from John Rambo on the condition that she have sex with him. After becoming pregnant, Bridgett and her father Peter began the legal proceedings by charging breach of promise. As in Massachusetts, the Pennsylvania court enjoined the couple either to marry or to pay a fee, only in this case the money was to be paid by both Bridgett and John to the court. John, in addition, was charged with support of the child. After the child was born and John ignored the ruling, Bridgett went to court again, this time without her father. John claimed never to have promised marriage and even alleged that he was willing to raise the baby, but Bridgett prevailed and apparently collected 150 pounds in damages.[78]

In sharp contrast to nineteenth-century cases, men as well as women charged breach of promise. In Maryland in1657, Robert Harwood claimed the right to marry Elizabeth Gary on the grounds of her verbal agreement. Evidently Robert Harwood began courting Elizabeth Gary without her mother's permission in 1654 (she was then around 21). Her mother had then been a single widow, but she remarried to Peter Sharpe sometime between 1654 and 1657. Elizabeth claimed in court that Robert had followed her in the spring of 1656 into the garden and "forced me to yeild [sic] to lye with him," and that he then insisted that she had no choice but to marry him. She said that he told her that he had raped her because "he had no other way, to keep me but by that in lying with me."[79] Yet her friend Sarah Benson testified that the previous August Elizabeth had told her both that her mother was preventing the marriage and that Elizabeth herself "would not any other man for her husband, and that She was very Capable of what She did [meaning, one gathers, that she didn't regret the sexual intercourse and did it voluntarily]."[80] It is not clear from this record whose statements, if any, were truthful. Robert Harwood himself claimed that Elizabeth had promised to marry him "upon a Mutual declared affection."[81] The marriage was, in any case, blocked, either by Elizabeth's second thoughts or by her disapproving parents, and Robert proceeded to publicly slander Elizabeth and her family. Then Peter Sharpe, Elizabeth's stepfather, sued for reparations.[82]

In the end, no damages for either slander or breach of promise were collected. Robert Harwood, however, clearly expected the court to consider the admissibility of his claim, and the justices took his argument seriously enough to arrange that Elizabeth be given another chance to marry him. Instead of fining Elizabeth or her parents for breach of promise — or punishing Robert for slander — the court intervened in this courtship in a still more extreme manner. In a complicated compromise arrangement, Elizabeth Gary was sent to live in the home of a neutral third party for several weeks. There, Robert would be allowed to court her under the supervision of chaperones, and she would have the freedom to decide about marrying him without undue pressure from either him or her parents. This remarkable and creative solution shows not only the credence of the claim of breach of promise but the extraordinary lengths to which an early Maryland court would go to regulate the practice of courtship.

Although Robert Harwood's action shows that men in the seventeenth-century colonies could present themselves as victims of breach of promise, the crime of seduction was from the outset defined specifically as male. Unlike breech of promise, it always involved sexual intercourse, and in certain respects can be understood as a lesser version of rape.[83] Indeed, one reason for the appearance of seduction was the severity of the penalty for rape, which was, in several colonies, death. Rape was, moreover, then and now, difficult to prove. Understandably, women and their families hesitated to launch formal accusations of a capital crime without airtight evidence, and, as in the case of John Row and Martha Beale, settled on the less serious actions of seduction or breach of promise instead.

Whereas in England common law suits for seduction and breach of promise were mainly employed by the nobility, becoming more popular middle-class actions only in the late eighteenth century, in America they had a continuous history among people of common status going back to the seventeenth century.[84] The criminal prosecution of fornication and irregular marriage declined over time in the colonies, illustrating both the difficulty of enforcing the stringent statues passed in the seventeenth century and the growing acceptance of consensual unions that failed to conform to prescribed procedures such as parental consent and a public ceremony. Yet to conclude from this evidence that the state had withdrawn from the regulation of courtship and marriage would be to ignore the civil side of the law.

Actions against seduction and breach of promise remained a part of American law through the eighteenth century and beyond, emanating not from legislative acts but from developments in the common law. Colonial cases are less well known than post-Revolutionary ones for essentially two reasons: first, the colonial cases typically fused with other charges, like fornication, trespass, and rape; second, it was only after the Revolution that legal authorities codified and compiled United States appellate decisions as precedents for American national law and made

them easily accessible to historians. As in the case of England, the scholarship on such cases has concentrated on the nineteenth century.[85]

Cases involving accusations of seduction and breach of promise were
brought to colonial courts already in the mid seventeenth century and
continued to be litigated into the nineteenth century. These charges were
heard even when the evidence failed to conform to the technical conditions of British civil law. The illegitimate mother Margaret Flin of
Chester County, Pennsylvania, for example, in 1731 testified in the context of a bastardy charge against her former lover Christopher Gore,
claiming that he had "through fair promises of marriage over Came her
and had then and there Carnal Knowledge of her body."[86] How much
the issue of breach of promise figured into Gore's fine of 80 pounds is
uncertain, but Margaret was clearly using this evidence to plead extenu-
ating circumstances to her own guilt. In Massachusetts a similar case
involving fornication, bastardy, and breach of promise was heard by the
Inferior Court of Common Pleas at Concord in 1730 and then appealed
to the Superior Court of Judicature in Charlestown the following year.
The plaintiff, spinster Susanna Holding of Watertown, filed a suit against
Joseph Bright, yeoman and father of her illegitimate child, for the large
sum of 500 pounds on the grounds that he had "ruined her Reputation
and Fortunes."[87] Bright plead that her evidence of his promise to marry
her was inadequate, since "the Facts alledged were private." Holding
responded by mobilizing townsmen as witnesses, who swore they
thought Bright had, "in his courting of her . . . designed to make her his
Wife."[88] The record contains no conclusion to the case, but the higher
court definitely heard Susanna Holding's appeal despite the lack of a
written promise by Bright.[89]

In Virginia in 1784 a case resembling a seduction suit, mixing together
abduction and rape, was presented by legislative petition of the woman's
father. He argued, unsuccessfully, that the marriage of twelve-year-old
Susannah Brown to Peter Hopwood, her former tutor, had been forced,
and that she should be permitted to testify against her husband during his
trial and accuse him of having raped her prior to the marriage.[90] Later,
Hopwood was again brought to trial for the lesser crime of abduction.
Although this request was denied, the Virginia legislature in 1789 and
1792 reaffirmed and strengthened its colonial abduction statute of 1696,
calling for both the imprisonment and the disinheritance of a man who
"deflowered" or contracted matrimony with a woman under age without her father's permission.[91] The early American acceptance of suits for
seduction and breach of promise is, in addition, indicated by the appear-

ance of a precedent-setting seduction and breach-of-promise case in the New Jersey Supreme Court already in 1791, immediately after the Revolution.[92] Compared to the cases in the earlier period, late-eighteenth- and early-nineteenth-century courts no longer mixed together civil and criminal charges, the difference between seduction and breach of promise received closer attention, and evidential requirements gained more emphasis.

As the law applied itself increasingly to sorting out these technical distinctions, it also made greater gender distinctions in judgments of men and women. To suggest that suits for seduction and breach of promise had a continuous history in colonial America is not, then, to claim that their legal and moral implications remained the same over time. The increased care taken by post-revolutionary courts to discriminate between types of legal actions had the effect of grounding even more firmly in the law the attempts of aggrieved women to seek redress from male suitors. Whereas some earlier breach-of-promise suits had been brought by men as well as by women, by the late eighteenth century breach-of-promise, like seduction, was an exclusively female action. While in America such cases had always involved issues of personal reputation more than property, now the law applied itself especially to the protection of the reputation of women.

Behind this change in the gender composition of plaintiffs was a still more fundamental and widespread cultural development — the growing presumption of female innocence. Whereas in the seventeenth century women were more likely to be thought morally deficient to men, the tide turned in the following century. The reasons for this transformation are complex. In intellectual circles, medieval scholastic beliefs that reason was the seat of natural morality began to give way to new ideas, emanating primarily from England and Scotland, theorizing that virtue was instead derived from sentiment.[93] While on the one hand this Enlightenment philosophical debate between rationalists and sentimentalists was gender-neutral, on the other hand the newfound tendency to privilege the emotions implicitly enhanced the moral status of women.

Women had traditionally been regarded as more emotional than men, a quality that now began, at least partly, to be interpreted in their favor. A similar and more visible sign of this reevaluation of female morality occurred in religion, as evangelical preachers of the mid eighteenth century began to celebrate female examples of piety and encouraged the highly emotional reception of grace.[94] Even the more liberal and Enlightened anti-revivalists veered toward a sentimentalist understanding of virtue as based on a divinely implanted innate moral sense. Women, like children, deemed at once more emotional and closer to nature than men, increasingly took on the glow of moral innocence. This image received still greater reinforcement in popular sentimental novels. The epic works of Samuel Richardson and other eighteenth-century British writers, widely read in America and imitated in the 1790s by Charles Brockden Brown and Susanna Rowson, told tales of pure and naïve women being ruined by unscrupulous, selfish men.

Judges presiding in American courts around the turn of the nineteenth century at once reflected and perpetuated these new attitudes towards morality and gender. In civil cases, especially, where they were unhampered by old statues and relatively free to reinterpret the common law, they began to bring these diffuse cultural currents into their judicial thinking. As courts reconsidered the standards of evidence in breach-of-promise actions, for example, they relieved the aggrieved women of the necessity of proving mutual promise. The only effective defense left to men charged with seduction and breach of promise was to assemble witnesses to attack the character of the woman. As long as the woman was held in good repute, the law almost always sided with her.[95]

This presumption of female innocence is perhaps best shown in the judges' open expression of moral outrage against irresponsible male lovers and their vocal sympathy for the emotional suffering of women. These attitudes, typically associated with nineteenth-century courts, had already developed over the course of the eighteenth century. A 1795 treatise on the laws of Connecticut, for example, made explicit allowance for female plaintiffs who sued their seducers for breach of contract, maintaining that "the most exemplary damages ought to be given, to make all possible reparation for the greatest injury that a woman can sustain."[96] Men, to the contrary, while also technically able to sue under the same law, carried a higher burden of proof.[97] Two appellate cases, one tried in New Jersey in 1791 and the other in Massachusetts in 1807, strikingly illustrate the new judicial leanings towards aggrieved women. In the New Jersey case, the man who was being charged with breach of promise had already been found guilty of seduction in a case brought by the woman's father. The follow-up breach of promise action was initiated by the woman herself.[98] Pointing to the injustice of being charged twice for the same crime, the accused pled poverty and maintained that he could not afford two separate sets of fines. The Chief Justice of New Jersey, however, rejected this argument, defending the right of the woman to add her own suit to her father's. Using highly moralistic language to instruct the jury, the Chief Justice emphasized "that the injury complained of was of the most atrocious and dishonorable nature, and called for exemplary damages. . . . He repeated in very strong terms his detestation of such conduct . . . that poverty was no . . . extenuation of a crime like this." In the most forceful terms, this highest representative of the state's law objected to the idea that such a man should "be let loose on society" and characterized the court as involved in the "protection of innocence."[99]

The second case, brought before the Massachusetts Supreme Court in the following decade, stemmed as well from a joint seduction and breach-of-promise case in which the defendant sought to lower or remove the penalty imposed by the lower court. He claimed that the woman possessed a bad character, using as evidence her extramarital sexual relations with him. As in New Jersey, the Massachusetts Court decided against him, on grounds that he himself bore responsibility for her bad reputation. As Chief Justice Sedgwick put it, the Court could not accept evidence of her character, "injured and degraded as it necessarily was by the treatment she had received from the defendant." To do so "would be placing the other sex absolutely in the power of ours. It is not to be endured, that a man should seduce a female, and ruin her character and standing in society; and when she comes to ask compensation for the injury under which she is suffering, avail himself of her humiliation and disgrace."[100] In an uncanny example of life imitating art, the victim in this case was named Clarissa Harlowe Boynton. Like Samuel Richardson's heroine, the original Clarissa Harlowe, after whom she had been undoubtedly named, Clarissa Harlowe Boynton had suffered at the hands of a male predator and was ultimately vindicated in the court of sentimental public opinion. Judge Sedgwick, the father of the future American sentimental writer Catherine Sedgwick, had learned his Richardsonian lesson well. The older common law actions of breach of promise and seduction were transformed in the late eighteenth and early nineteenth centuries by judges and juries like him.

Colonial historians focusing on fornication have overlooked the significance of these civil suits of seduction and breach of promise, as well as the evolving American moral code they reveal. A number of legal scholars have argued that there was a shift from moral to property issues in American courts during the eighteenth century.[101] They have pointed to the decline of criminal fornication cases and the simultaneous increase in supposedly financially-motivated bastardy and paternity cases aiming to secure child support. This argument fits into a more general argument about shift in American social values toward contractual individualism at the time of the Revolution and the rapid development of the commercial economy. Other social historians interested in women and sexuality have likewise seen a lessening in community control of sexual behavior as family life became increasingly viewed as "private."[102]

A more negative variation of this view, recently advanced by historian Cornelia Dayton, is that at least part of this change was bad for women. As Dayton shows in detail for Connecticut, fornication remained criminalized for women for many years after it ceased being so for men. Whereas in the mid-seventeenth century, men typically confessed to the crime and married mothers of their illegitimately conceived children, toward the end of the century they increasingly refused to admit complicity in fornication and were usually acquitted. Gradually, during the first half of the eighteenth century, fornication was in essence decriminalized for men, becoming a "woman's crime."[103] These developments meant, presumably, that women were less protected by their families and communities against rape and seduction and from the burden of unwanted children. No longer would the threat of criminal prosecution of the man serve to deter male sexual exploitation; no longer could the man be made to marry the woman. The fact that women were still charged with crime, and men not, suggests that the courts had become more misogynist, viewing women as chiefly responsible for illicit sex. The only redress women had was to sue, or have their fathers sue, for the child's support.

All of this, however, ignores the critical moral importance of the civil suits, and the way they reflected and promoted changing ideas about gender relations, courtship, and marriage. The social regulation of courtship through the law neither ceased nor significantly declined. It only changed, albeit in important ways. On the one hand, consenting couples faced fewer obstacles in the way of sex and marriage. Illicit sexual acts between single men and women that were not harmful to anyone — especially those that led to either formal or common-law marriage — were now generally ignored by the courts. But, on the other hand, the law still played a vital role in regulating sexual morality. This is especially true in cases of failed or broken courtships in which no marriage resulted and in which the woman was left with a damaged reputation and an illegitimate child. The prosecution of seduction and breach of promise cases, typically associated with the nineteenth century, suggests that already in colonial British America the common law had been pressed into the service of moral regulation.

The rise of paternity suits during the same period similarly illustrates this shift toward civil suits and the appearance of judicial decisions based upon the presumption of female innocence. These cases, by definition the result of extramarital sexual activity, have already received considerable attention from historians concentrating upon fornication. Because paternity suits aimed directly to provide illegitimate offspring with financial support, historians have interpreted their increasing frequency as evidence of courts moving from moral to economic priorities. Yet a reexamination of this development suggests that moral sanctions were operating in paternity cases even in the absence of criminal prosecution. Like cases of seduction and breach of promise, paternity suits involved far more than money alone; they, too, reflected the changing status and representation of women, especially as mothers.

One of the most interesting features of eighteenth-century paternity actions is that they were increasingly initiated by the women themselves rather than by either their fathers or the government.[104] Seen in this context, women's ability to seek legal redress for the immoral behavior of men may have actually been improving, not declining, despite the seemingly contradictory fact that in Connecticut, at least, women were being charged with fornication more often than men.[105] It may be, as Laurel Thatcher Ulrich has suggested for Maine, that the growing proportion of women charged with fornication stemmed from the legal requirement that a woman admit to illicit sexual relations before she was able to launch a paternity suit.[106] Ironically, what from one perspective looks the misogynist "feminization" of the crime of fornication, from another looks like an indication of women's ability to manipulate the law, albeit for limited purposes.

Scattered evidence gleaned from county courts outside New England similarly suggests that men, not women, increasingly fell victim to laws against extramarital sexual activity. Indeed, in Chester County, Pennsylvania, where no clear distinction between fornication and bastardy cases was made, only men, not women, were charged after 1780, whereas before 1760 men and women were both charged.[107] A similar shift occurred in Frederick County, Virginia during approximately the same period. Whereas in the 1750s the parish churchwardens sued the fathers of bastard indigent children, took the money for the parish, and removed custody from the mother, by the 1780s the money went directly to the mother, who retained custody.[108] Women as single and deprived mothers of dependent children, like women as pitiful victims of male lust, seem to have gained some standing under the law over the course of the eighteenth century.

What occurred was not a simple transition from criminal prosecution to civil suits. The morality reflected in the later judicial decisions was based on a different conception of male-female relations than had earlier been common, even in civil cases. Whereas courts in the seventeenth century assumed that women were as guilty of sexual crimes as men, in the eighteenth century they increasingly took the view of young women as aggrieved victims of deceitful male predators. This image of female virtue conformed closely to the pitiful female characters in sentimental fiction and to the female exemplars of piety featured in the preaching of ministers.

As the laws regulating courtship moved from legislature statutes to judicial decisions and from criminal law towards civil cases, courts also switched from imposing restrictions upon consensual marriages — especially the requirements of parental consent and public ceremony — to redressing the grievances of single women abused by unfaithful suitors. Taken as a whole, these changes reflected neither a shift from moral to economic preoccupations nor a shift from a more sexually egalitarian to a more sexually hierarchical society. The state, through the law, remained intimately engaged in establishing moral codes throughout the period. Even though the courts were less involved in reinforcing paternal authority and controlling access to marriage, they were still actively involved in adjudicating disputes when relationships broke down prior to marriage. The examples of suits for seduction, breach of promise, and paternity all illustrate this point. Even though criminal cases of fornication receded, civil ones with clear moral overtones persisted and became even more common over time. The very fact that the courts heard such cases and sought to set communal standards of personal behavior belies the notion that morals were truly private or that the state opted out of moral disputes.[109]

To be sure, the remedy for damages in civil court was, by definition, money, and there was surely a difference between seventeenth-century public humiliation and the paying of a financial settlement. The moral transgressor who earlier would have faced the entire community, later on typically faced a single victim and perhaps her father. But money in this evolving commercial and contractual society was not simply a material resource but a symbol of honor and reputation. The court still represented the public interest, and the awarding of damages still signified the enforcement of reciprocal human obligation. At a time when women had relatively few opportunities to litigate for financial damages in civil court, the fact that the beneficiaries of such payments were almost always single women or their families indicates that civil courts had partly taken on the task of disciplining sexually irresponsible men. Rather than reflecting the growth of a money-minded, individualistic culture, this legal change reveals changing assumptions about the moral underpinnings of gender relations. Contrary to earlier beliefs, by the late eighteenth century women were increasingly taken to be more morally pure than men. Paternity, seduction, and breach-of-promise cases all show that legal authorities came to perceive unmarried women as having justifiable claims against their former male lovers. The only effective defense mustered by the men accused of these courtship violations was defaming the sexual reputation of the female plaintiff, thereby undercutting the presumption of her innocence.[110] All this points not only to the persistence of the state's attempt to regulate sexual morality, but, more significantly, to the influence upon the law of wider cultural changes in the understanding of gender.

This underlying moral transformation — a transformation evident not only in the law but in religion, popular literature, and moral philosophy — cannot be categorized in any simple way as good or bad for women. To see in this period the rise of equal, companionate relationships misses the gender asymmetry and presumption of female passivity. To see it as a time of greater misogyny misses the growing assertion of female moral authority. What is clear, however, is that the definitions of masculinity and femininity were undergoing a historical change in eighteenth-century American civil courts as well as in other cultural venues, prefiguring "Victorian" morality long before Victoria mounted her throne.[111]

Women, Love, and Virtue in the Thought of Edwards and Franklin

PREFACE   Among intellectual historians of British colonial America, comparing Jonathan Edwards and Benjamin Franklin is a timeworn pedagogical exercise. The two men's canonical stature and intriguing contrasts in style, vocation, values, and belief system typically situate them on opposite ends of a continuum representing eighteenth-century American thought: Franklin the rationalist, Edwards the Calvinist; Franklin the practical doer, Edwards the otherworldly idealist; Franklin the humorist, Edwards the preacher of hellfire. The list goes on. In this essay, however, I seek to press these classic differences into the service of gender analysis by changing the terms of comparison. The essay focuses upon topics that, ironically, neither man addressed very much in his writing: women and romantic love. My purpose is partly to reveal the hidden linkages between "high" intellectual history and the social history of women by reexamining each of these men's own biographical connections to members of the opposite sex. Beyond that, the essay integrates Edwards's and Franklin's familiar and often antithetical ideas about virtue into broader cultural trends of the era, which were reshaping definitions of gender.

* * *

As major American intellectuals in the midst of the transition from Puritanism to the new Protestant middle-class morality of the late eighteenth and early nineteenth centuries, Jonathan Edwards and Benjamin

Franklin stood at an important juncture in the development of ideas about women and marital love. Although neither of them wrote extensively about relationships between men and women, their often implicit ideas reveal difficulties they had reconciling traditional Puritan with newer points of view. Their shared preoccupation with human morality, as well as their personal relationships with women, unavoidably raised basic questions about the role of human attachment in the generation of virtue. Their often internally contradictory answers to these questions at once resisted and encouraged broader changes in the American cultural understanding of women and love.

The Puritans before them, as many historians have shown, accorded marriage fundamental social value as the core of the "little commonwealth" of the family. Regarded as the basic unit of society, familial relationships served as the primary locus of religious education and the enforcement of the moral code. Love between men and women, defined largely in terms of duty, was conceived as a consequence rather than a precondition of marriage. Wives were deemed valuable as both economic and spiritual "helpmates," and traditional criticism of women as dangerously sexual and prone to sinful temptation was gradually giving way to a positive image of female piety and domestic devotion. Love of God, which was always, of course, to supersede conjugal love, was in the late seventeenth century increasingly symbolized in terms of marital bonds.[1]

During the eighteenth century, this earlier positive conception of women and marriage was transformed into a newly sentimental understanding of marital love. No longer stressing the tension between divine and human love, moral commentators increasingly viewed virtue as based on sympathetic connections between human beings. Influential British moral philosophers such as the Earl of Shaftesbury, Francis Hutcheson, and their popularizers rooted virtue in the emotions and posited the existence of an innate moral sense. A growing emphasis on the redemptive qualities of human love, including romantic love between men and women, as something distinct from sexual attraction, pervaded both religious and secular literature. Writings on courtship and marriage commonly attributed especially keen moral sensibilities to women, who as wives and mothers promised to cultivate benevolent emotions in men. According to this increasingly gendered ideal of virtue, feminine intuition and empathy balanced masculine industriousness and self-reliance. Whereas the earlier Puritans had typically characterized good wives as dependable assistants to men, late-eighteenth-century domestic moralists highlighted gender differences and the psychological interdependence of husbands and wives.[2]

On first impression, neither Edwards nor Franklin seems to have contributed to the development of this sentimental conception of women and human love. Neither was particularly concerned with the family as a social institution. Neither regarded virtue as either produced or realized in human relationships. Whatever their differences, the fundamental perspectives of both on the sources of human morality remained essentially individualistic. Virtue was never for either of them the result of emotional involvement with other people. It was instead a quality internal to the individual — for Edwards the product of the gracious awakening of one's spiritual sense, and for Franklin the disciplined quest for worldly happiness. Each in his own way assumed benevolent social relationships to be a necessary outcome of virtue, but neither regarded marriage or the family as distinctive or especially valuable arenas for the expression of virtue.

Both Edwards and Franklin found relations between men and women more problematic, however, than the ostensible clarity of these positions suggests. While biographers have, of course, paid attention to each of their relationships with women, they have made little effort to relate their personal attitudes and experiences to the general framework of their thought.[3] The dominant tendency of both men was to disregard or to trivialize the issues of gender difference and domestic attachments. Yet they each employed gender imagery and periodically sought to define the moral status of marriage. Inasmuch as their thinking did touch on these issues, they both played unwitting but significant parts in constructing the sentimental outlook toward women and marriage that was emerging in the middle of the eighteenth century. Their sporadic and often inconsistent comments about these matters also reveal underlying tensions in their moral theories. These tensions point to the intrusion of their complex personal relationships and deep-seated cultural assumptions about women into the seemingly gender-neutral structure of their thought.

· · ·

To my knowledge, Edwards left no sustained discussion of his views on women or love between the sexes. What documentation exists consists of several pieces of indirect evidence: his philosophical speculations about the relationship of the so-called "natural affections" and "instincts" to true virtue; his use of examples of women and sexual transgressions in his evangelical writings and ministry; and a few moving expressions of his love for his wife, Sarah. Taken together and set against the backdrop of major events in his life and the general development of his thought, these scattered bits and pieces fall into a discernable pattern.

Edwards was essentially of two minds about the moral status of love between women and men. He held, on the one hand, that love between human beings could be spiritual and, on the other, that such love was fundamentally selfish and instinctual. At times he elevated love above sex and self-interest, at other times he reduced it to them. Similarly torn between an idealization of female spirituality and an abhorrence of female seductiveness, he vacillated in his religious use of feminine symbolism. His overt position was always, of course, to maintain the genderless and transcendent quality of grace. Toward the end of his life, partly in response to pivotal experiences in his own marriage and ministry, this insistence finally drove him to assume a more absolute position equating love between the sexes with sinful self-love. This position was never, however, entirely consistent, and, despite all his efforts to differentiate love of God from human love, an ambiguous and suggestive connection remained between them.

No concept was as fundamental to Edwards's thought as love. The "first and chief" affection propelling the will, love caused desire, hope, joy, and gratitude; the negative affections of hatred, fear, and anger resulted from the absence of love.[4] Love was, he wrote in his "Notes on the Bible," "the sum of all saving virtue."[5] The most holy affection, love of God, was for him the essence of religious experience, the source of beauty, and the basis of virtue. The all-inclusive object of this spiritual love, which Edwards termed "being in general," of course rendered it different in kind from the mundane and unregenerate love of fellow human beings. Indeed, as Norman Fiering has argued, one of Edwards's major intellectual projects was to distinguish himself from the Scottish sentimentalists by denying the moral sufficiency of mere natural affections.

Yet, despite these clear intentions, problems of definition remained. On the one hand, Edwards consistently maintained that love of other human beings — whether of the opposite sex, one's children, neighbors, or humanity generally — arose from self-love rather than from true benevolence. Only love of God, which he variously called spiritual love or Christian love, was essentially selfless. On the other hand, he wavered considerably in his assessment of the morality of self-love, especially when it involved love of other people.[6] Until the early 1740s he often wrote eloquently in defense of the value of love between human beings, even allowing for an intermixture of divine and human love. Around the time of his engagement to Sarah he maintained that love between the sexes was the same "inclination" as Christ felt toward his spouse, the church. Far from hindering one's attraction to the opposite sex, "love of God only refines and purifies it."[7] Although love between human beings remained for him fundamentally an expression of self-love, it was not, he reasoned in 1732, the "simple" self-love that delights only in one's own exclusive good. Instead, the "compounded" self-love, which delights in the good of another, "is not entirely distinct from love of God, but enters into its nature."[8] In a 1738 sermon entitled "The Spirit of Charity the Opposite of a Selfish Spirit," he similarly argued that the personal happiness derived from seeking the good of others "is not selfishness, because it is not a confined self-love."[9] "The self which he loves is, as it were, enlarged and multiplied, so that in those same acts wherein he loves himself he loves others. And this is the Christian spirit . . . divine love or Christian charity."[10] Condemning the wickedness of the heathen who lacked natural affection, he strenuously objected to the "notion that no other love ought to be allowed but spiritual love, and that all other love is to be abolished as carnal, . . . and that therefore love should go out to one another only in that proportion in which the image of God is seen in them."[11] To the contrary, he advocated love on the natural basis of family ties, even at one point claiming "the nearer the relation, the greater is the obligation to love."[12]

Edwards's dual perspective on human love as distinct from, and yet infused by, the love of God, shifted significantly sometime prior to 1755, when he published *True Virtue*. Earlier he had simply insisted that love of other people be "well-regulated" or kept "under the government of the love of God."[13] In *True Virtue*, however, he emphasized a direct antagonism between natural and religious affections. Love of other people, as he now put it, "is contrary to the tendency of true virtue" and "will set a person against general existence, and make him an enemy to it."[14] The only virtuous love was directly dependent on love of God.[15] For the regenerate, love of other human beings varied in proportion not to the nearness of their familial relationship but to the degree of their holiness: "When anyone under the influence of general benevolence sees another being possessed of the like general benevolence, this attaches his heart to him, and draws forth greater love to him."[16] Mere natural, particular love for one's children or for one's husband or wife Edwards classified as narrow and instinctual self-love, in opposition to "a principle of general benevolence."[17]

This shift in focus within his theory of human love can, as Norman Fiering has suggested, be partly explained by Edwards's increased intellectual efforts to refute the naturalistic premises of sentimental philosophy.[18] Whereas his earlier discussion of human love assumed the presence of grace, he now turned to refute the benevolists' argument for a natural, universal principle of love independent of grace. The difference between his earlier and later perspectives reflects these different intellectual premises. Yet there was a personal dimension to Edwards's intellectual development as well, involving two critical experiences of his middle age: the growing disaffection of his parish and the spiritual crisis of his wife, Sarah. Patricia Tracy's study of his pastoral life shows Edwards to have been singularly preoccupied with the danger of youthful sexual transgressions, a concern that may well have reflected a painful history of adultery and divorce in his own family.[19] His sermons during the revival of 1734–1735 passionately denounced both parental negligence and the "sensual filthiness" and "abominable lasciviousness" of the town's young.[20] The practices of premarital "bundling" and late-night "frolicking" received his particularly strenuous criticism.[21] Indeed, one of his chief objectives as a minister was to purify souls by divesting religious affections of dangerous sexual tendencies: "Certainly the mutual embraces and kisses of persons of different sexes, under the notion of Christian love and holy kisses, are utterly to be disallowed and abominated, as having the most direct tendency quickly to turn Christian love into unclean and brutish lust."[22] For this reason, he made it his policy during the revivals that informal religious meetings be sexually segregated. In his account of the 1735 Northampton revivals he focused on the conversion of a young woman, "one of the greatest company-keepers of the town," whose change of heart "seemed to be almost like a flash of lightning, upon the hearts of young people all over the town and upon many others."[23]

Successful in the short run, Edwards's efforts to arouse the consciences of the wayward young men and women of Northampton almost immediately resulted in a wave of youthful conversions. Later on, however, his tenacious efforts to enforce strict moral discipline apparently cost him the support of much of his original youthful constituency. In the "bad books" incident, he infuriated many parishioners by publicly humiliating a group of young men who had surreptitiously examined anatomical drawings of women in a midwife's manual and then knowingly jeered at a female companion.[24] In another case, Edwards tried hard to force the marriage of parents of an illegitimate child, despite the fact that their sexual affair was over and their families had already agreed on a financial

settlement.[25] In these episodes Edwards acted in part to defend the reputation of women victimized by irresponsible young men, as well as to
serve, as he put it, "the well being of society."[26] But instead of awakening
religious consciences, these disciplinary efforts only contributed to the
growing resentment of his ministry. Edwards's later categorization of
love between men and women as unregenerate instinct can be understood in part as a response to his failed pastoral exertions.

The second development in his personal life that throws light on
Edwards's shifting theories about human love was his wife Sarah's religious experience of 1742. In sharp contrast to his response to the sexual
impulses of parish youth, his relationship with Sarah Pierrepont had
from the beginning an otherworldly quality. His well-known lyrical
description of her written shortly after they met, sets her in blissful soli-
tary communion with nature and God: "She loves to be alone, walking in
the fields and groves, and seems to have someone invisible always con-
versing with her." [27] However much sexual passion may have permeated
their marriage, Edwards left no written record of his attraction to her.
His few recorded words about their relationship stress only their attachment through faith. As he poignantly assured her on his deathbed, "The
uncommon union that has so long subsisted between us has been of such
a nature as I trust is spiritual and therefore will continue forever." [28]
Unlike earlier Puritans who worried lest marital love become obsessive
desire and thereby displace the love of God, Edwards seems to have distinguished sharply between examples of illicit sexuality and the spiritual
love of his marriage.

His idealization of Sarah's spirituality took extensive written expression only once, in *Some Thoughts Concerning the Present Revival of
1743*. Borrowing from her account of her recent religious crisis, he
described it as a model spiritual experience. To a degree, his use of her as
an ideal of religious piety was continuous with the promotion of female
examples of faith in his previous evangelical writing. In *A Faithful
Narrative* of 1736, the most salient illustrations of the glorious work of
the spirit were women: the notorious loose young woman whose reformation catalyzed a round of conversions, an "aged woman" who sud-
denly saw scripture in a new light, the invalid Abigail Hutchinson, and
the four-year-old Phoebe Bartlett. In this earlier choice of female exemplars, Edwards conformed to a growing tendency among New England
ministers to associate women with religious faith. [29] But what distinguished Edwards's depiction of Sarah in 1743 was precisely his refusal to
identify her as a woman. His description meticulously omitted all men-

tion of gender. The exemplary character modeled after Sarah became in print simply "the person," rupturing Edwards's earlier pattern of associating piety with femininity.

Heavily editing Sarah's own written account of her experience, Edwards expunged all references to the intimate interpersonal context of her crisis. Her version poignantly reveals her dependency on his approval of her, confessing her special sensitivity to "the esteem and love and kind treatment of my husband."[30] As she tells her story, the sources of her spiritual anxieties of 1742 were twofold, both resulting from her deep attachment to Edwards: she became upset because he reprimanded her for being tactless in a conversation with a relative and she felt acutely jealous of the visiting minister Samuel Buell, who proved to be a more popular preacher than he.[31] After her conversion experience, she described herself as having reached a greater spiritual distance from Edwards. "If the feelings and conduct of my husband were to be changed from tenderness and affection, to extreme hatred and cruelty, and that every day, I could so rest in God that it would not touch my heart, or diminish my happiness."[32] Edwards's published rendition, to the contrary, omits this entire emotional context, only reporting briefly that the joys of grace removed the "person's" former melancholy and censoriousness.[33]

These deletions go far beyond an understandable effort to maintain anonymity. They reveal Edwards's refusal to accord the experience of human love a role in spiritual regeneration, evidence from his own marriage notwithstanding. Whereas he might well have used the occasion to expound upon the way that mortal attachments are superseded by the love of God, he eliminated the marital drama altogether. Sarah's account commendably affirmed the transcendent quality of divine love, but it also more ambiguously pointed to the religious repercussions of mundane human attachments. Edwards left out the entire interpersonal emotional process and chose to endorse only the spiritual conclusion.

Indeed, Sarah's successful disengagement from Edwards may well have pushed him still further toward disparaging the moral value of natural human love, the position he articulated most clearly in his later treatise on *True Virtue*. The scarce evidence permits only the most tentative interpretation of their emotional relationship, but Sarah's experience of religious transcendence seems to be linked to an unusual degree of tension between them. As Patricia Bonomi has suggested, perhaps 1742 marked a period of crisis in their marriage, which led to their assuming a greater emotional distance. Without expressing overt hostility, Sarah's account, written exclusively for Jonathan, dwells repeatedly on his rival's superior preaching, and in it she claims to have finally "rejoiced" over Buell's success. The spacing of the births of their children also suggests the possibility of increased estrangement. Only in 1742 did they not conceive a child within two years of the previous birth — a pattern Bonomi has found otherwise unbroken during more than twenty years of childbearing.[34] On a personal level, Sarah's religious experience and the possibly related change in their marriage can be placed alongside Edwards's disappointment in the revivals and his increased antagonism to the optimistic philosophical arguments of the British sentimentalists.[35] What he most disliked in the moral philosophers — their confidence in the benign quality of human relationships — his wife's inspiring (and perhaps also painful) emotional detachment from him had already powerfully and intimately challenged.

Corresponding to Edwards's growing pessimism about the value of human love was a revealing shift in his use of gender imagery. His earlier description of subjective religious experience had used the passive, often implicitly feminine and sexual metaphors of taste, sight, physical incorporation, and infantile dependency: "an inward sweetness," "the light of the sun," the soul "swallowed up," "intercourse . . . as a child with a father."[36] While this passively sensual language continued to be used in his later accounts, in the 1746 *Religious Affections* he employed far more aggressive and explicitly male symbolism to convey the intensity of religious affections. "The business of religion is . . . compared to those exercises, wherein men are wont to have their hearts, and strength greatly exercised and engaged; such as running, wrestling or agonizing for a great prize or crown, and fighting with strong enemies that seek our lives, and warring as those that by violence take a city or kingdom."[37] And, whereas his earlier evangelical writings had highlighted female conversion experiences, his *Life of David Brainerd* of 1749 exalted a singularly male model of piety. Bravely forsaking the comforts of family and community to venture into heathen lands, pushing himself to the point of death in the service of God, Brainerd's life of continuous "striving and violence in religion," as Edwards put it, could hardly contrast more with the childishness of Phoebe Bartlett or the sickbed confinement of Abigail Hutchinson.[38]

Despite these notable changes in both his perspective on natural affection and his use of gender symbolism, Edwards never fully resolved the thorny moral and spiritual questions posed by human love. Insisting upon the centrality of love in religious life, he equivocated in his judgments about the value of love between people, particularly in relationships between men and women. For a time he assumed an ambiguous compromise position in which human love occupied a kind of middle ground between love of God and base self-love. During the same period he publicly elevated examples of female piety, while consistently express-ing abhorrence of female physical seductiveness and sexual desire. In these ways, Edwards can even be seen as indirectly contributing to the more positive evaluation of romantic love and female morality that was gradually developing in the eighteenth century. Yet, in his insistence on the absolute superiority of divine love, he powerfully resisted these senti-mental implications. In the 1740s, in response to a combination of intel-lectual and personal experiences, he began moving toward the more extreme position taken in *True Virtue* in 1755. Uncompromising in his moral castigation of all forms of human attachment, he finally relegated love between men and women simply to the category of instinct. By instinct he first and primarily meant sexual drive. But even in this passage he equivocated, agreeing with Hutcheson and Hume that the "kind affec-tions between the sexes" arose not only from "sensitive pleasure" but from "a disposition both to mutual benevolence and mutual compla-cence." He acknowledged that God implanted such affections not just to reproduce the race but to provide, more diffusely, for "the comfort of mankind."[39] The notion that human beings instinctively promote the comfort of mankind through their love of the opposite sex is not a view ordinarily associated with Edwards. For all his efforts to deflate the moral and spiritual status of human love, Edwards still left a small open-ing for the sentimental naturalist arguments about marriage that were gaining currency by the middle of the eighteenth century.

· · ·

Franklin's relationship to the wider development of middle-class domes-tic morality is in many respects more straightforward. According to his basic moral philosophy, the pursuit of private, this-worldly happiness promoted rather than undermined the larger moral good. As Poor Richard once expanded on the image of a pebble thrown in a lake, he described self-love as benignly radiating outward to encompass "Friend, Parent, Neighbor, . . . all [the] human Race."[40] For Franklin there was no intrinsic conflict between promoting one's own happiness, benevolently promoting the happiness of others, and pleasing God. As he outlined strategies for achieving success, moreover, he frequently designated mar-riage as a key to both personal happiness and a beneficial social life.

"The good or ill hap of a good or ill life," the almanac put it, "Is the good or ill choice of a good or ill wife."[41] Repeatedly, he characterized single men as "the odd halves of scissors" or as lone volumes "of a set of books."[42] "A Man without a Wife, is but half a Man."[43]

For Franklin, of course, virtue inhered not in one's inner disposition but in one's outward acts. Just as Edwards drew from a side of Puritanism in his emphasis upon the emotional experience of grace, Franklin enlarged upon the Puritan commitment to vocations. His writing on women and marriage stressed above all the practical affairs of the domestic economy and the larger social benefits of reproducing the race. As wives, frugal and hardworking women served as invaluable assistants to upwardly mobile men. Franklin frequently drew the equation between a good wife and money. "A good Wife and Health," read one of Poor Richard's typical aphorisms, "Is a Man's best Wealth."[44] Commenting in a letter to his sister on his nephew Benny's bride, he wrote, "If she does not bring a fortune she will help to make one. Industry, frugality, and prudent economy in a wife, are . . . in their effects a fortune."[45]

As mothers, women possessed perhaps even greater value, for in Franklin's view fertility was an index to social happiness. Linked to inexpensive tastes, a high birthrate such as that found in America, he argued, stemmed from the affordability of early marriage made possible by frugal women.[46] Deploring the single life of many English acquaintances, he reported, "The great Complaint is the excessive Expensiveness of English Wives."[47] Franklin's spirited speech in the persona of the unwed mother Polly Baker satirically underscores her "natural and useful Actions" in adding citizens to the commonwealth. Far from attacking marriage, she boasts all her Franklinesque qualifications to marry, "having all the Industry, Frugality, Fertility, and Skill in Oeconomy appertaining to a good Wife's Character."[48]

For all Franklin's appreciation of the economic and reproductive aspects of marriage, he made considerably less room for intimate relationships than Edwards. His standard of moral judgment was not feeling but behavior. The ultimate goal of personal happiness inhered, in his view, in material success, sound health, and good reputation.[49] He used the term love in a highly diffuse manner. "Love and be loved," advised an aphorism he included twice in his almanac.[50] In letters home he sent love to his wife, family, and friends with no effort to discriminate among them, once jokingly acknowledging his wish to have "everybody" love him.[51] Benevolence and efforts to make others happy ranked high for him as human virtues, but he always described the recipients of these acts impersonally. His famous discussion of the "art of virtue" altogether dispenses with such traditional interactive virtues as charity, mercy, kindness, and fidelity. The thirteen virtues included on his list were instead all purely instrumental, chosen for their usefulness in the attainment of happiness for the autonomous self.[52]

Franklin's quality of individual detachment permeated not only his moral theory but his personal attitude toward his own life. The *Autobiography*'s well-known accounts of his own singularly unromantic courtships perhaps best illustrate this point. He indignantly broke off one engagement when he suspected the family of cheating him out of a dowry. His eventual marriage to the penniless Deborah Read, whom he had several years earlier planned to marry but had forgotten about, as he tells it, during his trip to England, came only after his painful discovery that he could command no better price on the marriage market.[53] A similarly utilitarian perspective on marriage led him much later to oppose as "a very rash and precipitate step" the engagement of his daughter Sarah to the debt-ridden Richard Bache.[54]

The repeated effort to secure financial position through marriage was consistent with his apparently affectionate but doggedly practical relationship with his wife. His praise of her centered on her helpfulness in his business, her frugal and efficient housekeeping, and her unwavering loyalty. The song he composed about her for a club of male friends, entitled "I Sing My Plain Country Joan," expressed appreciation of her down-to-earth qualities in an implicit critique of more exalted ideas of romance.[55] However genuine his regard for her, the emotional content of their marriage clearly dwindled to next to nothing through the fifteen years of separation while he was negotiating for America abroad. Their correspondence was mainly about household matters. He professed homesickness, and doubtless meant it, but was at the same time able to lead a largely satisfying life without her. She claimed that the reason she stayed home was her fear of the sea, but one suspects that both he and she preferred that "plain country Joan" not risk embarrassment by joining him in the polite social circles of England and France.

In the meantime, beginning already prior to his departure, Franklin developed a series of personal relationships with younger people, particularly young women, to whom he freely gave paternalistic advice. Late in life, during his years in France, he especially cultivated the role of fatherly flirt. Even in his most effusive and charming moments, however, "Cher Papa," as he was known among his female admirers, characteristically used humor to keep his emotional distance.[56] An ironic tone even permeates what we know of his ostensible efforts to proposition Madame Brillon and to propose marriage to Madame Helvetius. Madame Helvetius commented to a friend that Franklin "loved people only as long as he saw them."[57]

Yet beneath Franklin's evasive humor and cool utilitarianism vied deeply conflicting conceptions of women. His scattered comments on sexuality, courtship, and marriage presented dichotomous images of women as irrelevant and invaluable, undermining and uplifting. His focus remained, of course, on men, with himself as the primary model. In the fundamentally male quest for virtue and economic success, women played a profoundly ambiguous role. For Franklin, individual self-reliance was an essential value, the key to the attainment of happiness. Yet within the context of his culture women unavoidably represented the opposite qualities of dependency and attachment. Faced with this basic problem, Franklin wavered between praising women as productive assistants and criticizing them as wasteful spendthrifts. In neither capacity could they comfortably fit into a theory extolling the achievements of autonomous males.

Just as Edwards's ideas about human love played themselves out in his portrayal of Sarah Edwards, Franklin's ambivalence about women is perhaps best revealed in his conflicting assessments of Deborah Franklin. True to his public admonitions about the financial value of a well-chosen wife, the dominant image he conveyed of Deborah was that of "a good & faithful Helpmate," hard-working and economical.[58] Toward the end of his life he fondly recalled in a letter to one of his young female correspondents, "Frugality is an enriching virtue; a Virtue I never could acquire in myself; but I was once lucky enough to find it in a Wife, who thereby became a Fortune to me."[59] The main passage about Deborah in the *Autobiography*, illustrating the proverb, "He that would thrive/Must ask his Wife," similarly counts his good fortune in having a wife "as much dispos'd to Industry & Frugality as myself."[60] Yet immediately following this proud depiction of their mutual parsimony, Franklin relates the famous anecdote about finding his breakfast one day "in a China Bowl with a Spoon of Silver." Presenting this episode as an example of the way "Luxury will enter Families, and make a Progress, in Spite of Principle," he describes his wife as having "no other Excuse or Apology to make but that she thought *her* Husband deserved a Silver Spoon & China Bowl as well as any of his Neighbors."[61] This contrary, critical view of his wife as a frivolous consumer appears most vividly in his private correspondence. His letters from England periodically remind her to be "careful of your Accounts," warning her of his declining income and even raising the specter of poverty.[62] "I know you were not very attentive to Money-matters in your best Days," he chastised her.[63] He gave her a memorandum book and pressed her, unsuccessfully, to keep a close record of her expenses.[64] In the last years of her life, while she suffered from partial paralysis and deteriorating memory, Franklin put her on an inadequate allowance and refused to acknowledge her financial difficulties, even though she was borrowing from friends.

Vacillating between his proud appreciation of Deborah's economic value and his harsh criticism of her excessive expenditures, Franklin seems to have been genuinely unsettled in his basic evaluation of her worth as his wife. This double image of her as both frugal and extravagant expressed Franklin's ambivalence about women generally. Especially in his relatively youthful writings of the 1720s and 1730s, women often appear as vain, lazy, irresponsible, and hopelessly addicted to the latest expensive fashions.[65] His essay on the industrious Anthony Afterwit, driven to despair by his wife's status-seeking and luxurious taste, seems modeled, in part, in his own experience with Deborah's purchase of the china bowl and silver spoon.[66] Repeatedly, in his public and private writings, he juxtaposed the symbols of tea tables and spinning wheels: "Many estates are spent in the getting/Since women for tea forsook spinning and knitting."[67] Often Franklin issued his warning against female acquisitiveness in the context of a comic battle of the sexes. In the opening issues of *Poor Richard's Almanack,* for example, Richard's wife Bridget, whom he regards as "excessive proud," carps at him about their poverty and the necessity of her "spinning in her shift of tow" while he uselessly gazes at stars.[68] In addition to impugning them for their vanity, Franklin frequently caricatured women as malicious gossips, overly talkative, and domineering.[69] He ridiculed the sexual pride of aging, unwanted spinsters who had found too many faults with suitors when young and poked fun at the unfulfilled needs of frustrated widows and old maids.[70]

Taken together, these numerous misogynist pieces depict women as sexually demanding, haughty, and contentious. In keeping with these images, Franklin himself occasionally used the comic mask of a female pseudonym in order brazenly to publicize controversial opinions and attack adversaries.[71] At one point, following Defoe, the young Franklin even had the forceful widow Silence Dogood argue for better female education on the grounds that female failings were mostly due to ignorance, a position that, however, Franklin never espoused elsewhere.[72]

Instead he insisted that the proper antidote to overbearing women was male domination. As Poor Richard put it, "Ill thrives that hapless Family that shows/A Cock that's silent and a Hen that crows."[73] Objecting in the *Pennsylvania Gazette* to a recent critique of marriage as a form of slavery for women, Franklin responded, "Every Man that is really a Man is Master of his own Family; and it cannot be Bondage to have another submit to one's Government."[74]

Later on, beginning in the 1740s, Franklin increasingly developed a less hostile (if also less humorous) outlook on women and marriage. Whereas in the early issues of *Poor Richard,* only lawyers receive as much ridicule as wives, after 1738, and especially after 1748, the number of verses and aphorisms that comment on women or marriage dramatically declined.[75] The few that are printed are notably less misogynist as well, giving way to practical recommendations to marry and sensible bits of advice about the prudent choice of a spouse.[76] By 1746 even the acrimonious Richard and Bridget had settled into an idyllic, harmonious, and prosperous married life.[77]

Occasionally in this later period Franklin even espoused a more sentimental attitude. One verse extolled women's benign, civilizing influence; another claimed that men were drawn to women not by their bodies but by their "souls."[78] Deploring the destructive influence of sophisticated taste and high fashion, pieces that dispensed marital advice idealized uncorrupted wives for their "native Innocence," being "form'd in Person and in Mind to please."[79] In other writings as well Franklin increasingly underscored the benign aspects of innate gender differences. "It is the Man and Wife united that make the compleat human Being," he wrote in his famous 1745 letter on the choice of a mistress: "Separate, she wants his Force of Body and Strength of Reason; he, her Softness, Sensibility, and acute Discernment."[80] Women, he variously observed in the later decades of his life, were less rivalrous and more impressionable than men.[81] In a letter to Madame Brillon of 1780 he went so far as to claim to trust feminine intuition more than male intellect, "for women, I believe, have a certain feel, which is more reliable than our reasonings."[82]

In the end, however, for all these lighthearted concessions to a sentimental ideal of women, Franklin remained as much opposed to idealized expressions of romantic love as Edwards. As he wrote characteristically in a spoof on hot air balloons in the Parisian press, "an element ten times lighter than inflammable air" can be found "in the promises of lovers and of courtiers and in the sighs of our widowers."[83] The dominant tendency of his thought held that virtue was a quality of autonomous males, an attitude well illustrated by the membership restriction in his proposed United Party of Virtue to "young and single Men only."[84] According to his proverbial expression, "it is hard for an empty Sack to stand upright," virtue hinged on the achievement of economic independence.[85] As dependents, women were at best aides, at worst parasites, in this prototypically masculine quest. The fundamental lack of clarity in Franklin's view of women — the vacillation among images of vain and impulsive consumers, industrious helpmates, intuitive innocents — suggests the underlying difficulty he had determining the relationship of women to his model of the self-reliant, upwardly mobile man. For Edwards, to the contrary, virtue was a quality of genderless saints in communion with God, extended diffusely to all people as part of "being in general." Both men stopped well short of a sentimental conception of women or of love between human beings. In this, though in sharply contrasting ways, both remained faithful to their common Puritan past.

Yet, in other respects, each of them unwittingly helped set the stage for the transformed gender ideology of the late eighteenth century. In his depiction of female exemplars of piety, Edwards took measured steps in the direction of upholding a female standard of virtue. Even the elderly Franklin did so briefly in his extravagant statements about female moral intuition and judgment. Still more importantly, however, Edwards's insistence upon the centrality of love in religious life, coupled with his ambiguous description of the spiritual and moral status of human attachments, point toward more positive interpretations of marital love. Franklin's most decisive contribution lay instead in the formulation of a new male utilitarian standard of virtue. Although he himself only vaguely and inconsistently endorsed an alternative feminine ideal, he defined the male standard against which the sentimental female one was quick to emerge.

Despite the fact that neither of these figures systematically addressed the issue of gender or romantic love, their sketchy and often contradictory depictions of women and marriage point to their troubled ambivalence as much as their intellectual indifference. To a degree, their difficulties with the subject can be understood biographically as the product of their very different relations to women. When considered from a wider historical perspective, however, both the omissions and the inconsistencies point to their transitional position as theorists of human psychology and morality. Edwards's towering achievement consisted in integrating modern moral philosophy with Calvinist pietism, an accommodation that problematized the relationship between religious and natural affections despite his own repeated efforts to draw a sharp distinction between them. Franklin, too, was poised between Puritanism and contemporary secular thought, in his case balancing a traditional commitment to hard work and frugality — norms he applied to men and women both — against a more resolutely masculine and utilitarian endorsement of the value of individual economic success. Romantic love between men and women, I would suggest, symbolized the ambiguous and even threatening element of human interdependence and emotional fusion. While these two intellectuals managed for the most part to avoid this increasingly troublesome issue, it would emerge with full force in the sentimental literature and religious moralizing of the following generation.

PART THREE

Revolutionary Syntheses

Religion, Literary Sentimentalism, and Popular Revolutionary Ideology

PREFACE   This essay, the first of three on the American Revolution, situates the changing discourse of gender within the larger frameworks of fictional narratives, religious expression, and political thought. It takes issue with recent historians' tendencies to divide revolutionary ideology into two opposing sets of values: the individualistic, associated with liberalism, and the collectivistic, associated with classical republicanism. Instead it points to the ways in which this apparent contradiction was mediated outside the boundaries of explicit political argument within the realm of popular culture. The seemingly apolitical symbolism of religion, gender, and family helped to bring together the antistatist individualism and the collective solidarity so deeply fused within American political thought.

■   ■   ■

Not since the disputes of Progressive and Consensus historians more than two decades ago have the dividing lines between scholars interpreting the ideology of the Revolution been so clearly drawn. To summarize a complex historiography in admittedly oversimple terms, the central debate concerns conflicting judgments about the relative strength of classical republican and liberal ideas in American revolutionary ideology. Those historians stressing classical republicanism have situated American patriots in the framework of an older civic humanism and have highlighted their commitment to checks and balances and their fear of change.[1] Those emphasizing liberalism have, to the contrary, underscored the Revolution's newfound optimism about the prospects of a society of free individuals regulated only by a minimal government.[2] In different ways each interpretation has challenged both the early-twentieth-century Progressive theories about ideology as a simple reflection of economic interest and the later neo-whig views about the importance of rational legal principles in the Revolutionary movement. Despite impressive recent efforts to reassert the centrality of constitutional rights in patriot arguments, the main thrust of contemporary scholarship has been to downplay the specialized legal issues of concern to some Revolutionary leaders and to emphasize instead the broad social and economic values underlying the public debate over the Revolution.[3]

What has divided those historians who stress the importance of classical republicanism from those who insist on the emergence of liberalism is essentially a disagreement over the substance of these broad underlying values. Classical republicanism has been associated with an ethic of civic- or community-mindedness, in particular its celebration of public-spirited individuals willing to sacrifice their own interests on behalf of the common good. Such model citizens, according to the classical republican ideal, would display their virtue through service to the state, chiefly as statesmen and soldiers. Liberalism, on the other hand, has been identified with the promotion of free trade and arguments for limited government. Whereas for classical republicans the realization of liberty depended on disinterested, harmonious citizens acting within the state, for liberals it depended on self-interested, competitive individuals acting outside the state in the market economy. The central question posed by recent historians of the American Revolution is which of these two ideological tendencies predominated.[4]

One reason for the intensity of the debate is that the flexible concept of "ideology" has been stretched to embrace far more than ideas about government per se. Looking beyond patriots' specific discussions of legitimate rule, political systems, duties to the state, and constitutional rights, historians frequently have found broader meanings pertaining to other important aspects of American social life. What has especially concerned such scholars as J. G. A. Pocock and Joyce Appleby, who have argued about the relative strengths of liberalism and republicanism, is the relationship between political ideas and attitudes toward economic development. Their contrasting perspectives on the economy have been phrased in terms of alternatively communitarian or individualistic values: the historians of classical republicanism have pointed to communal values harkening back to a precapitalist past, those of liberalism to the economic individualism of the commercial market.

In following this historical debate, one is repeatedly left asking how, if at all, Americans of the Revolutionary generation reconciled these conflicting social values. Part of the answer, to be sure, is that even some of the most articulate ideological spokesmen — such as Thomas Jefferson — were, to our minds, often frustratingly contradictory, perfectly capable of entertaining seemingly opposite sets of convictions at the same time. Another way to address this problem is to note that the political elite and public commentators were internally divided along regional and partisan lines, with some inclining more toward classical republicanism (most typically Federalist New Englanders) and others more toward liberalism (Democratic-Republican Philadelphians, New Yorkers, some southern planters). Whatever these internal logical inconsistencies, regional differences, and political disagreements among the revolutionary political leadership, however, the interpretive debate among historians over the relative importance of liberalism and republicanism has given surprisingly little attention to the transmission of such conflicting sets of values outside of explicitly political arguments. By concentrating on the ideological convictions of those most centrally engaged in the numerous political debates between the 1760s and the 1790s, historians of classical republicanism and liberalism have scarcely begun to explore the permeation of these basic ideological orientations into other dimensions of cultural life in the Revolutionary period.

Working on the periphery of the central debate about the political economy of republicanism, some historians have injected arguments about the ideological importance of contemporary commentary about religion and the family. Although when compared to the subjects of politics and economics, these topics may appear somehow less "public," religious and familial values pervaded the popular understanding of public life. Far from merely reflecting the ideological convictions of either classical republicanism or liberalism, moreover, the social values expressed in popular writings about religious and domestic life embodied the competing strains of individualism and communalism in ways that significantly muted the conflict between them. Only by looking beyond the explicitly political debate of the period can we come to appreciate better the manner in which these seemingly opposite sets of values were both absorbed and at least partly resolved on the level of popular ideology.

Whereas most historians of Revolutionary ideology have focused on the public debates about British imperial legislation, independence, the Constitution, and the partisan struggles of the 1790s, historians concentrating on religious and familial issues have dug deeply into the popular literary forms of published and unpublished sermons, domestic advice books, novels, and periodical fiction. There is little doubt that the audience for such works was extensive throughout the Revolutionary period. Indeed, among the imported books listed in late-eighteenth-century northeastern library and booksellers catalogues, both Samuel Richardson's novel *Pamela* and Thomas Newton's *Dissertations on the Prophecies* were held in far greater numbers than either of the two basic texts articulating classical republican and liberal perspectives on government, John Trenchard and Thomas Gordon's *Cato's Letters* and the *Independent Whig* and John Locke's *Treatise on Government*.[5] Cheaper, unbound sermons by American clergymen and lay religious exhorters spoke to an even wider public, and since some of these works were originally delivered orally, they might therefore have reached the illiterate as well as the educated. Literacy was high, in any case, especially in the northeast, where the popular revolutionary movement was strongest, and it is doubtful that there was a wide gap between oral and print cultures. Plenty of inexpensive broadside, pamphlet, and periodical publications spoke to high and low alike. Even the first American magazines, which were certainly expensive by modern standards, were distributed through a remarkably broad spectrum of northern urban society.[6] While there were components of the culture of the educated elite that were not shared by ordinary Americans — perhaps including an understanding of some of the more complex constitutional issues at stake in the struggle with Britain — the reverse is less true. With few exceptions, the popular culture of revolutionary America was popular more in the sense of being widely shared than in the sense of being the distinctive culture of the illiterate. And this popular culture was particularly preoccupied with both religious and domestic concerns.

Arguments for the centrality of religion to American revolutionaries have a long history, of course. Before the emergence of the current republicanism-liberalism debate, as formidable a spokesman as Perry Miller insisted on the fundamental connection between Puritan covenant theology and the revolutionary pronouncements of patriot clergymen.[7] The earliest formulations of the republican perspective by Bernard Bailyn were, indeed, written in part to challenge this religious interpretation.[8] Since then several works have appeared that further clarify the relationship of religious ideas to the ideology of the Revolution. Taken together these present a broad range of arguments for the basic affinity of American Protestantism to classical republicanism, for an implicit connection between religion and liberalism, and for the independent ideological contribution of religious beliefs.[9] So far, no one has attempted to untangle the strands of individualism and communitarianism within the dominant forms of revolutionary religious expression, however, or to relate them to other currents within popular culture.

The case for the importance of religion to the American Revolution builds on a long history extending back to the seventeenth century. Among patriot New Englanders, especially, and to a lesser extent among Presbyterians and Baptists elsewhere, connections between religion and revolution can be traced to the English revolutionary Puritanism of the seventeenth century. Whereas in England the radicalism of the 1640s and 1650s was driven underground after 1660, in America many ideas associated with the English Revolution stayed closer to the surface, gaining a kind of legitimacy among orthodox Protestants. American writings of the eighteenth century suggest that even the memory of Oliver Cromwell was not entirely tarnished by the shift to the right after the Glorious Revolution.[10] Transforming the pro-monarchical English holiday of Guy Fawkes Day, New England's alternative of "Pope's Day" annually ritualized hatred for both Catholics and the Stuart kings.[11] Meanwhile milder and more conventionally whig formulations about the blessings of English liberty had already found their way into Congregational sermons in the wake of the Glorious Revolution.[12] On the level of religious belief, other elements of the English revolutionary tradition were sustained in the colonies — criticisms of sacerdotal authority, the idea of an elect nation, expectations of a millennial future — even though they did not always take an explicitly political form.[13] In the middle of the eighteenth century, the religious revivals of the Great Awakening reinforced and further disseminated these themes in many parts of the colonies.[14] It is no accident that popular support for the American Revolution came disproportionately from the Congregational, Presbyterian, and Baptist denominations most powerfully affected both by the Puritan past and by the evangelical movement of the mid-eighteenth century. Of course influential nonrevivalist Congregational and Presbyterian ministers — such as Charles Chauncy, Jonathan Mayhew, and John Witherspoon — also joined in the religious attack on British tyranny, similarly drawing on a history of New England and Scottish mistrust of English rule that was rooted in the revolutionary seventeenth century.

An appreciation of the familial themes in Revolutionary ideology is more recent among scholars, related above all to the rise of interest in the history of the family and the history of women.[15] This ideological dimension surfaces above all in the debate of the 1780s and 1790s over female education and in the emerging genre of popular sentimental fiction. As a leading literary historian has recently argued, the American Revolution coincided with the onset of another, "reading" revolution.[16] Not only were Americans, especially women, becoming increasingly literate, but popular literary taste was shifting away from purely devotional religious literature to sentimental fiction.[17] Standing somewhat between these two genres and also in great demand in the late eighteenth century were numerous conduct books written by English and Scottish moralists that prescribed the appropriate education, behavior, and demeanor of young women and men facing prospects of marriage. After midcentury, newly established American magazines such as the *Boston Magazine,* the *American Museum,* and the *New York Magazine* also featured innumerable sentimental short stories, as well as pieces of practical domestic advice. French and English novels were imported into the colonies in growing numbers, and by the end of the century the prodigious production of indigenous American sentimental literature had begun.[18]

The themes of this fiction and didactic literature almost inevitably involved courtship and seduction. The stock characters of novels and short stories consisted of dictatorial fathers sabotaging the marital choices of their daughters and sons, aristocratic rakes bent on exploiting maidens deceived by false promises, and, of course, the innocent common young women and men themselves, who were egalitarian and trusting, representative of simple, bourgeois virtue. What united the bulk of this literature and gave it an implicitly revolutionary meaning was its protest against the arbitrary control of fathers and the decadence of a hereditary elite.[19] Building on the model of Richardson's *Clarissa,* which along with his *Pamela* was itself one of the best-sellers of Revolutionary America, story after story either written or reprinted in late-eighteenth-century America told of the cruelty of authoritarian, status-seeking fathers forcing their sacrificial offspring to reject true love or to accept odious suitors against their will.[20] So pervasive was this basic narrative structure that a character in one novel proclaims, "I hate almost all fathers in novels, because their poor daughters must suffer so much for their stubbornness."[21]

Such protests against oppressive patriarchal authority were seconded by equally strident objections to corrupt and artificial manners associated with aristocratic fashion and foreign taste. In fiction, innumerable foppish rogues, like the character Dimple in Royall Tyler's play *The Contrast* or Montraville in Susanna Rowson's *Charlotte Temple*, illustrated the moral dangers hidden within seductive genteel refinement. The prescriptive literature written by popular moralists also repeatedly warned against the dissipated pursuit of frivolous fashionable amusements at the expense of the simple virtues of domestic life. "If I wished a lady's picture to appear to advantage, it should not be taken when she was dressing for an assembly, a levee, or a birth night," counseled the English clergyman John Bennet in the many American editions of his instructive *Letters to a Young Lady*. "She should be holding *one* lovely infant in her arms, and presenting a moral page, for the instruction of *another*."[22] The goal of female education, he insisted, was not the showy, polite accomplishments of foreign languages, musical skills, or learned conversation, but "the culture of the heart."[23]

The readers of this fictional and prescriptive literature about family life were no doubt typically more educated, genteel, and religiously liberal than the evangelical Protestants, but the messages of evangelical religion and sentimental literature were in many respects similar. Both endorsed expressions of emotion and both criticized traditional authority in its ecclesiastical and patriarchal forms. The fact that prominent clergymen launched a vigorous campaign against novel reading is often regarded as evidence of a gap between the worlds of religion and literature.[24] Yet this very competition also suggests that these worlds considerably overlapped.[25]

No less an orthodox New Light than Jonathan Edwards took notice of favorable reviews in the British press of recent romances by Fénelon, Fielding, and Richardson, and found the writing of the latter, in the words of his son, "wholly favourable to good morals and purity of character."[26] Ebenezer Parkman, a theologically conservative minister from Westborough, Massachusetts, similarly read both volumes of *Pamela* with great interest, expressing in his diary his intention to "draw up . . . some Remarks" on the work.[27] Nor were these instances of novel reading on the part of eighteenth-century American clergymen exceptional. The innumerable foreign and domestic variations on Richardsonian tales of innocent virtue pitted against worldly vice, with their characters ineluctably led from moral temptation to repentance and reform, met with widespread clerical approbation. In Samuel Miller's *Brief Retrospect of the Eighteenth Century* this New York Presbyterian offered an extensive survey of contemporary novels in which he scrupulously distinguished between the commendable writings of Richardson, Fielding, Goldsmith, Henry MacKenzie, Fanny Burney, and Charlotte Smith and the objectionable works of such writers as Smollet, Sterne, Diderot, and Voltaire.[28] Characterizing the prevailing "morbid appetite" for fiction as a disease, Miller nonetheless recommended the reading of selected novels, acknowledging that fiction is "one of the most powerful means of exciting curiosity, of awakening sympathy, and of impressing the understanding and the heart."[29] On the liberal end of the theological spectrum, the universalist minister Enos Hitchcock, while similarly expressing reservations about most novels, himself wrote a work of didactic sentimental fiction on the themes of domestic harmony and childhood education.[30] Much of the imported literature offering advice on education, including the popular Mrs. Chapone's *Letters on the Improvement of the Mind* as well as other well-known works by the respectable Scottish clergymen James Fordyce and Hugh Blair, reconciled an emphasis on piety with the approval of certain moralistic works of fiction.[31]

The conflicting religious attitudes of hostility and sympathy towards the novel stemmed, in part, from the clergy's own growing preoccupation with domestic themes similar to those found in fiction. Not since the seventeenth-century Puritans had so many ministers preached and written about the subjects of child rearing and family life.[32] And, like many of the novelists they so vociferously condemned, they too preached about the dangers of illegitimate pregnancy and the morally beneficial effects of feminine sensibility on men.[33] For all the animosity occasionally unleashed by clergymen against fiction, the culture of domestic sentimentality was religious as much as literary in its inspiration and form.[34] The clerical attack on the novel at the end of the eighteenth century can be seen in many ways as a quarrel among siblings, each committed to similarly sentimental conceptions of personal morality and the larger social good.

Just as the religious works and sentimental literature of the late eighteenth century were complementary components of the same larger culture, each bore directly on popular political understanding. Despite their seemingly apolitical content, many of the same themes that dominated religion and sentimental literature permeated the ritual activism and the polemical literature of the American Revolution. Biblical and familial imagery saturated revolutionary arguments, especially in appeals aimed at a large popular audience. The patriot movement repeatedly dramatized a religious perception of Great Britain as the agent of the Antichrist, beginning as early as the Stamp Act crisis of 1765 and continuing into the Revolutionary War. Colonial crowds, for example, hanged British ministers in effigy alongside the devil and turned the traditional anti-Catholic holiday of Pope's Day into a celebration of the American cause.[35] The polemical pamphlet and newspaper literature of the Revolution repeatedly associated the British with the Antichrist and the Americans with the ancient Israelites resisting tyrannical oppression.[36] One of the mostly widely reprinted revolutionary pamphlets of the entire period, the lay Baptist John Allen's *Oration upon the Beauties of Liberty,* modeled its plea for resistance directly on that of the Old Testament prophet Micah.[37] With increased frequency as the colonists moved towards independence, patriot literature portrayed the Americans not only as oppressed Israelites but as the historical forces of Christ destined by Providence to usher in the glory of the millennial kingdom of God.[38]

Often such explosive religious imagery was combined with equally emotional references to the dynamics of family life. Thomas Paine's best-selling *Common Sense* wove into its argument for independence both an appeal to the Old Testament prophets' indictment of monarchy and a characterization of America as a stifled, overprotected adolescent coming of age.[39] In an influential printed sermon of 1776, the Boston minister Jonathan Mayhew even more thoroughly mixed together religious and familial metaphors in his argument for American independence: Liberty was "a celestial Maid, the daughter of God, and, excepting his Son, the firstborn of heaven."[40] The conception of America as a virtuous youth was, of course, encoded in the name of the early patriot organization, the Sons of Liberty, and later on applied as well by the female Daughters of Liberty. Conversely, just as Great Britain assumed the diabolical stature of the Antichrist, the mother country and the King were both repeatedly cast in the image of oppressive, cruel parents.[41] By no means coincidentally, at the conclusion of the Revolution its consummate symbol of authority and stability, George Washington, became known as the benign father of the nation, the good parent replacing the bad.[42]

On the one hand, this religious and familial imagery can be seen as the means by which revolutionary leaders conveyed their political message to ordinary colonists. Whereas Americans outside the educated elite might have had some difficulty committing themselves to the constitutional issues underlying the patriot cause, most Americans were Protestants well versed in a Providential understanding of history and were also members of families familiar with generational struggles between parents and children. The implication of such an interpretation is that the religious and familial symbolism was itself politically neutral, only to be infused with revolutionary meaning by effectively drawing analogies to the imperial struggle at hand. This point of view would suggest that the ideological power of this symbolism was emotional rather than substantive, that it lacked political content of its own and served primarily as a rhetorical flourish conveying revolutionary ideas to an unsophisticated public.

On the other hand, the religious and familial images that so often appeared within Revolutionary arguments need to be understood within the broader context of religious and literary culture, for the underlying ideological meanings embedded in the use of this imagery were more thoroughly articulated in religion, domestic advice literature, and fiction than in the explicitly political polemic itself. From this perspective, seemingly apolitical symbolism takes on a new significance as the source as well as the carrier of political outlooks. Many of the deeper social and psychological issues confronted by the Revolutionary generation — issues of authority, equality, autonomy, and interpersonal moral obligation — were central themes in religious exhortations about salvation and in sentimental and didactic writings about family life.

The relationship between communal and individualistic values comprises one of these basic themes, and it is also an issue at the heart of the current debate over the ideology of the American Revolution. Just as the political literature of the Revolutionary elite displays elements of both ideological tendencies — with communitarianism typically associated with classical republicanism and individualism with liberalism — one can find both tendencies within religious and sentimental literary culture. Yet the ways that communitarian and individualistic elements were combined within religion and fiction significantly deviate from both the liberal and the classical republican understandings of the political culture of the Revolution. A look at this broad cultural context reveals a fundamentally different way in which these core values of Revolutionary ideology may have been understood by this wider public. The simultaneous commitment to individualism and to the community appears from this perspective to be not so much contradictory as complementary. For while popular religious and sentimental culture incorporated aspects of both the classical republican and liberal points of view, a relatively cohesive social vision emerged despite the tension that existed within more explicitly political ideology.

Religion in eighteenth-century America is usually, if not exclusively, understood as communitarian, as wedded to a backward-looking ideal of social cooperation as opposed to the competitive individualism of the

modern, secular, commercial world. It is well known that in popular
evangelical exhortations, especially, the selfish pursuit of personal wealth
and social prestige were repeatedly denounced as terrible sins. Revivalists
preached on the superior morality of Christian self-sacrifice and loving
benevolence. The religious awakenings of the mid eighteenth century
were themselves collective events, the first truly mass conversion rituals
of American religious history, and the shared experience of the revivals
bound evangelicals together in community against their unregenerate
foes. Adherence to codes of simple dress and conspicuous abstention
from frivolous entertainment were among the many ways that evangelical Protestants shaped what has been called a "counterculture" of opposition to the worldliness of the elite.[43] These communal characteristics of
popular religious culture found repeated expression in the identification
of the patriot cause with the united forces of Christ and in the definition
of Revolutionary virtue as ascetic self-sacrifice on behalf of the whole. As
the Connecticut army chaplain David Avery phrased his millennial hopes
for the Revolution, while simultaneously denouncing selfish sinners who
succumbed to the temptations of avarice and covetousness, "Should pure
and heavenly love pervade through all these states, quicken all our
hearts, and unite us in the glorious interest of the REDEEMER'S KINGDOM;
should we love our neighbors as we love ourselves . . . then *America* will
become IMMANUEL'S *land*."[44]

Yet there were individualistic elements to American religious culture
as well, and they were more compatible with liberal notions of natural
rights than with classical republican appeals to public virtue. Core doc-
trines of Reformation Protestantism had always upheld the primacy of
the individual believer's relationship to God, and in the early American
colonies church covenants were formed out of essentially contractual
relationships among individuals. In different ways both the Arminian liberals and the Calvinist evangelicals of the eighteenth century developed
this individualistic side of colonial Protestantism. In their emerging critique of the Calvinist assumption of human depravity and their increased
emphasis on the power of individuals to effect their own salvation, the
so-called liberal Protestants, such as Chauncy, Mayhew, and Alexander
Garden, were in harmony with the individualism of political and economic liberal theory if not necessarily with its acceptance of material self-
interest or its belief in limited government. Evangelical Protestantism
also had its individualistic features, based on its very emphasis on conversion, which accorded primary value to individual spiritual experience
as opposed to either sacerdotal and secular authority. During the Great

Awakening, moreover, the conflicts between revivalist and nonrevivalist clergymen meant that many individuals were confronted for the first time with a choice between competing religious alternatives. In her recent history of colonial religion, Patricia U. Bonomi has gone so far as to suggest that the Great Awakening produced "a new spirit of defiant individualism" in the face of the collapse of the unitary religious ideal.[45] Other historians have presented evangelical culture as uneasily balanced between contradictory individualistic and communitarian tendencies, as implicitly sanctioning the rise of a complex market economy and rising standard of living while at the same time offering a critique in the name of a primitivistic communal ideal.[46] Whereas the latter tendency merged with the classical republican plea for self-sacrificial virtue, the revivalists' defense of minority rights against religious establishments provided religious reinforcement for the more general liberal rights theories of the Revolution.

Just as religion contained both individualistic and communitarian elements, so did sentimental literature. Whereas the religion of this period is generally associated with communal solidarity, however, the fiction and domestic advice literature are usually described as individualistic. One reason for the religious reaction against the novel, argues a recent literary critic, is that it enabled readers individually to interpret the printed word without the intervention of clerical middlemen.[47] The same might well be said about the proliferation of domestic advice books, including even the many that were written by clergymen. Not only were individual consumers of literature thus freer to make their own judgments about the didactic messages being delivered to them, but the moral predicaments presented in this literature were typically those faced by individuals with little or no protection from family or community. The images of young women and men encountering the temptation of a dissipated high life, or of impressionable virgins confronting deceptively charming seducers, encapsulated a social vision in which the self-contained individual is pitted against a turbulent, competitive, and self-interested world. A standard interpretation of the rise of the novel links the emergence of sentimental literature to the rise of the liberal bourgeoisie.[48] Not only were aristocratic rakes a common target of this fiction, but the theme of youthful rebellion against patriarchal authority expressed the Lockean values of individual autonomy as against filial obedience.[49] Both the class and the generational dynamics of this fiction, then, seem to celebrate a kind of liberal, anti-authoritarian individualism.

Yet at the same time the culture of sentimentality insisted on the necessity of human interaction and extolled the virtues of domestic life, partly in the interests of the greater social good.[50] Even in fiction the gender dynamics illustrated in these plots reveal both the authors' sympathies with the hapless heroines victimized by male vice and their simultaneous inability to endorse female self-assertion.[51] Clarissa's rebellion leads her to ruin. Pamela, for all her heroic assertiveness, speaks in the name of cross-class mutual responsibility and familial bonds. Similarly, in one of the best works of American fiction in this period, Hannah Foster's *The Coquette,* the sympathy one feels with the plight of miserable Eliza, who holds out for love and is deceived by the false charm (and false riches) of Sanford, is balanced by the subplot of the successful, sentimental marriages of her more sensible friends Lucy Freeman and the Richmans.[52] While freer to act than the women, even the men portrayed in sentimental fiction were ultimately bound to the conjugal unit, dependent on women and marriage for the realization of their virtue.[53] No less popular than the plot of the pathetic young woman destroyed by status-seeking parents and predatory men was that of the selfish rake reformed by triumphant female purity.[54] Even the didactic literature on courtship and marriage, while occasionally warning against the adage "a reformed rake makes the best husband," urged women to "civilize" their suitors and husbands, "inspite of early vicious habits, [to] compel them to a behavior of tenderness and love."[55] Nor were children depicted as ideally independent of all parental authority: good parents — like Richardson's triumphantly maternal Pamela or the crestfallen parents of Rowson's disobedient Charlotte — exercised benign and legitimate authority over their young.[56] In all these ways, then, the fictional endorsement of individualism was partial — qualified by its concurrent celebration of the solidarity, interdependence, and even the gender and generational hierarchy of what was portrayed as the ideal family.

Upon first impression, these images drawn from the religion and sentimental literature of the Revolutionary era seem a jumble of contradictions. One might be tempted to conclude that fundamentally irreconcilable tendencies collided within popular culture, with individualistic tendencies supporting a liberal ideological outlook and communitarian tendencies supporting a classical republican view. Surely the coexistence of these values was, in part, an expression of tension. However, from another perspective these contradictions can be resolved, at least to a point. Rather than being simply torn between liberal and classical republican values, Revolutionary popular culture defined the relationship between individualism and communitarianism in a significantly different

way. The individualism of evangelical religion and sentimental literature
was not that of economic liberalism. Far from endorsing the competitive
free market, this was an individualism opposing the arbitrary authority
of state churches and coercive fathers in the name of personal spiritual
and emotional experience. It surely upheld the freedom of individual
choice, but the choices described within these religious and sentimental
frameworks were not those of individual autonomy but of identification
with the communal groups of the church and family. Evangelicals
insisted on the "right" of individuals to join churches without the consent of their families or their social superiors, but they also assumed the
"right" of converts to regulate the behavior of their families and fellow
church members.[57] Similarly, sentimental fiction accorded adolescents
the "right" to resist tyrannical patriarchal authority, but at the same
time it sanctioned the authority of truly loving parents and husbands and
celebrated the virtues of emotional interdependence within a family life
that was deemed the foundation of social order itself. Thus, an anonymous essayist writing on love in a 1791 issue of the *New York Magazine*
linked the individual romantic emotion to the collective good: "Perhaps,
in the moment of its highest power, it may occupy the whole soul: But the
moment of delirium will pass. . . . The lover becomes a husband, a parent, a citizen."[58]

Nor was this ethic of social solidarity the same as public spirit in the
classical republican sense. The church and the family, unlike representative government or the military, were institutions located outside the
republican state. Yet increasingly in the 1780s and 1790s, clergymen and
educators claimed that these institutions were the moral foundation of
the American republic. Good citizenship or patriotism, so the argument
went, depended less on direct political participation than on the personal self-discipline and the emotional identification with the American
republic that was taught in churches and families.[59]

Communitarianism and individualism can thus be interpreted as compatible as well as antagonistic themes within American Revolutionary
ideology, particularly if one looks beyond explicitly political debate to the
level of religious and literary popular culture. The dominant political language that emerged within American religion and sentimental literature
was neither of public service nor of individual self-interest; rather, it spoke
of diffuse patriotic sentiment. This sentiment was perceived to be rooted
in interdependent social relationships symbolized by church and family.
Ideally these institutions were at once internally communitarian while
separate from the collective order of organized political life — private and

increasingly voluntary while set apart from the competition of the market economy.

Rather than simply reflecting either classical republican or liberal political ideologies, these themes within Revolutionary popular ideology anticipate the emergence of nineteenth-century voluntary, benevolent, and social reform associations, groups with extensive support among white middle-class Protestants that also drew heavily upon the language of religion and sentimental domesticity. Movements espousing a variety of causes ranging from temperance to the abolition of slavery profoundly shaped the course of American history, while typically remaining critical of both competitive capitalism and partisan politics. Alexis de Tocqueville recognized this peculiar mixture of antistatist individualism and social communitarianism when he described Americans as both libertarian and conformistic.[60] One can see this peculiar juxtaposition of values already in much of the popular ideology of the American Revolution. The religious and familial symbolism within Revolutionary discourse at once helps to explain popular allegiance to the patriot cause and suggests ways that important tendencies within revolutionary popular culture — significantly different from both the liberal and the classical republican traditions — shaped the future development of American democracy. However useful the categories of liberalism and classical republicanism have proved in the analysis of Revolutionary political debate, these ideological tendencies were not polar opposites but overlapping parts of a cultural whole that historians have misleadingly torn asunder.[61]

CHAPTER 7

The Gendered
Meanings of Virtue
in Revolutionary America

PREFACE   First appearing in 1987 in the wake of Joan Scott's pathbreaking article, "Gender: A Useful Category of Analysis" of 1986, this essay
seeks to uncover the latent assumptions about gender informing American
Revolutionary thought. Like the previous essay in this volume on "Religion, Literary Sentimentalism, and Popular Revolutionary Ideology," it
moves away from the limited arguments about republicanism and liberalism that have dominated recent historical work on Revolutionary ideology, stressing instead the multiple and divergent connections between the
Revolution and notions of ideal masculinity and femininity. Underscoring
the merger of evangelical and radical Enlightenment ideals of motherhood, "The Gendered Meanings of Virtue" expands upon the conceptual
framework developed in the earlier "American Feminine Ideals in Transition." It refines general references to the Enlightenment by concentrating
upon the moral theories of Scottish philosophers as well as upon religion,
fiction, and the polemical works of the American Revolution.

. . .

In its contemporary colloquial usage, "virtue" is usually a term for
female sexual prudence and benevolent activity with old-fashioned connotations. It evokes traits like chastity and altruism and, in a cynical
post–sexual revolution world, prudery and hypocritical do-goodism.

On the one hand, these connotations are very old in Western culture.

The sexual meaning of the word "virtue" dates back to medieval and ancient times, when the virtues were symbolized as virgins.[1] The Catholic ideals of celibacy and charity also reinforced the association of Christian virtue with sexual purity and personal sacrifice. On the other hand, the Protestant Reformation placed less emphasis on these qualities, criticizing the monastic ideal of celibacy and denying the spiritual èfficacy of church offerings. It stressed other individual virtues — piety, temperance, frugality, and work in a useful calling.

The view that women were capable of greater sexual self-control and generosity than men arose later, in the eighteenth and nineteenth centuries, at different times and to different degrees in different places and social groups. This transformation was, at most, only indirectly a consequence of the cultural changes brought on by the Reformation. In middle-class America, where both Calvinism and early evangelical Protestantism were particularly strong, it was not until the end of the eighteenth century that women were commonly idealized as selfless and pure. According to the quintessentially Victorian view, intrinsically feminine traits — traits eventually satirized as "motherhood and apple pie" — lay at the base of the American nation. It is the echo of this nineteenth-century culture that we hear in the colloquial use of the word "virtue" today.

Among historians identified with the recent interpretation of the American Revolution known as the "Republican synthesis," the word "virtue" has, however, been invested with an older political meaning.[2] Resurrected in its classical and early modern republican forms, the term refers not to female private morality but to male public spirit, that is, to the willingness of citizens to engage actively in civic life and to sacrifice individual interests for the common good. Is virtue, then, to be understood as a word with two different meanings — one personal and female, the other political and male? Or is there a deeper historical and symbolic connection between the two definitions?

An appreciation of the eighteenth-century political use of the term is essential to an understanding of the American Revolution, but it is becoming increasingly clear that such an appreciation must also take into account the history of masculine and feminine symbolism. Conceptions of politics and of gender were tied together in late-eighteenth-century America in ways that historians have only begun to unravel. The transition toward the personal and feminine definition of "virtue" was a development already occurring during the Revolutionary period, partly in response to political events and partly in response to changes in gender-based symbols that had already begun.

The experiences and perceptions of women during the American Revolution have attracted considerable scholarly attention from historians of women. So far, most studies point to the importance of women's activity during the Revolution and to the ways in which their social status was affected, for good or ill.[3] Here the relationship of women to the Revolution will be approached from a somewhat different angle. Pursuing insights contained in a few recent writings, I would suggest that conceptions of sexual difference — views that were at once deeply held (often only implicit) and highly unstable — underlay some of the most basic premises of the Revolution and shaped important ideological changes in the early Republic.[4] However much the meaning of "virtue" changed over the course of this period, it remained a word laden with assumptions about gender.

The focus of this essay, in other words, is less on the Revolution's impact on women and more on the influence of gender-based symbols in the formation of Revolutionary thought. To trace the late-eighteenth-century changes in this symbolism contributes to our understanding of gender as a cultural — and, therefore, historical — construct. The connections between the constructions of gender and politics point to the importance of women's history in exploring the conventional questions of political history.[5]

Some of the most influential recent intellectual historians of Anglo-American political thought have considered individual words — liberty, tyranny, corruption, and especially virtue — as keys that unlock the meaning of the broadly consensual historical "discourse" of classical republicanism.[6] A few others have only just begun to challenge the overly static and holistic conception of culture that this "republican synthesis" implies.[7] I argue here that an examination of the multivalent meanings embedded in the term virtue leads to a more complex and dynamic understanding not only of gender but also of Revolutionary ideology itself.

The work of Caroline Robbins, Bernard Bailyn, Gordon Wood, and J. G. A. Pocock outlines the extent to which American patriots conceptualized the American Revolution within the intellectual framework of classical republicanism. As we now understand this intellectual background, the revival of ancient republican theories — first in the city-states of the Italian Renaissance, then in seventeenth-century England — was kept alive into the eighteenth century by a small, disunified, yet vociferous group of political dissidents in England. The distinctive structural conditions of politics in the colonies, in combination with the values of

American Protestantism, led the colonists of the mid eighteenth century to embrace many of the tenets of classical republicanism.

According to the basic constitutional theory of classical republicanism, the preservation of liberty depended on a mixed and balanced government. Such a government consisted essentially of three parts, each representative of a different social order: the king in the monarchy, the aristocracy in the House of Lords (or the colonial Councils), and the property-holding populace in the elected legislature. The hallmark of a free republic, according to this theory, was the autonomy of a legislature with institutionalized power to tax. The social base necessary to sustain this arrangement, described most fully by James Harrington in the seventeenth century, was a large class of arms-bearing freeholders — fairly equal and independent property owners, able to defend themselves, and sharing a regard for the public good — whose common voice would be expressed in their elected legislature.[8] When in the 1760s and 1770s the British imperial government challenged powers traditionally exercised by the elected colonial legislatures, including the power to tax, colonists interpreted the new policy in the terms of republican theory — as a fundamental assault on their liberty.

Even then, however, the political ideas espoused by the American Revolutionaries were a hybrid mixture. Some of these derived not from the classical republican tradition of Machiavelli and Harrington but from constitutional ideas about individual rights and from Protestant theories about the providential purpose of government. For American Revolutionaries, as for those English opposition writers, such as John Trenchard and William Gordon, who were most widely read in the colonies, the ideas of egalitarian individualism and Nonconforming Protestantism were blended with classical republican notions about the sovereignty of the popular legislature.

Throughout the Revolutionary period, virtue was the most valued quality defining individual commitment to the American republican cause. One reason for its salience was that both the classical republican and the Protestant traditions emphasized the value of public virtue. According to both, virtue reconciled otherwise contradictory commitments to both individual political freedom and the greater public good, because virtue would prompt otherwise selfish individuals to actions on behalf of a just and harmonious social order. The main difference between these traditions lay in their assumptions about the source of virtue: within orthodox Protestantism, it was bestowed by Providence or faith; within classical republicanism, it was obtained through independent property holding and mixed government. Each tradition, moreover, had its own way of describing the relation of virtuous citizens, high and low, to the body politic. Within orthodox Protestantism political virtue was primarily a trait of good rulers who, with God, tended the political order. Ordinary members of the covenanted community assumed the more limited responsibility of obeying good rulers and living according to the moral code. Within classical republicanism, also, the few and the many exercised their virtue in dissimilar ways: the titled and the propertied were to rule; the people were to rise against threats of foreign invasion and political corruption. Yet according to each of these traditions, the virtue of both the rulers and the populace was indispensable to preserving the good health of the polity.

The orthodox Protestant and classical republican traditions also fundamentally agreed that public virtue was an inherently masculine trait. Patriarchal analogies pervaded seventeenth-century English and American Protestant political thought, which drew heavily on Old Testament models: a good leader, like a good father, was wise, caring, and firm.[9] In 1637, the New England Puritan governor John Winthrop defended the power of the Massachusetts magistrates against Henry Vane, a supporter of Anne Hutchinson, by insisting on the superior judgment of the "fathers of the commonwealth." The Aristotelian notion of virtue, as always "united with a rational principle" — a notion that continued to dominate American Puritan ethical theory until the late seventeenth century — by definition favored men since men were deemed more rational than women.[10]

Not that women were ever regarded as incapable of all kinds of virtue. Women were thought to be as rational as men in exercising the private, Christian virtues — temperance, prudence, faith, charity. It was specifically public virtue — active, self-sacrificial service to the state on behalf of the common good — that was an essentially male attribute. While there were a few exceptional early American women who won recognition for their heroic defense of the wider community, these were the kind of exceptions that proved the rule. Public virtue was indeed possible for exceptional women, but it was never an inherently feminine characteristic.

Among the most renowned examples of exceptional women were the New Englanders Hannah Dustin and Mary Rowlandson, who bravely withstood Indian attacks.[11] Hannah Dustin, who won her fame by brutally scalping her assailants, demonstrated qualities of physical courage and strength that conformed to a typically male model of virtue. What distinguished her as a heroine was precisely her ability to step out of her femininity. Mary Rowlandson, to the contrary, never overtly violated the Puritan conception of a virtuous woman. Her heroism consisted in her pious adherence to Puritan faith and in her shrewd use of domestic skills to earn the protection of her enemies. Yet it was the very fact that she was an *exceptional* woman — a woman who kept her faith and maintained her wits amid heathens — that largely accounts for the sensational popularity of her captivity narrative. Despite the striking differences between them, Hannah Dustin and Mary Rowlandson won public acclaim precisely because they, as women, went so far beyond typical expectations: they proved themselves neither weaker nor less capable than men of absorbing and retaining the standards of civilization.

In the classical republican tradition, the masculine attributes embedded in the concept of public virtue are even more pronounced than those in American Puritanism. The ancient origins of this highly gendered concept can be traced as far back as the Homeric idea of *aretē,* or human excellence (later translated as "virtue"), which stressed the physical strength and bravery displayed in athletic contests and in battles. This emphasis on courage remained a basic component of the classical tradition and later fused with Greek and Roman ideas about the intellectual and cooperative virtues (such as judgment, justice, and friendship) that bind men in citizenship within the polis.[12] According to the revitalized Renaissance republicanism of Machiavelli, virtue was, again, best displayed in acts of military heroism and civic activism. Exemplary citizens were above all daring soldiers and inspired orators — those who risked danger and won glory in valiant defense of liberty. As Pocock has defined it, the Machiavellian *virtù* that proved so influential in America consisted in "the skill and courage by which men are enabled to dominate events and fortune."[13] Hannah Pitkin examined the gender implications of the word in her book on Machiavelli's political theory: "Though it can sometimes mean [Christian] virtue, *virtù* tends mostly to connote energy, effectiveness, virtuosity. . . . The word derives from the Latin *virtus,* and thus from *vir,* which means 'man.' *Virtù* is thus manliness, those qualities found in a 'real man.'"[14] The political realm was constituted by the actions of fathers and sons — patriarchal founders and fraternal citizens. Typically, women appeared in this symbolic matrix as the dangerous, unreliable force of *fortuna* (or, later, according to Pocock, public credit), threatening to sabotage the endeavor of virtuous men.[15]

On the face of it, the masculinity embedded in ideas of public virtue appears trivial, the simple reflection of the male domination of political institutions. In fact, property requirements guaranteed that statesmen, soldiers, and enfranchised citizens would be, by definition, men. The intrinsic maleness of the term "virtue" could be seen, then, as the logical, even automatic, cultural consequence of male political hegemony. But there is more to it.

These notions of masculinity were fundamental to the concept of public virtue in a way that would change in Revolutionary America without bringing corresponding changes in military recruitments, property holding, or franchise requirements. As ideas about the political order underwent a profound transformation during the Revolutionary period, so did the understanding of virtue. Even as political institutions continued to be essentially male, underlying shifts in the gendered meaning of virtue expressed (even, perhaps, helped to make possible) a new understanding of republican politics.

. . .

In the mid 1770s, with the outbreak of revolution and war, the specifically masculine qualities embedded in conceptions of public virtue received, if anything, still more emphasis. The model patriot was frequently described according to classical republican ideals as a heroic orator or citizen-soldier.[16] In a widely distributed 1775 oration commemorating the Boston Massacre, Joseph Warren envisioned "fathers/ looking/. . . with smiling approbation on their sons who boldly stand forth in the cause of virtue."[17] Virtue was above all the mark of "the uncorrupted patriot, the useful citizen, and the invincible soldier."[18] Even as military enthusiasm began to flag in subsequent years, calls to "virtuous Americans" to give "firm and manly support" to the war effort continued.[19] According to a minister preaching before Virginia troops in New Jersey in 1777, virtue was inextricably associated with glory and fame: "Glory is the reward of honourable toils, and public fame is the just retribution for public service; the love of which is so connected to virtue, that it seems scarcely possible to be possessed of the latter without some degree of the former."[20]

If the virtues of heroic courage, glory, and fame were inherently male, the opposites — cowardice, idleness, luxury, dependence — were, not surprisingly, castigated as the "effeminate" weaknesses of unpatriotic men. Whereas the Americans were "a hardy virtuous set of men," proclaimed a patriot orator in 1776, their corrupt British enemies had succumbed to "that luxury which effeminates the mind and body."[21] But what about women themselves? Was there any model of female public virtue consistent with the glorification of male heroism in the Revolution? The most famous examples were the legendary "Molly Pitcher" of the Battle of Monmouth and Deborah Sampson Gannett, a young woman subsequently glorified for disguising herself as a man in order to enlist in the Revolutionary army.[22] More typical were the women gathered in such organizations as the Daughters of Liberty and the Ladies Association, who abstained from tea drinking, boycotted loyalist shops, made homespun clothing, and raised money in support of the Revolutionary cause.[23] Neither the courage of Gannett nor these women's less heroic — Protestant as well as republican — virtues of industriousness, abstention, charity, and frugality differed markedly from what was expected of patriotic men. Essentially the only distinctively feminine images of Revolutionary virtue during the 1770s were those of a mother passively donating her sons to the struggle or of a helpless virgin physically abused by the enemy.[24]

It was later, in the 1780s and 1790s, that a significantly separate image of female public spirit began to appear. During the period in which the exigencies of warfare gave way to the politics of state, women were increasingly presented as indispensable and active promoters of patriotism in men. As mothers, young social companions, and wives, women came to be idealized as the source not only of domestic morality but also of civic virtue itself.

Historian Linda Kerber has already drawn attention to the emerging idea of the "republican mother" in the late eighteenth century.[25] It was already a cliché of the age that mothers, not fathers, were particularly responsible for inculcating children with the piety, benevolence, and self-discipline that compose virtue.[26] By the turn of the century, several patriotic commentators had extended this responsibility to include the public virtue deemed necessary to sustain the republic. Women, according to this view, would serve the new nation by making good citizens of their sons despite formal exclusion from institutional political life. A few even justified the education of women on these grounds as a patriotic necessity. A young female graduate of Susanna Rowson's Academy foresaw the day when "future heroes and statesmen," having learned "the love of virtue" as children, "shall exaltingly declare, it is to my mother I owe this elevation."[27] In the words of one minister preaching in 1802, "How should it enflame the desire of the mothers and daughters of our land to be the occasion of so much good to themselves and others! — You will easily see that here is laid the basis of public virtue; of union, peace and happiness in society. . . . Mothers do, in a sense, hold the reins of government and sway the ensigns of national prosperity and glory."[28]

Though they held this responsibility as mothers, women were to instill public virtue in men through courtship and marriage perhaps even more.[29] It was repeatedly claimed, by American and English moralists both, that women's influence over men gave them the power to reform the manners and morals of society.[30] In the writings of American patriots, this notion took on a distinctively republican coloring. "Love and courtship, it is universally allowed, invest a lady with more authority than in any other situation that falls to the lot of human beings," declared a Columbia College orator in 1795. Describing American women as "patriots and philanthropists," he insisted that it was up to them to withstand "the deluge of vice and luxury, which has well nigh overwhelmed Europe, . . . [and] to save, to aggrandize your country! . . . The solidity and stability of the liberties of your country rest with you; since Liberty is never sure, 'till Virtue reigns triumphant."[31] Another writer similarly insisted that "female virtue," by which he essentially meant chastity, was the key to "national prosperity and the honour and happiness of posterity," because "the profoundest politicians, wisest statesmen, most invincible champions, greatest generals, ingenious artists, and even pulpit orators" spent so much of their time with women.[32] American men were advised that good republican citizenship, as well as personal happiness, would follow ineluctably from true love and marriage.[33]

∎ ∎ ∎

To understand the origins of this transformation of ideas about public virtue, it is necessary to look not only at Revolutionary political discourse but also at the seemingly nonpolitical ideas about human psychology, education, and women that were current in the eighteenth century. In this broader intellectual history one finds the origins of a long-term redefinition of gender distinctions already well underway by the 1770s and intimately connected to changes in the nonpolitical understanding of virtue. Over the course of the Revolutionary period, particularly as debates surrounding the Constitution formulated a new conception of republican government, these nonpolitical ideas about virtue came to assume political significance. Changes in the gender-based meaning of public virtue in the late eighteenth century owed as much to these earlier intellectual developments as to the influence of Revolutionary politics.

It is possible to identify at least three understandings of virtue that emerged in the American colonies during the eighteenth century — not one of which was derived from traditional Protestant or classical republican ideas of public virtue. The first, most pronounced in New England, was essentially religious. It concerned, above all, the relationship between virtue and grace. American Puritans, like Reform theologians in general, had long sought to balance the Calvinist belief in faith as the free gift of God with the view that individuals could voluntarily take certain steps to prepare for salvation. Acts of virtue themselves, the offspring of the human will and the intellect, could never lead to redemption. Yet at the same time a life of virtue would be the likely consequence of a predisposition toward grace.

Recent scholarship emphasizing the emotional, experiential aspects of Puritan piety has pointed to the continuities between developments within seventeenth-century Puritanism and the new forms of eighteenth-century evangelical Protestantism.[34] Even among seventeenth-century Harvard students of moral philosophy, the idea of virtue gradually became inseparable from a positive evaluation of the emotions.[35] In the middle of the eighteenth century, Jonathan Edwards used his formidable intellectual talent to reconcile this increasingly naturalistic conception of virtue with an uncompromising Calvinist belief in the sovereignty of God. An articulate proponent of religious revivalism, Edwards preached that only saving grace, experienced through the affections, could give rise to the real virtue of "disinterested benevolence." Unregenerate self-love could, he acknowledged, give rise to behavior in conformity with a narrowly utilitarian moral law. But "true virtue," as he defined it, consisted in a selfless "love to Being in general."[36]

When Edwards distinguished between sinful self-love and the virtue of "public benevolence," he did not mean public virtue in the classical republican sense.[37] He measured virtue by the disposition of the will and heart rather than by the performance of civic duty. Yet, for all his denial of the importance of external behavior, his ideal individual, like the classical republican one, would disregard narrow self-interest when it conflicted with the common good. Not surprisingly, during the American Revolution individuals combined elements of his nonpolitical conception of virtue with classical republicanism. In 1774 a Marblehead minister defined patriotism as "the grand law of love," explaining that "disinterested benevolence" led to "the support of virtue; the controul of vice, and the advancement of the best interests of [the] country." For many Revolutionary clergymen, the words "virtue," "piety," and "righteousness" were basically interchangeable.[38]

This type of religious virtue was not, of course, regarded as distinctively feminine. Yet there is, beginning in the late seventeenth century, a steady climb in the number of sermons that celebrate models of female virtue and piety. Women, long regarded as morally encumbered by their supposedly excessive emotionalism, were beginning to be regarded as particularly receptive to grace. The first vigorous proponent of this view was the third-generation Puritan pietist Cotton Mather. He explained that the greater tendency of women to experience religious conversion was a response to the distinctively female "difficulties both of *Subjection* and of *Child bearing.*"[39] Over the course of the eighteenth century, evangelical and liberal Protestant ministers alike increasingly preached on the theme of female piety.[40]

A second, though related, conception of virtue that emerged in eighteenth-century America came from the psychological theories of John Locke and the Scottish moral philosophers. Medieval faculty psychology, which had survived even the Protestant Reformation, became a subject of controversy in the late seventeenth and the eighteenth centuries. Among the many points at issue was the status of the "moral sense": Was it a rational or an emotional faculty? Some figures of the British Enlightenment, including John Locke and Thomas Reid, agreed with the older scholastic position that it was rational. Virtue was the chief object of Locke's educational theory and was, for him, still an essentially masculine trait. He wrote, above all for the fathers of sons, emphasizing not only reason, but other qualities culturally associated with men as well: stoicism, self-sufficiency, and physical hardiness.[41]

Another wave of Enlightenment opinion, represented in Scotland by Francis Hutcheson and in England by Lord Shaftesbury, claimed morality for the emotions.[42] It was, argued Hutcheson, not the offspring of reason but an inborn principle of sociability, "an instinct toward happiness."[43] If innate, however, moral sense was dependent, especially in infancy and early childhood, on parental nurturance. In their emphasis on education, if not in their epistemology, Locke and the Scots agreed: they all stressed noncoercive child rearing, saw children as corruptible but not corrupt, and posited innate qualities — whether reason or moral sense — which, if cultivated, would lead to virtue.[44] Although these particular philosophers envisioned men as the principal educators, their ideas about the importance of early childhood education gradually led to a greater emphasis on the motherhood role in didactic and medical literature.[45]

The question of whether reason or emotion was the more important source of virtue was never, of course, fully answered, but it is clear that the eighteenth century was a time of particular confusion and conflict over these basic epistemological issues.[46] Albert O. Hirschman has argued, for example, that avarice, previously regarded as a sinful "passion," was elevated to the status of a rational "interest" in this period.[47] This realignment coincided, more or less explicitly, with a revision of binary gender distinctions: rationality, long associated with men, was linked to interest; the emotions, long associated with women, to morality. Scottish philosophy and evangelical Protestantism, each occupying a kind of middle ground between the atomistic individualism of Locke and Hobbes and the communitarian ethos of classical republicanism, were particularly important in establishing these new connections.

Yet a third cultural movement — literary sentimentalism — contributed to this eighteenth-century reassessment of emotional life. Indeed, the intellectual boundaries between British moral philosophy, evangelical Protestantism, and sentimental fiction are impossible to draw clearly. As Norman Fiering has recently emphasized, the new moral philosophy of Hutcheson and Shaftesbury owed its origins to Puritan piety.[48] Edwards, determined to discourage a belief in a natural moral sense, nonetheless shared many of the ideas of the new moral philosophy. Edwards read sentimental fiction, and the Scottish moralists, also known as "sentimental philosophers," influenced those works through the writings of popularizers like Lord Kames.[49]

Yet, despite these historical interconnections, literary sentimentalism had a different orientation, style, and audience than either evangelicalism or moral philosophy. It concentrated on neither salvation nor epistemology, but on the quest for personal happiness through domestic relationships. Like exhortatory evangelical writings, but unlike moral philosophy, sentimental fiction was a relatively popular literary form in America (though largely imported from Britain). And, of all three movements, it was clearly literary sentimentalism that had the most to say specifically to and about women.

According to literary sentimentalism, virtue was above all a feminine quality. In the chain of being, women were the link between men and angels; they "ennoble human nature" by being not only "the fair" but also the "cherishing," "pious," "pacific," "sympathetic," and "reverential" sex.[50] The chief female virtues were "modesty," "tenderness," "delicacy," and "sensibility."[51] Women have a "superior sensibility of their souls," read one piece that appeared in several late-eighteenth-century American magazines. "Their feelings are more exquisite than those of men; and their sentiments greater and more refined."[52] Others summed up this idealized impression of women by stressing the female "qualities of the heart."[53] According to one American work of didactic fiction, women were best equipped to teach what Lord Kames had taught was "the chief branch" of learning, "the culture of the heart."[54]

If women were idealized for the supposedly innate qualities of emotionalism, tenderness, and delicacy, so too were they valued for a kind of self-discipline. The sentimental conception of female virtue was closely linked to chastity and the maintenance of simple tastes and manners. Often the word "virtue" was used simply to mean chastity, and in the didactic literature of the period women were repeatedly enjoined to protect their sexual purity.[55] In the midst of the early Revolutionary fervor a patriot magazine instructed its readers, "What Bravery is in man, Chastity is in Woman." Among the dominant themes in the popular fiction of the period, best exemplified in such works as Samuel Richardson's *Clarissa* and Susanna Rowson's *Charlotte Temple,* was that of the innocent virgin ruined by male lust. Another variation on this theme of seduction was that of the adulterous husband redeemed by his faithful and forgiving wife — also a plot developed by Richardson in *Pamela.*[56]

As Ian Watt stressed many years ago in his *Rise of the Novel,* this literature conveyed a specifically middle-class version of personal morality. Typically, the lustful men were aristocratic rakes, and the women were wholesome commoners. In America, especially after the Revolution, such plots took on an additional patriotic significance. The villains could be seen as representing not only aristocratic but European decadence as well. While the idea that women should abstain from sexual temptations and ornamental refinements was scarcely new in this period — American Protestant teachings had traditionally instructed housewives to be sexually self-restrained, frugal, and industrious — the equation of female virtue with chastity, modest dress, and useful knowledge became more pronounced in the late eighteenth century as women were increasingly deemed the moral instructors of men.[57] The numerous proponents of a practical education for women repeatedly made this point.[58] No longer were the traditional ascetic and self-sacrificial virtues regarded as more easily achieved by men. The older view of women as more closely tied to base physical nature than men had been gradually displaced by an image of women as particularly receptive to moral education. On the one hand, female virtues were themselves regarded as essentially natural. On the other hand, such virtues in women needed cultivation, and still more important, women were needed to cultivate virtue in men. In these respects, the late eighteenth century can be seen as a time in Western history when the nearly universal association of women with nature, and men with culture, was disrupted.[59]

. . .

Each in a different way, then, American Protestantism, Scottish moral philosophy, and literary sentimentalism opened the way for the feminization of ideas about public virtue. During the course of the Revolutionary period, these seemingly nonpolitical ideas began to displace the earlier idea of public virtue as military courage and civic glory. Royall Tyler's *The Contrast,* a popular play of the late 1780s, publicized as the first dramatic work by a "Citizen of the United States," conveniently marks the transition. The hero, appropriately named Colonel Manly, combines the new and old ideals of virtue. On the one hand, he is depicted as an old-fashioned New Englander and former Revolutionary War officer, who believes, in classical republican fashion, that the reason for the decline of ancient Greece was that "the common good was lost in the pursuit of private interest." His heroic manliness stands in contrast to the foppish and self-indulgent effeminacy of the English villain. Yet, the virtuous Manly himself, like the woman he loves, exudes "tenderness" and speaks "the language of sentiment."[60]

The changing meaning of virtue at once facilitated and reflected a transformation within American political thought. Several historians of political culture have noted that American Revolutionaries gradually revised their conceptions of public virtue. Earlier classical republican ideas increasingly competed with a more instrumental theory of government in which virtue played a much less conspicuous part.[61] Already in 1776 Thomas Paine's *Common Sense* argued that human cooperation and happiness were rooted in "society," not "government." Far from being the arena for the expression of virtue, a minimal state was necessary only because of the "inability of moral virtue to govern the world."[62] By the late 1780s, in the argument for the U. S. Constitution in the *Federalist Papers,* the maintenance of the Republic no longer depended on a conception of goodness within collective social life. Instead, the most realistic and necessary conditions of liberty were the competition of conflicting factional interests and the balance of governmental powers. Such conditions ideally would encourage the rise of a "virtuous" elite of political representatives, but the conception of virtue implied here was not the classical republican one.[63] The word virtue itself scarcely appeared in the *Federalist Papers*. Instead of being based in a self-sacrificial public spirit, the moral underpinnings of good government were reason, justice, and enlightenment — all qualities presumably embodied in the "natural aristocracy" that would emerge to lead the Republic. Good leadership was in this view fully compatible with "true" or "enlightened" self-interest.[64]

Not that the republican belief in disinterested public virtue altogether vanished with the creation and ratification of the Constitution. This classical idea continued to find expression in opposition movements well into the nineteenth century.[65] Moreover, even in the late-eighteenth-century ideological mainstream, a revised notion of republican virtue remained very much alive on the periphery of political debate. The demise of classical conceptions of virtue did not simply give rise to purely individual and utilitarian standards of morality devoid of reference to the common good.[66] Unlike the early Revolutionary virtue, the public virtue that remained was for the most part located outside rather than inside the state — the virtue of a diffuse, patriotic public whose allegiance was not to particular rulers or to the common interest of a homogeneous property-holding social order but to a large and impersonal republican nation. The institutional basis of this collective identification was to be found not in the military or in participatory government but in churches, schools, and families. Women — as social companions, wives, and mothers — assumed a major role in instructing men to be virtuous.

This transition can be seen in part as a response to political events between the 1770s and 1790s. By the late 1780s, Revolutionaries had generally given up the quest for heroic mastery that was associated with the early war effort and had taken on the task of political reform involved in the process of state building. The early ethic of public service called on the presumably voluntary participation of free and independent (male) individuals. It was, at bottom, deeply anti-institutional — hostile to established churches, to government bureaucracy, to standing armies, to banks. The movement toward a more personal, domestic, and feminized definition of morality in the 1780s and 1790s was linked to a greater acceptance of institutionalized public order. A similar transformation, also expressed in the substitution of female for male Revolutionary symbolism, has been recently traced in the French Revolution by historian Lynn Hunt.[67] In America, this transitional phase in the Revolution coincided with the creation and establishment of the American Constitution in the late 1780s.

The *Federalist Papers* insisted on strengthening national government —

giving it, in Alexander Hamilton's words, the "energy" the decentralized Confederation had previously lacked — while at the same time denying that the government had the power to interfere with natural rights or to eliminate inevitable factional conflict. Gone was the assumption that citizens would unite around a common conception of the public good. This false hope had only given rise to the specter of "majority tyranny" under the state constitutions of the 1770s and 1780s. In the words of an especially hard-bitten Federalist newspaper polemicist, *"virtue,* patriotism, or love of country, never was nor never will be till men's natures are changed, a fixed, permanent principle and support of government."[68]

The political order produced by the Constitution was designed more to protect private virtue than to be the arena for the expression of manly *virtù.* Despite the increased power of the national government in relation to that of the states, a continuing hostility to formal political institutions remained a major theme in American reform efforts well into the nineteenth century. The Constitution's provision of stable, limited government opened the way for the proliferation of voluntary associations, which enlisted significant numbers of women as well as men. These associations, often formed for the "benevolent" purposes of moral and social reform, were repeatedly justified on patriotic grounds, as vital to the preservation of the liberty and harmony of the American nation.

The Revolution had in effect accelerated a long-term cultural process that began well before the outbreak of the imperial conflicts with Britain. A transition in the meanings of virtue, associated with changes in ideas about sex difference, meant that women and the emotions became increasingly associated with moral activity, while men and reason became more exclusively associated with the utilitarian pursuit of self-interest. By the end of the eighteenth century, most people were beginning to believe that these were complementary contributions to the common good.[69]

These changes in themselves owed little to the American Revolution or to republican thought. The underlying cultural transformation was already underway by the 1770s, and it was, from the beginning, transatlantic in scope. What did change as a specific consequence of the American Revolutionary experience was that the feminine notion of virtue took on a political significance it had previously lacked. Americans never altogether abandoned the idea that the populace of the republic should be virtuous. Instead, they relegated the production and maintenance of public virtue to a new realm, one presided over largely by women. Women, as Lester Cohen and Linda Kerber have observed about the Revolutionary writer Mercy Otis Warren, continued to embody the

collectivist values of classical republicanism after they had ceased to resonate in national politics.[70] The transformation in conceptions of femininity and masculinity, the emotions, and self-interest that had occurred
in the eighteenth century made it possible to preserve the notion of public virtue while at the same time divesting it of its former constitutional
significance. Virtue, if still regarded as essential to the public good in a
republican state, became ever more difficult to distinguish from private
benevolence, personal manners, and female sexual propriety.[71]

Subsequent developments among the early-nineteenth-century middle
and upper classes deepened these symbolic associations.[72] The declining
birth rate in the nineteenth century may have been a result of the growing ability of women to discipline male sexuality.[73] As the American
polity became more democratic and expansionist, women, as teachers in
the school system, played an increasingly important role in service to the
republican nation — a role often seen as an extension of the practice of
maternal virtue.[74] The fervent religious revivalism of the Second Great
Awakening, along with the birth of romantic literature, furthered the
connections between morality and the emotions already perceived in the
previous century by evangelicals, moral philosophers, and sentimental
writers. As eager supporters and occasional leaders, women were active
participants in both the revivalist and the romantic cultural movements.[75]

From the late eighteenth century onward, the conflation of the virtuous with the feminine produced tensions. Looking back over the
Revolutionary period with characteristic pessimism, John Adams once
commented, "The people are Clarissa."[76] Public virtue had, for him,
become associated with the passive virtues of female chastity — destined
to be deceived and violated by unscrupulous men in power. Indeed, the
representation of public virtue as a feminine trait hinged on the exclusion
of women from institutional public life. If virtue was regarded as outside
politics, what better way to conceive of it than as feminine? In an increasingly competitive male political system, the distinction faded between virtuous men committed to public service and unvirtuous men pursuing
narrow self-interest. The new distinction between feminine virtue and
masculine self-interest eased the process by which all white men (whether
rich or poor, individually "virtuous" or not) could become political
actors and all women could not.[77] That the ideal of female virtue was
typically extended to upper- and middle-class women but not to poor
women — who, as Christine Stansell has shown, continued to be characterized in the new nation in blatantly misogynistic terms — reveals the

extent to which the older republican emphasis on both virtue and social rank remained particularly strong within conceptions about women.[78]

The transformation in the meaning of virtue during the Revolutionary period sharpened the social boundaries between the sexes in ways that continue to deny power to all classes of women. The deep cultural connections between American patriotism and female middle-class domesticity persist to the present day, most conspicuously among conservative evangelical groups. Yet the increasing participation of early-nineteenth-century women in the teaching profession, religious benevolent associations, and voluntary reform societies — activities that led directly to the early women's rights movement — suggests another side to the story. Virtue, even if domesticated, still contained residues of *virtù*, which for a long time helped to legitimate women's activities in American public life.

CHAPTER 8

Gender and the Public/Private Dichotomy in American Revolutionary Thought

PREFACE   This concluding essay, published for the first time in this volume, refines several issues that have been addressed in the preceding essays. Like the two other essays in Part 3, it explores the relationship of the Revolution to changes in feminine ideals and views of woman's role in society. Expressing uneasiness about according too much causal significance to the Revolution as a singular event, however, this essay departs from the others in advancing a more subtle, multi-faceted account of changing notions of domesticity. The essay elucidates several alternative ways that late-eighteenth-century Americans conceived of the public/private distinction in relation to gender, presenting them all as products of developments in Anglo-American culture that predate the Revolution. The crucial role of the Revolution in framing the public/private divide, and, with it, the new emphasis on female domesticity, lay in channeling these earlier trends through its varied ideologies. The essay also questions the monolithic stature usually accorded by historians to early-nineteenth-century middle-class Anglo-American ideas about "separate spheres." Instead, by focusing as well on the interrelationship between liberal commercialism and notions of romantic love, the essay suggests that post-Revolutionary Americans articulated at least two, conflicting conceptions of gender, which remain with us today.

. . .

Historians used to say that the American Revolution had virtually no impact on the position of women. Thanks to the generation of women's historians working since the 1970s, this claim is no longer made. Some revolutionary developments affecting women were legal ones, including the spread of legal divorce on the state level and the short-lived expansion of the franchise in New Jersey. These were, however, mostly made without benefits to women explicitly in mind. Linda Kerber, Jan Lewis, myself, and others have tended to stress instead more subtle changes affecting the definition of women's familial roles.[1] Newly respectful attitudes toward the authority of women, we have argued, enabled mothers and wives to be valued as the inculcators of republican political values in children and men.[2]

I have always been uneasy about this line of interpretation even though I myself have contributed to it. Very few of the documents used to make the case that women assumed a new moral role had anything much to do with politics, the state, or the Revolution per se. Even the use of the word "republic" was rare in writings about women, and it was often nothing more than a synonym for the new nation. Benjamin Rush's oft-quoted essay on female education did maintain the special need for an informed female citizenry in a republic, but this was only one of many reasons given by him and others for advocating the education of women.[3] One can, moreover, find similar kinds of documents emphasizing women's moral role in England and Scotland, where no revolution occurred. In fact, some of the sources American historians have cited were writings imported from Britain and, to a lesser extent, France.[4] Taking all this into account, it seems fair to question both what the American Revolution really had to do with the emergence of the so-called "Republican Mother" or "Republican Wife" and how "republican" she really was.

A second, related set of questions emerges. How can we explain the paradox of a "politicized" domestic realm developing at same time as the doctrine of "separate spheres" with its strict demarcation of the private and public realms? We have been content to leave it at that, a paradox. We dwell upon the irony that the ideas of the Republican Mother and Wife accorded women political purpose in relation to their family members but at the same time kept them out of real politics. How, if at all, can the concurrence of these two intellectual developments — the attribution of public virtue to women and the separation of the private domain of the family from the public worlds of work and politics — be accounted for, given what we know about the intellectual and cultural history of the period?

Part of the answer lies in a twofold reconfiguration of the public and private dichotomy in late-eighteenth-century America, a reconfiguration closely connected to a shift in conceptions of women. The idea of women as uniquely virtuous, in the sense of morally disciplined and self-sacrificing, did not arise from Revolutionary thought in itself. Instead, its intellectual roots lie in the quite apolitical formulations about human psychology and morality within evangelical Protestantism, Scottish moral philosophy, and sentimental fiction.[5] All of these formulations antedated the Revolution; most of them were not uniquely American but familiar to American colonists. Why they became so important in America during the late eighteenth century, and why they mixed together in the way that they did, however, cannot be understood without the intervention of the American Revolution. The product of this combustible mix was not so much one or another type of feminine ideal, Republic Mother or Republican Wife. Rather, two fundamentally different notions of the relationship of gender to public life emerged from the American patriot resistance to Britain. Only by analyzing shifts in the distinction between public and private can we better understand the Revolution's impact upon perceived differences between men and women.

To address these concerns, it is necessary first to review certain intellectual premises of the revolutionary movement beginning in the 1760s. As historians have recently come to appreciate, there is no easy way to generalize about the origins of American revolutionary thought. Attempts to argue for the supremacy of the Enlightenment, for classical republicanism, for Protestantism, and for legal traditions, have all been made and have all been found wanting. Instead of evaluating each of these perspectives, the most useful way of surveying how early patriots thought about the relationship between public and private is to select the relevant ideas apparent in all of them. What follows is a brief distillation of these four very important and more-or-less distinguishable intellectual traditions, concentrating on what each had to say about this relationship and how each of them viewed gender differences. To distinguish among these traditions is not to imply that they existed in pure form isolated from one another in the minds of one or another revolutionary. Rather, in most revolutionary discourse they were merged into ideological hybrids. The reason to pull them apart is to explore their analytical differences, differences that help explain underlying tensions within Revolutionary thought on the subject of women.

The most ancient of the sources of Revolutionary thinking came from Greece, mediated by the influence of the English Revolution of the seventeenth century. Historians since the 1960s have underscored the influence of classical thinking on the American Revolution, typically with little or no attention to ideas about women. According to this originally Aristotelian outlook, later reinforced by Aquinas and revived in the Renaissance, the most laudable human practice was the leading of a virtuous civic life. The male citizen possessed property in order to have the freedom from work necessary to engage in political pursuits. The Greek word for property, *oikos* (the root of the modern word "economics") referred to the household as the place of production, occupied by women, children, and slaves. The categories of public and private thus simultaneously distinguished men from women and politics from the economy. To value either property relations or relations with women in themselves would be a violation of the civic ideal. The mundane world of the economy contained women; the higher world of politics did not. Sexual desire and avarice were deemed the two vices particularly destructive to the public good.

While classical republicanism upheld an ideal of disinterested public service, a very different ideal was also espoused by American revolutionaries: that of natural rights, derived from a legal tradition originated by Roman jurists and natural-law theorists. In this view, the goal was not a virtuous civic life but rather the proper ordering of the world according to a sacred law of nature. The right to property, like the right to life, was one such natural right. In contrast to the classical republican perspective, property was not merely the lowly means to an exalted political end. Rather than seeing freedom as realized by citizens engaging in politics, natural law theory held that rights were protected by rulers who controlled their subjects through law. Natural rights were private — in the sense that they originated outside of government — and public institutions served at best to defend them against threats of tyranny. Subsumed within these notions of property and life were unstated rights to the sustenance provided by the household economy and to men's patriarchal authority over women.[6]

The classical republican and natural-law theories differed markedly in how they assessed the relative value of public and private. Natural-rights theory privileged private property; classical republican theory privileged active citizenship. However, while neither set of ideas questioned gender hierarchies and both of them peacefully coexisted with monarchical rule, each of these traditions contained seeds of revolutionary egalitarian thought. The ideals of participatory government and natural rights ran against absolutist notions like the divine right of kings. By the time of the

American Revolution, each of these two traditions had taken root in English political radicalism and had spread from there into the colonies.

Still more conspicuous on the colonial stage was a third tradition, that of dissenting Protestantism. As most clearly articulated by New England Puritans and their descendants, this tradition blurred the public/private distinction by conceiving of the family as a microcosm of the state. Such a conception could be traced back to God's covenant with Abraham; his seed were to be the people of Israel. In certain respects Puritans agreed with royalists, who similarly held that the father's rule in the family was a model for the king's rule of the state. But the dissenting Protestant formulation had an egalitarian edge: it was rooted in the idea of consent.[7] Early Massachusetts used to enjoy the reputation of being the seedbed of American democracy because its government officials were elected by adult male church members. Still, while this remarkably large electorate determined who would be chosen to lead, once elected, the governor and other magistrates were expected to receive the deference due to fathers and husbands. The submission of subjects to rulers was seen as analogous to marriage, Governor John Winthrop explained, in which a "true wife," once having chosen her husband, "accounts her subjection her honor and freedom."[8] Further collapsing the private/public distinction, Massachusetts' first body of laws closely regulated family life and set limits on free trade in the name of both the divine covenant and the social good. Although by the end of the seventeenth century these laws were no longer in force, American Protestant thinking nonetheless continued to straddle the line between public and private that had been drawn by both the classical republican and the natural-rights traditions.[9]

Enlightenment liberalism comprises the fourth and most modern intellectual influence upon American revolutionaries' views of the public/private dichotomy. There is a debate among intellectual historians of the seventeenth and eighteenth centuries about whether "liberal" ideas about property and the state derived the most from civic humanist, natural-rights, or Protestant traditions.[10] What is clear is that Locke, disputing the royalist patriarchal theories of Filmer, justified the Glorious Revolution of the late seventeenth century by shrinking the role of government and sharply distinguishing public from private life. The patriarchal family was no model for the state, he insisted. To the contrary, he envisioned the family and private property as having both existed already in the state of nature, hypothetically before the invention of government. And even after the creation of civil society they both properly remained outside the duly limited political realm.

The Lockean state of nature thus posited the existence of a society separate from government, an idea elaborated in subsequent liberal theory about the economy and the state. Eighteenth-century intellectuals like Daniel Defoe and Montesquieu began defending the morality of commercial relations and the reliability of the market economy. As economic historian Albert Hirschman has shown, the market grew alongside a new way of understanding human psychology. The rational egoism behind the pursuit of material gain, formerly understood as a destructive "passion," was converted by economic theorists into a socially desirable "interest." These eighteenth-century thinkers increasingly placed trade, not politics, at the center of freedom and social life. Combining inherited notions about the natural right to property and the value of pursuing the public good, they viewed the state as consisting of propertied male citizens who, through taxes, voluntarily supported a government that was limited to defending their rights.

Whereas the older, natural-rights theory held that the physical world itself had a moral significance expressive of divine will, liberalism redefined natural rights as the property of individuals. Liberal citizenship was established by owning property, which women could not do.[11] The "natural" power of husbands and fathers within Lockean theory is quite distinct from the artificially constructed power of the magistrate.[12] As Carole Pateman and other feminist theorists have argued, despite Locke's permissive ideas about divorce, women were just as subsumed and invisible in the liberal state as they were in the classical or monarchical ones. No one put this more dramatically than Mary Astell in her *Reflections Upon Marriage* of 1700: "If all Men are born free, how is it that all Women are born Slaves?"[13]

American revolutionaries drew from all four of these traditions. Whereas in the more radical phase of the revolutionary movement, in the 1760s and 1770s, the Protestant and classical republican ideals of public service and material self-sacrifice comprised the dominant motifs, by the 1780s concerns about the preservation of individual rights and the need to limit government gained precedence. A decidedly masculinist ethos ran through both phases of the revolutionary movement. The decadence and corruption that was thought to plague Britain was often represented in feminine form as an extravagant or overly domineering woman.[14] The mounting disillusionment of the inflationary postwar period took expression in denunciations of female consumers of luxurious imported goods. A woman who stoically withstood hardships for the sake of the republican cause was commended for her unusual "masculine virtue."[15] Whereas early revolutionaries invested their hopes in the idealistic public spirit of the patriot movement, in the postwar period doubts about the virtue of the new nation began to emerge. While at the beginning of independence from Britain Americans favored unicameral legislative governments because they were understood to reflect popular will, later on these were replaced by new constitutions that featured checks and balances and bills of rights. The virtue of the citizenry was no longer an adequate foundation for representative government. James Madison's defense of the U. S. Constitution in Federalist #10 assumes the inevitability of self-interested factional politics, arguing that the Constitution's best safeguard of freedom lay in its ability to render the unending competition among them politically fruitless. The widespread political disillusionment of the 1780s, reinforced in many quarters by disappointments in the French Revolution of the 1790s, propelled many formerly idealistic patriots to withdraw from political activism and to insist on a sharp divide between public and private life. Still, these same decades witnessed a strong emergent nationalism and a continuing desire to foster the common good. How, if not through politics?

The answers to this question stressed the roles of commerce, the family, and religion. To some extent these were old answers, drawing from both the liberal and the Protestant traditions. What was new, however, was the way in which the invocations of commerce, family, and religion came together in changed conceptions of public and private, and, at the same time, changed relations between men and women. During the late eighteenth century, the "public" in essence lost its primarily political meaning. When Americans spoke of the common good or the general welfare or the nation, or even the "republic," they no longer necessarily had government in mind.

The word "private" for nongovernmental property of course remains in use even today, and we still differentiate between "private" and "public" sectors in that sense. However, liberal thinkers of the eighteenth century reconceived the world of commerce as a social world, a world of harmonious reciprocity and ever-expanding voluntary human relations. Scottish theorists of capitalism like Adam Smith even objected to contractual theories of government on the grounds that society, and with it economic relations, was a natural rather than an artificial creation.[16] Just as "public" no longer referred especially to a political world, the economy lost much of its classical association with private life.

Conceptions of the private sphere contracted in turn. At most, the "private" came to encompass sexual and domestic relations alone, and the public/private dichotomy was reconfigured by making the family the quintessentially private institution. Always highly gendered, this conception of the family defined the realm of child rearing and homemaking as the proper place of women. Men, to the contrary, were to venture out into the public world, now defined partly as economic and only secondarily as political. These masculine public activities were given positive moral value in their supposed collective utility. However, enough of the older Protestant and classical republican suspicions of self-interest remained to raise troubling questions about the morality of both the economy and politics. Persistent worries about unscrupulous creditors, irresponsible debtors, greedy merchants, and power-hungry politicians — anxieties driven as well by the winds of post-revolutionary social change — cast shadows over much of the supposed domain of men.

The emergent ideology of "separate spheres," which valorized female domesticity, found little to commend in public life. Virtue was instead increasingly located in the family. Already in 1778 the political pessimist John Adams asserted in his diary that "the foundation of national morality must be laid in private Families," rather than in state law or state churches.[17] The "private," a quality formerly equated with selfishness, became newly emblematic of heartfelt human compassion, kindness, and loyalty. Women, especially in their role as mothers, were endowed with newfound moral authority. The public/private distinction was in this manner redrawn, turning the classical ideal of male civic virtue on its head. As has been frequently observed by historians of women, the rigid ideological boundaries between male and female spheres in the early republic helped to carve new opportunities for American women, especially in education. Yet the doctrine of separate spheres was undeniably also a conservative formulation, reinforcing the male-female divide and unabashedly maintaining the legal, political, and economic superiority of men. Behind the idealization of motherhood was a didactic model of service, dedicating dutiful women to perpetuating conventional social and political values.

But another, less familiar and, I believe, more subversive formulation of the relationship of public to private and of male to female arose simultaneously alongside the notion of separate spheres. Post-revolutionary Americans drew at least two, differently situated, conceptual lines differentiating public from private, both of them new. In contrast to the idealization of private morality, an alternative view held that the general good was produced through minute human interactions and exchanges among equals. Instead of the private serving the public, no clear boundary existed between them. These ideas partly came from the liberal political economy and moral philosophy of the Scottish Enlightenment, according to which commerce not only bred wealth but produced an interdependency among people that cemented social ties. Adam Smith viewed both the pursuit of self-interest in the free market and the sympathetic interaction of individuals in small groups as essential to the making of a good society.[18] One can find ingredients of this liberal commercial thought in the more democratic-minded American revolutionaries of the late eighteenth century, most notably Thomas Paine and the Jeffersonians of the 1790s.

What is less well known is that these ideas about commerce applied to gender relations as well. Language itself suggested the connection: the words "intercourse," "commerce," and "conversation" were used synonymously to denote economic, cultural, and sexual relations.[19] Liberal thinkers in Scotland, especially, who were well-known writers in America, elaborated on the Lockean idea of marriage as the first society. Instead of demarcating natural from civil society, they saw relations between men and women, especially the institution of love-based marriage, as the basis of social harmony and public morality. "Why then exclude the highest satisfactions of life, those of mutual love in such tender relations," asked Francis Hutcheson, objecting to Plato's disparagement of marriage, "[marital relations] which have always been found the chiefest springs of industry, and an incitement to zeal for our country's defense, and to all honorable services?"[20] David Hume concurred, describing relations between men and women as the "original principle of human society," a bond that then extended to their children and eventually to the wider community.[21] Often described as the first sociologists, these writers looked at history to understand the progressive evolution not of government but of society. They developed a four-stage theory of history beginning with hunters and ending with merchants; in the modern world, commerce and relations with women played equivalent roles in civilizing the passions and fostering mutual benevolence.[22] New psychological values of introspection and empathy were in essence eroticized, part of a complex cultural process that historians have recently called the transformation of the self.[23]

For most proponents of love-based marriage, love was sharply distinguished from mere lust. Erotic desire was not denied but transformed by moral sentiments, which drew the heart to the inner soul of the beloved.[24] David Hume, for example, characterized amorous passion as a compound of sexual drive, pleasure in beauty, and "a generous kindness or good-will."[25] Marital love, in his view, "chiefly subsists in friendship," and the "marriage-knot" uniting husband to wife should therefore be drawn "the closest possible."[26] Commenting upon the progress of humanity from savagery to civilization, the popular moralist Henry Home maintained that once "the more delicate senses are unfolded, the peculiar beauties of the female sex, internal as well as external, are brought into full light; and women, formerly considered as objects of animal love merely, are now valued as faithful friends and agreeable companions."[27] As these themes translated into sentimental fiction, writers often deplored "false love" based on vanity and self-interest, contrasting it with the true love of "native sociability."[28]

There is nothing inherently revolutionary or republican about this perspective on love. The Scots themselves were socially elitist, and typically moderately promonarchist in their politics, despite the liberalism of their economic theory. Hume impugned the coarse morals of ancient republics and asserted "the superiority in politeness" and "gallantry" towards women, which he saw as characteristic of courts and monarchies.[29] For these thinkers, sentimental attitudes about marriage and female society were subsumed within a model of gentility. Colin Campbell, in his study *The Romantic Ethic and the Spirit of Consumerism*, presents an analysis of the English commercial revolution in which an imaginary quest for pleasure, embedded at once in Protestant spirituality and popular fiction, stimulated the rise both of consumer spending and romantic love. In England as in Scotland, these mutually reinforcing ideas about love and commerce carried no particularly radical overtones.

But in America such ideas had far more egalitarian implications. As the revolutionary war officer James Tilton repackaged them in his 1790 argument for the importance of women:

> The men possess the more ostensible powers of making and executing the laws . . . [but] the women, in every free country, have an absolute control of manners: and it is confessed, that in a republic, manners are of equal importance with laws.[30]

The ideals of reciprocal commercial and romantic relationships permeated Revolutionary ideology and were generally expressive of strong anti-aristocratic, anti-imperial sentiments. Paine opened *Common Sense* with a paean to the possibilities of free trade, a vision that cannot be separated from his attack on monarchical government and his confidence in the youthful energy of the American nation. Similar narratives of young couples breaking free of parental constraints permeated the romantic fic-

tion that was widely published in revolutionary America.[31] Whatever
else Thomas Jefferson may have meant in the preamble to "The
Declaration of Independence" when he substituted the brilliantly evoca-
tive "pursuit of happiness" for "property," he had transformed individual emotional experience into a natural right and a revolutionary
republican cause. [32]

Jefferson's intellectual indebtedness to Scottish moral philosophy, as
well as to Locke, is well known. So are his ardently sentimental ideas
about marriage and women — his commitments to rationalism and his
problematic affair with his slave Sally Hemings notwithstanding.[33]
Looking beyond the ideas of towering intellectuals like Jefferson and
Paine, it is more of a challenge to unravel the intellectual roots of the
emerging ideal of romantic marital love. On the level of popular culture,
evangelical religion and sentimental fiction seem to have played especially important roles in the dissemination of a romantic notion of marriage beginning in the middle of the eighteenth century. Each in its own
way elevated the moral value of love and undercut the age-old stereotype
of women as overly emotional and therefore less virtuous than men.[34] By
the turn of the nineteenth century, evangelical religion more vigorously
promoted an ideal of feminine domesticity and benevolent religious
activity. A renewed emphasis upon the import of familial religious obser-
vance also contributed to the more conservative formulation of separate
spheres.[35] Sentimental fiction had a less obvious impact on thinking
about the public/private dichotomy. Inasmuch as it too presented an ideal
of family life insulated from the social and economic world and depicted
women as the moral bulwarks of men, it also reinforced the developing
notion of separate spheres.[36] However, inasmuch as fiction concerned
itself more with courtship and romance than with the duties of married
life, it interplayed with the more egalitarian model of mutual emotional
exchange and fusion of identities.

Beginning already with the novels of Samuel Richardson in the 1740s,
the plots of eighteenth-century British and American literature featured
conflicts between romantic love and the social hierarchies that limited the
choice of a spouse. One of many fictional representations of this tension
can be found in the first American novel: William Hill Brown's aptly titled
The Power of Sympathy of 1789. The young protagonist Harrington has
resolved to marry the virtuous Harriot despite her poverty and the objections of his father. In a letter to her at the height of his ardor, Harrington
aims to prove to her that he is, in his words, a "man of sensibility" who
has a "soul." He recounts an encounter he had, while on a tour of the

South, with slave woman who had just undergone a terrible whipping in order to save her child. Exulting in his sympathy with the slave, Harrington reports, "I felt my heart glow with feelings of exquisite delight."[37] He then closes his love letter with the exclamation:

> Hail *Sensibility!* Sweetener of the joys of life! . . . From thee! Author of Nature! from thee, thou inexhaustible spring of love supreme, floweth this tide of affection and Sympathy."[38]

God and sensibility, love supreme and sympathy, the wealthy young man and the miserable slave, the mother and the child, Harrington and Harriot — all are one. Later the lovers discover that they are brother and sister, a fact that not only dooms them to death but explains the intensity of their sympathetic attraction and mutual identification. The many romances in the novel are virtually all about incestuous or semi-incestuous couples who have known each other well since childhood. *The Power of Sympathy,* like much eighteenth-century fiction, dramatizes an ideal of love that requires the dissolution of individual boundaries.

A quote from the diary of a young single woman named Mary Guion in the town of North Castle, New York, illustrates the dissemination of romantic ideas of marriage in revolutionary America:

> I always anticipated to myself great satisfaction should I ever enter a connubial life, wich [sic] I never shall unless the person entirely meets my aprobation [sic], and one that I think would know how to comprise a real friend 'True social pleasure is founded on unlimited confidence, on an affectionate and reciprocal interchange of sentiments and opinions . . . where the gentle hand of Love conducts us along the path of truth and virtue; where every thought is anticipated before it escapes from the lips. [39]

This ideal of marital love, one of "unlimited confidence" in which "every thought" of the other is anticipated, amounts to a romantic fusion of identities. According to this view, the realization of the self depends on communion with the other. Not surprisingly, the idealistic Mary Guion also prides herself on never considering the wealth of a suitor.[40]

We have inherited some of today's definitions of romantic love from the eighteenth century, including in particular the notion that true love and social status are somehow in opposition. It is always tempting to see romantic love as the consummate expression of individualism, for that is the way it is subjectively experienced. We tend to naturalize and universalize it as a basic human emotion. Even scholars who seek to historicize the emergence of love-based marriage as having occurred in the modern West tend to present love-based marriage as the inevitable consequence of the removal of oppressive conditions.[41] Unless otherwise fettered, this argument implies, men and women will fall in love, and true love will lead to enduring unions. The actual collapse of many such unions fails to shake the common assumption that romantic love is a natural feeling. The fact that in the history of the modern world the popularization of the ideal of romantic love has more or less coincided with revolutions against authoritarian states only further obfuscates the issue. Romantic love, like freedom and equality, has come to be viewed as a kind of natural right.

Yet to view it instead as a fundamentally socializing experience, as a foundation of social cohesion and public good, is to gain a different type of insight from the eighteenth century, a less individualist one. A reconsideration of this history also points to cultural changes that have, over time, redefined people's objects of desire to accentuate romantic ideals of mutual identification and the dissolution of emotional boundaries.[42] While there are always tensions over sex roles and confusions about gender boundaries, certain periods of history display more fluidity than others. In revolutionary America, I have tried to suggest, profound changes in gender relations merged with the redefinition of public and private. Two new symbolic configurations of male/female and public/private began to take shape.

The one that has left the most obvious and enduring impression is the dualistic ideology of separate spheres and the related conviction that private rights need to be protected against the intervention of the state. It has largely been forgotten that another strand of revolutionary thought worked against these dichotomous formulations. Gender dichotomization has been a constant target of modern liberal feminism, but the public/ private distinction has proved far more intractable. Even the contemporary argument for abortion rights hinges on a defense of the right to privacy; the National Organization for Women and other women's organizations rallied in defense of President Clinton during the impeachment scandal by drawing a firm line between the so-called political and so-called private life. This insistence on the public/private distinction has not, however, always been characteristic of contemporary feminism. In the early years of the movement in the 1960s, the phrase, "the personal is political" collapsed this very dichotomy on behalf of the liberation of women. Perhaps this contrary — more radical and presently less visible — current within modern American feminism also owes something to the transformations of the Revolutionary period.

Notes

INTRODUCTION

1. The scholarly literature on the nineteenth century is voluminous. See especially Nancy F. Cott, *The Bonds of Womanhood* (New Haven, Conn.: Yale University Press, 1977); Carl Degler, *At Odds: Women and the Family in America* (New York: Oxford University Press, 1980); Peter Gay, *The Bourgeois Experience — Victoria to Freud*, esp. vol. 2, *The Tender Passion* (New York Oxford University Press, 1986); Barbara Welter, "The Cult of True Womanhood," *American Quarterly* 18 (Summer 1966). Michel Foucault, *The History of Sexuality,* trans. Robert Hurley (New York: Pantheon, 1978) and *The Use of Pleasure,* trans. Robert Hurley (New York: Pantheon, 1985) sees what appears as sexual repression as sexual obsessiveness. Perspectives from the vantage point of the working class and minorities include Christine Stansell, *City of Women: Sex and Class in New York, 1789–1860* (Urbana: University of Illinois Press, 1986); Burt James Loewenberg and Ruth Bogin, eds., *Black Women in Nineteenth-Century American Life* (University Park: Pennsylvania State University Press, 1976).

2. The theme of refinement has in recent years been further pursued, although not with gender centrally in mind. See Richard L. Bushman, *The Refinement of America: Persons, Houses, Cities* (New York: Random House, 1992); and David S. Shields, *Civil Tongues and Polite Letters in British America* (Chapel Hill: North Carolina University Press, 1997).

3. For the supremacy of the authority of male heads of household in colonial America, see the brilliant synthesis by Carole Shammas, "Anglo-American Household Government in Comparative Perspective," *The William and Mary Quarterly,* 3d ser., 52 (January 1995): 104–144. Patriarchal household governance is related to the strength of nonconforming religion, since the Puritans and most other dissenting Protestants transferred much of what had been ecclesiasti-

cal authority into the domestic realm of patriarchical authority. On this transformation, see Christopher Hill, *Society and Puritanism in Pre-Revolutionary England* (London: Secker E. Warburg, 1964) and Gordon J. Schochet, *Patriarchalism in Political Thought: The Authoritarian Family and Political Speculation and Attitudes, Especially in Seventeenth-Century England* (New York: Basic Books, 1975).

4. On marriage and romantic love, see Ruth H. Bloch, "Changing Conceptions of Sexuality and Romance in Eighteenth-Century America," *The William and Mary Quarterly,* 3d ser., 60 (forthcoming, January 2003).

5. See for example: William Goode, *World Revolution and Family Patterns* (Glencoe, Ill., 1963); Neil J. Smelser, *The Family and the Industrial Revolution;* Gerda Lerner, "The Lady and the Mill Girl: Changes in the Status of Women in the Age of Jackson, 1800–1840," *Midcontinent American Studies Journal* 10 (1969): 5–14. Nancy F. Cott's pathbreaking work on domesticity, *The Bonds of Womanhood,* also gives primacy to similar economic processes. For a telling critique of the view of male/female "spheres" as geographically based, see Linda K. Kerber, "Separate Spheres, Female Worlds, Woman's Place: The Rhetoric of Women's History," *The Journal of American History* 75 (June 1988): 9–39.

6. Mary Beth Norton, *Liberty's Daughters: The Revolutionary Experience of American Women, 1750–1800* (Boston: Little Brown, 1980); Linda K. Kerber, *Women of the Republic: Intellect and Ideology in Revolutionary America* (Chapel Hill: University of North Carolina Press, 1980). Also see Bloch, "Linda Kerber's Republican Mother" in *Locating American Studies: The Evolution of a Discipline,* ed. Lucy Maddox (Baltimore: Johns Hopkins, 1999), pp. 162–166; Margaret Nash, "Rethinking Republican Motherhood," *Journal of the Early Republic* 17 (Summer 1997): 171–191.

7. Niel McKendrick et al., *The Birth of a Consumer Society: The Commercialization of Eighteenth-Century England* (Bloomington: Indiana University Press, 1985); Paul Langford, *A Polite and Commercial People, 1727–1782* (Oxford: Oxford University Press, 1989). On women's declining activity in household manufacturing, see Ivy Pinchbeck, *Women Workers and the Industrial Revolution, 1750–1850* (London: G. Routledge, 1930); Bridget Hill, *Women and Work in the Eighteenth Century* (Oxford, Eng.: Blackwell, 1989).

8. T. H. Breen, "An Empire of Goods: The Anglicization of Colonial America, 1690–1776," *Journal of British Studies* 25 (1986): 467–499; and Breen, "Narrative of a Commercial Life: Consumption, Ideology, and Community on the Eve of the American Revolution," *William and Mary Quarterly,* 3d. ser., 50 (July 1993): 471–501; Bushman, *The Refinement of America.*

9. Elaine Forman Crane, *Ebb Tide in New England: Women, Seaports, and Social Change, 1630–1800* (Boston: Northeastern University Press, 1998). This interpretation runs against the grain of those interpretations that see progress instead. Cf. Mary Beth Norton, "The Evolution of White Women's Experience in Early America," *The American Historical Review* 89 (1984): 593–619.

10. On the Revolution specifically, also see Elaine Forman Crane, "Dependence in the Era of Independence: The Role of Women in a Republican Society," in Jack P. Greene, ed., *The American Revolution: Its Character and Limits* (New York: New York University Press, 1987); Joan Hoff-Wilson, "The Illusion of

Change: Women and the American Revolution," in Alfred Young, ed., *The American Revolution: Explorations in the History of American Radicalism* (De Kalb, Ill.: Northern Illinois University Press, 1976): 383–445.

11. Kerber, *Women of the Republic*; Norton, *Liberty's Daughters*.

12. Jan Lewis, "The Republican Wife: Virtue and Seduction in the Early Republic," *William and Mary Quarterly*, 3rd. ser., 44 (1987): 689–721; Carroll Smith-Rosenberg, "Dis-Covering the Subject of the 'Great Constitutional Discussion,' 1786–1789," *Journal of American History* 79 (1992): 841–873; Rosemary Zagarri, "Morals, Manners, and the Republican Mother," *American Quarterly* 44 (1992): 192–215; and Norma Basch, *Framing American Divorce: From the Revolutionary Generation to the Victorians* (Berkeley: University of California Press, 1999).

13. These essays also seek to revise the debate over liberalism and republicanism, the terms of which are usefully described in Joyce Appleby, *Liberalism and Republicanism in the Historical Imagination* (Cambridge, Mass.: Harvard University Press, 1992); James T. Kloppenberg, "The Virtues of Liberty: Christianity, Republicanism, and Ethics in Early American Political Discourse," *Journal of American History* 74 (1987): 9–23; and Daniel T. Rodgers, "Republicanism: The Career of a Concept," *Journal of American History* 79 (1992): 11–38.

14. For contemporary commentary on this problem, see Alice Kessler-Harris, "The Just Price, the Free Market, and the Value of Women," *Feminist Studies* 14 (Summer 1988): 235–250; Joan W. Scott, "Deconstructing Equality-Versus-Difference," *Feminist Studies* 14 (Spring 1988): 33–50.

15. For an example of this debate, compare Mary Beth Norton, "The Evolution of White Women's Experience," and Elaine Forman Crane, *Ebb Tide in New England*.

16. Nancy F. Cott, *The Bonds of Womanhood*, and Norma Basch, *The Framing of American Divorce*, both see continuity but take different views.

1. A CULTURALIST CRITIQUE
OF TRENDS IN FEMINIST THEORY

I would like to thank Joyce Appleby, Anne Lombard, Anne Mellor, Carrie Menkle-Meadow, and Debora Silverman for their helpful readings of an earlier draft.

1. The recent debate in *Contention* over Nicky Hart's article also addresses this issue. As Juliet Mitchell, Elizabeth Fox-Genovese, and others have pointed out, some of the reproductive processes that Hart regards as given, such as the mother's primary role in childrearing, others would view as the products of society and subject to feminist transformation. See Nicky Hart, "Procreation and Women's Oppression," *Contention* 1 (Fall 1991) and 2 (Winter 1992); Juliet Mitchell and Elizabeth Fox-Genovese reply in *Contention* 3 (Spring 1992). All are reprinted in *Debating Gender, Debating Sexuality*, ed. Nikki Keddie (New York: New York University Press, 1996).

2. There are some fine studies of the women's liberation movement, most notably Alice Echols, *Daring to Be Bad: Radical Feminism in America, 1967–*

1975 (Minneapolis: Minnesota University Press, 1989), but they do not take this theoretical perspective.

3. See, for example, the examples and discussion of the "culturalist" approach within social anthropology in Sherry B. Ortner and Harriet Whitehead, eds., *Sexual Meanings: The Cultural Construction of Gender and Sexuality* (New York: Cambridge University Press, 1981). Among historians, perhaps the most salient examples are the writings of Natalie Davis and Carroll Smith-Rosenberg. See Natalie Zemon Davis, especially "Women on Top," in *Society and Culture in Early Modern France* (Stanford, Calif.: Stanford University Press, 1975); Carroll Smith-Rosenberg, "The Female World of Love and Ritual," and other essays reprinted in *Disorderly Conduct: Visions of Gender in Victorian America* (New York: Oxford University Press, 1985).

4. Most notably, Kate Millett, *Sexual Politics* (Garden City, N. Y.: Doubleday, 1970); Elaine Showalter, *A Literature of Their Own: British Women Novelists from Bronte to Lessing* (Princeton, N. J.: Princeton University Press, 1977).

5. One notable but much criticized exception is Sherry Ortner's classic article "Is Female to Male as Nature Is to Culture?" *Feminist Studies* 1 (Fall 1972): 5–31. Ortner presented a structuralist cultural analysis of dualistic and hierarchical symbols of men and women. The static and deterministic implications of her analysis have aroused objections from other feminists. For example, see Carol P. MacCormack, "Nature, Culture, and Gender: A Critique," in MacCormack and Marilyn Strathern, eds., *Nature, Culture, and Gender* (Cambridge: Cambridge University Press, 1980), pp. 1–25; and Ludmilla Jordanova, "Natural Facts," in her *Sexual Visions: Images of Gender in Science and Medicine Between the Eighteenth and Twentieth Centuries* (New York: Harvester Wheatsheaf, 1989), pp. 19–41.

6. The Foucauldian tendency to explain racist cultural formulations by referring to a material context of "power" has become increasingly common. See, for example, David Theo Goldberg, "The Social Formation of Racist Discourse," in Goldberg, ed., *Anatomy of Racism* (Minneapolis: University of Minnesota, 1990), pp. 295–318.

7. For works on opposite ends of this spectrum, see Jean Bethke Elshtain, *Public Man, Private Woman: Women in Social and Political Thought* (Princeton, N. J.: Princeton University Press, 1981) and Judith Butler, *Gender Trouble: Feminism and the Subversion of Identity* (New York: Routledge, 1990.

8. For example, Shulamith Firestone, *The Dialectic of Sex: The Case for Feminist Revolution* (New York: Marrow, 1970); Juliet Mitchell, *Woman's Estate*, 1st American ed. (New York: Pantheon, 1971); Susan Brownmiller, *Against Our Will: Men, Women, and Rape* (Washington: Simon and Schuster, 1975); Zillah R. Eisenstein, ed., *Capitalist Patriarchy and the Case for Socialist Feminism* (New York: The Monthly Review Press, 1979); Annette Kuhn and AnnMarie Wolpe, eds., *Feminism and Materialism: Women and Modes of Production* (Boston: Routledge and Kegan Paul, 1978); Lydia Sargent, ed. *Women and Revolution: A Discussion of the Unhappy Marriage of Marxism and Feminism* (London: Pluto Press, 1981).

9. Catherine A. MacKinnon, *Towards a Feminist Theory of the State* (Cambridge: Harvard University Press, 1989), p. 3.

10. Nancy Hartsock, *Money, Sex, and Power: Toward a Feminist Historical Materialism* (New York: Longman, 1983); Allison Jaggar, *Feminist Politics and Human Nature* (Totowa, N.J.: Rowman and Allenheld, 1983); Christine Stansell, *City of Women: Sex and Class in New York, 1789–1860* (New York: Knopf, 1986). Other especially notable and excellent works in this neo-Marxist, socialist feminist tradition include: Gayle Rubin, "The Traffic in Women," in *Toward an Anthropology of Women,* ed. Rayna Rapp Reiter (New York: Monthly Review Press, 1975), pp. 157–210. Heidi Hartman, "The Unhappy Marriage of Marxism and Feminism," in Sargent, ed. *Women and Revolution;* Sheila Rowbotham, Lynne Segal, and Hilary Wainwright, *Beyond the Fragments: Feminism and the Making of Socialism* (London: Merlin Press, 1979); Linda J. Nicholson, *Gender and History: The Limits of Social Theory in the Age of the Family* (New York: Columbia, 1986); Linda Gordon, *Heroes of Their Own Lives: The Politics and History of Family Violence, Boston, 1880–1960* (New York: Penguin, 1988); Jeanne Boydston, *Home and Work: Housework, Wages, and the Ideology of Labor in the Early Republic* (New York: Oxford University Press, 1990).

11. For a recent comparison of the theories of patriarchy and Marxism, see Sylvia Walby, *Theorizing Patriarchy* (Cambridge: Blackwell, 1990).

12. Kathryn Kish Sklar, *Catharine Beecher: A Study in American Domesticity* (New Haven, Conn.: Yale University Press, 1973); Nancy F. Cott, *The Bonds of Womanhood* (New Haven, Conn.: Yale University Press, 1977); Smith-Rosenberg, "Female World of Love and Ritual."

13. Patricia Meyer Spacks, *The Female Imagination* (New York: Knopf, 1975); Showalter, *Literature of One's Own;* Sandra Gilbert and Susan Gubar, *The Madwoman in the Attic: The Woman Writer and the Nineteenth-Century Literary Imagination* (New Haven, Conn.: Yale University Press, 1979).

14. Nancy Chodorow, *The Reproduction of Mothering: Psychoanalysis and the Sociology of Gender* (Berkeley: University of California Press, 1978); Carol Gilligan, *In a Different Voice: Psychological Theory and Women's Development* (Cambridge: Harvard University Press, 1982). Also see Juliet Mitchell, *Psychoanalysis and Feminism,* 1st American ed. (New York: Pantheon, 1974); Jean Baker Miller, *Toward a New Psychology of Women* (Boston: Beacon, 1976); Sara Ruddick, *Maternal Thinking: Towards a Politics of Peace* (Boston: Beacon, 1989); Mary Belenky, Blythe Clinchy, Nancy Goldberger, and Jill Terrle, *Women's Ways of Knowing: The Development of Self, Voice, and Mind* (New York: Basic Books, 1986); Dorothy Dinnerstein, *The Mermaid and the Minotaur* (New York: Harper and Row, 1976); Nell Noddings, *Caring: A Feminine Approach to Ethics and Moral Education* (Berkeley: University of California Press, 1984).

15. Luce Irigaray, *This Sex Which Is Not One,* trans. Catherine Porter with Carolyn Burke (Ithaca, N. Y.: Cornell University Press, 1985); Irigaray, *Speculum of the Other Woman,* trans. Gillian C. Gill (Ithaca, N. Y.: Cornell University Press, 1985); Toril Moi, ed., *The Kristeva Reader* (New York: Columbia University Press, 1986); Toril Moi, *Sexual/Textual Politics: Feminist Literary Theory* (London: Methuen, 1985). Also see selections by Hélène Cixous, Julia Kristeva, Luce Irigaray, and others in Elaine Marks and Isabelle de Courtivron, eds., *New French Feminisms: An Anthology* (Amherst: University of Massachusetts, 1980).

16. Mary Daly, *Beyond God the Father: Toward a Philosophy of Women's Liberation* (Boston: Beacon, 1973); *Gyn/Ecology: The Metaethics of Radical Feminism* (Boston: Beacon Press, 1978); Andrea Dworkin, *Woman Hating* (New York: Dutton, 1974).

17. Several critics of Gilligan made this point in the commentaries in *Signs* 11 (1986): 303–333 and *Feminist Studies* 11 (1985): 149–161. The conflicting and problematic meanings of "essence" itself are explored in Diana Fuss, *Essentially Speaking: Feminism, Nature, and Difference* (London: Routledge, 1989).

18. For the exchange between Hart and Fox-Genovese, see *Debating Gender, Debating Sexuality,* ed. Nikki Keddie (New York: New York University Press, 1996). Fox-Genovese, *Feminism Without Illusions: A Critique of Individualism* (Chapel Hill: University of North Carolina, 1991), p. 54. For a scathing critique, see Ellen DuBois, "Illusions Without Feminism," *The Nation* 254 (Jan. 20, 1992): 57–60.

19. Susan Faludi, *Backlash: The Undeclared War Against American Women* (New York: Crown, 1991).

20. Elizabeth V. Spelman, *Inessential Woman: Problems of Exclusion in Feminist Thought* (Boston: Beacon Press, 1988). For a similar perspective among literary critics and women's historians, as well as efforts to rectify the imbalances, see Judith Newton and Deborah Rosenfelt, eds., *Feminist Criticism and Social Change: Sex, Class, and Race in Literature and Culture* (New York: Methuen, 1985) and Ellen Carol DuBois and Vicki L. Ruiz, eds., *Unequal Sisters: A Multicultural Reader in U. S. Women's History* (New York: Routledge, 1990).

21. For example, Suzanne J. Kessler and Wendy McKenna, *Gender: An Ethnomethodological Approach* (Chicago: Chicago University Press, 1978); Emily Martin, *The Woman in the Body: A Cultural Analysis of Reproduction* (Boston: Beacon, 1987); Thomas Laqueur, *Making Sex: Body and Gender from the Greeks to Freud* (Cambridge: Harvard University Press, 1990); Butler, *Gender Trouble.*

22. Gayle Rubin, "Traffic in Women."

23. Ibid, p. 199.

24. On the broader phenomenon of the "linguistic turn," see, for example, the discussion and works cited in John Toews, "Intellectual History after the Linguistic Turn," *American Historical Review* 92 (October 1987): 879–907.

25. Irigaray, *Sex Which is Not One,* p. 186.

26. See, for example, Nancy Hewitt, "Beyond the Search for Sisterhood: American Women's History in the 1980s," *Social History* 10 (1985): 299–321; Stansell, *City of Women;* Gordon, *Heroes;* DuBois and Ruiz, eds., *Unequal Sisters.*

27. Jane Flax, *Thinking Fragments: Psychoanalysis, Feminism, and Postmodernism in the Contemporary West* (Berkeley: University of California Press, 1990), p. 28.

28. Linda Kauffman, ed., *Gender and Theory: Dialogues in Feminist Criticism* (New York: Basil Blackwell, 1989), p. 5.

29. The literature making this point is increasingly large. For a few examples, see: Elizabeth Fee, "Is there a Feminist Science?" *Science and Nature* 4 (1981): 46–57; Carolyn Merchant, *The Death of Nature: Women, Ecology, and the Sci-*

entific Revolution (New York: Harper and Row, 1980); Evelyn Fox Keller, *Reflections on Gender and Science* (New Haven, Conn.: Yale University Press, 1985); Sandra Harding, *The Science Question in Feminism* (Ithaca, N. Y.: Cornell University Press, 1986); Ruth Bleier, *Science and Gender: A Critique of Biology and Its Theories on Women* (Oxford: Pergamon Press, 1984); Genevieve Lloyd, *The Man of Reason: "Male" and "Female" in Western Philosophy* (Minneapolis: University of Minnesota Press, 1984); Carole Pateman, *The Sexual Contract* (Stanford, Calif.: Stanford University Press, 1988).

30. Lawrence Stone, "Only Women," *New York Review of Books* 32 (April 11, 1985): 21–22, 27; Helen Vendler, "Feminism and Literature," *New York Review of Books* 37 (May 31, 1990): 19–25.

31. Michel Foucault, "Body/Power," in *Power/Knowledge,* ed. Colin Gordon (New York: Pantheon Books, 1980), pp. 57–58.

32. Joan Wallach Scott, *Gender and the Politics of History* (New York: Columbia University Press, 1988), p. 45.

33. Butler, *Gender Trouble,* p. 136.

34. I owe this insight to a observation of Lucy White of the UCLA Law School during a discussion of poststructualist feminist theory.

35. Gayatri Chakravorty Spivak, *In Other Worlds: Essays in Cultural Politics* (New York: Methuen, 1987), p. 107.

36. Poovey, *Uneven Developments: The Ideological Work of Gender in Mid-Victorian England* (Chicago: University of Chicago Press, 1988), p. 17.

37. Nancy C. M. Hartsock, "The Feminist Standpoint: Developing the Ground for a Specifically Feminist Historical Materialism," in Sandra Harding and Merrill B. Hintikka, eds., *Discovering Reality: Feminist Perspectives on Epistemology, Metaphysics, Methodology, and Philosophy of Science* (Boston: D. Reidel, 1983), pp. 283–305; Also see Harding, *Science Question,* pp. 136–196; Dorothy E. Smith, "Sociological Theory: Methods of Writing Patriarchy," in Ruth A. Wallace, ed., *Feminism and Sociological Theory* (Newbury Park, Ca.: Sage Publications, 1989) pp. 34–64.

38. Deborah K. King, "Multiple Jeopardy, Multiple Consciousness: The Context of a Black Feminist Ideology," *Signs* 14 (1988): 42–72; Audre Lorde, *Sister Outsider: Essays and Speeches* (Trumansburg, N. Y.: Crossing Press, 1984), pp. 114–123; Patricia Hill Collins, *Black Feminist Thought: Knowledge, Consciousness, and the Politics of Empowerment* (Boston: Unwin Hyman, 1990).

39. Gerda Lerner, "Reconceptualizing Differences Among Women," *Journal of Women's History* 1 (Winter 90): 116.

40. See, for example, Bonnie Thornton Dill, "Race, Class, and Gender: Prospects for an All-Inclusive Sisterhood, " *Feminist Studies* 9 (Spring 1983): 131–150; Karen Brodkin Sacks, "Toward a Unified Theory of Class, Race, and Gender," *American Ethnologist* 16 (1989): 534–550.

41. Rita Felski, *Beyond Feminist Aesthetics: Feminist Literature and Social Change* (London: Hutchinson Radius, 1989), p. 8. For Felski's repeated use of the adjective "bourgeois" to describe and modify the noun "society," see especially pp. 155, 159–160, 164–167. Other excellent recent studies that draw (in my view too much) on Habermasian categories are Joan Landes, *Women and the Public Sphere in the Age of the French Revolution* (Ithaca, N. Y.: Cornell University

Press, 1988) and Nancy Fraser, *Unruly Practices: Power, Discourse, Gender in Contemporary Social Theory* (Minneapolis: University of Minnesota Press, 1989).

42. Bonnie S. Anderson and Judith P. Zinsser, *A History of Their Own: Women in Europe from Prehistory to the Present,* 2 vols. (New York: Harper and Row, 1988), 1: xv.

43. Ibid, p. xvii.

44. The Joan Scott–Linda Gordon exchange is in *Signs* 15 (1990): 848–859.

45. Nancy Chodorow, *Feminism and Psychoanalytic Theory* (New Haven, Conn.: Yale University Press, 1989), pp. 189–190. Also see Miriam Johnson on "expressiveness," *Strong Mothers, Weak Wives: The Search for Gender Equality* (Berkeley: University of California Press, 1988).

46. Flax, *Thinking Fragments,* p. 23.

47. Judith Butler, who calls for the performance of stylized "acts" that challenge gender conventions, is in this respect close to the mark. Yet without a broader theory of culture she both exaggerates the individual's freedom to improvise independently of broader systems of meaning and sells short the ability of collective as well as individual feminist "acts" to change conventional gender definitions. *Gender Trouble,* esp. pp. 128–141.

48. Compare the interpretations of Gerda Lerner, "The Lady and the Mill-Girl: Changes in the Status of Women in the Age of Jackson," *Mid-Continent American Studies Journal* 10 (1969); Nancy F. Cott, *The Bonds of Womanhood: Woman's Sphere in New England, 1780–1835* (New Haven, Conn.: Yale University Press, 1977); Mary Beth Norton, *Liberty's Daughters: The Revolutionary Experience of American Women, 1750–1800* (Boston: Little, Brown, & Co., 1980); Linda Kerber, *Women of the Republic: Intellect and Ideology in Revolutionary America* (Chapel Hill: University of North Carolina Press, 1980); and Chapter 7.

49. None of these writers advance my particular theoretical position, but their works can in part be seen as empirical demonstrations of this argument. See especially Caroline Walker Bynum, *Jesus as Mother: Studies in the Spirituality of the High Middle Ages* (Berkeley: University of California, 1982); Bynum, *Holy Feast and Holy Fast: The Religious Significance of Food to Medieval Women* (Berkeley: University of California Press, 1987); Evelyn Fox Keller, *A Feeling for the Organism: The Life and Work of Barbara McClintock* (San Francisco: Freeman, 1983); Keller, *Reflections on Gender and Science;* Donna Haraway, *Primate Visions: Gender, Race, and Nature in the World of Modern Science* (New York: Routledge, 1989).

2. UNTANGLING THE ROOTS OF MODERN SEX ROLES:
   A SURVEY OF FOUR CENTURIES OF CHANGE

The general ideas presented here first arose from discussions in a graduate seminar taught by Natalie Zemon Davis, whose instruction and example I gratefully acknowledge. I also wish to thank the anonymous readers for *Signs* for their helpful critiques of an earlier draft of this paper.

1. Many important works analyzing long-run changes in the history of the

family and sex roles cast their arguments in a unilinear framework, often utilizing a broad evolutionary historical theory, such as types of Marxism or modernization theory. Among the many examples that could be cited, perhaps the most notable are Frederick Engels, "The Origin of the Family, Private Property and the State," in Karl Marx and Frederick Engels, *Selected Works*, 2 vols. (Moscow: Foreign Languages Publishing House, 1962), 2: 185–327; Phillipe Ariès, *Centuries of Childhood: A Social History of Family Life*, trans. Robert Baldick (New York: Vintage Books, 1962); William Goode, *World Revolution and Family Patterns* (Glencoe, Ill.: Free Press, 1963): Fred Weinstein and Gerald M. Platt, *The Wish to Be Free: Society, Psyche and Value Change* (Berkeley: University of California Press, 1969); Edward Shorter, *The Making of the Modern Family* (New York: Basic Books, 1975); and Janet Zolinger Giele, "Centuries of Womanhood: An Evolutionary Perspective on the Feminine Role," *Women's Studies* 1 (1972–73): 97–110. Joan Kelly-Gadol, in "The Social Relation of the Sexes: Methodological Implications of Women's History," *Signs* 1 (Summer 1976): 809–823, offers a less unilinear, more variable model of historical change, which is in some respects more compatible with the interpretation offered here.

2. "*C. W.,*" the *Bespotted Jesuit* (1641), as quoted in Alice Clark, *Working Life of Women in the Seventeenth Century* (New York: E. P. Dutton & Co., 1919), p. 238.

3. There is considerable historical debate over the net effect of Protestantism on the status of women. For examples of works lining up on the positive side, see Giele, "Centuries of Womanhood"; William and Madeville Haller, "The Puritan Art of Love," *Huntington Library Quarterly* 5 (1941–42): 235–272; and Nancy I. Roelker, "The Appeal of Calvinism in French Noblewomen in the Sixteenth Century," *Journal of Interdisciplinary History* 2 (1972): 391–418. Examples of historians taking a more critical view of Protestantism's effect on women are Natalie Zemon Davis, *Society and Culture in Early Modern France* (Stanford, Ca.: Stanford University Press, 1975), pp. 65–95; and Keith Thomas, "Woman in Civil War Sects," *Past and Present* 13 (April 1958): 42–62.

4. Davis, *Society and Culture*, pp. 77–83; Thomas, "Woman in Civil War Sects"; and Roelker, "Appeal of Calvinism."

5. Margaret W. Masson, "The Typology of the Female as a Model for the Regenerate: Puritan Preaching, 1690–1730," *Signs* 2 (Winter 1976): 304–315.

6. On English Protestants' views of marriage, see Edmund S. Morgan, *The Puritan Family*, rev. ed. (New York: Harper & Row, 1966), pp. 29–64; Haller, "Puritan Act of Love"; Louis B. Wright, *Middle-Class Culture in Elizabethan England* (Chapel Hill: University of North Carolina Press, 1935), pp. 201–227; and Keith Thomas, "The Double Standard," *Journal of the History of Ideas* 20 (April 1959): 195–216. On Christian humanists, see Davis, *Society and Culture*, pp. 89–90.

7. John T. Noonan, *Contraception: A History of Its Treatment by the Catholic Theologians and Canonists* (Cambridge, Mass.: Harvard University Press, 1966), pp. 292–255, 305–330; Haller, "Puritan Act of Love"; and Edmund S. Morgan, "The Puritans and Sex," *New England Quarterly* 15 (December 1942): 591–607.

8. Davis, *Society and Culture*, pp. 88–89. For Calvin's attack on celibacy and

acceptance of male sexual nature, see his *Commentaries on the First Book of Moses Called Genesis,* trans. John King (Edinburgh: Edinburgh Printing Company, 1847), 1: 128–131. The distinguished seventeenth-century English physician Thomas Sydenham similarly played down sexual distinctions in his analysis of hysteria (see *Selected Works of Thomas Sydenham,* ed. John D. Comrie [New York: William Wood & Co., 1922], pp. 130–144).

9. David Hunt, *Parents and Children in History* (New York: Harper & Row, 1972), pp. 60–64; and Natalie Zemon Davis, "Ghosts, Kin and Progeny: Some Features of Family Life in Early Modern France," *Daedalus* 106 (Spring 1977), pp. 105–108. A rise in dowries also imposed external constraints on couples. Our best evidence for this is about the aristocracy (see Lawrence Stone, *The Crisis of the Aristocracy* (Oxford: Clarendon Press, 1965), pp. 612–631; and H. J. Habakkuk, "Marriage Settlements in the Eighteenth Century," *Transactions of the Royal Historical Society,* 4th ser., 32 [1950]: 23–26).

10. Morgan, *Puritan Family,* pp. 21–25.

11. M. W. Perkins, *Christian Oeconomic, or, A Short Survey . . . according to the Scriptures* (n.p., 1609), p. 10; as quoted in Haller, "Puritan Act of Love," p. 247.

12. Christopher Hill, *Society and Puritanism in Pre-Revolutionary England,* rev. ed. (New York: Schocken books, 1964), pp. 443–481; Morgan, *Puritan Family,* pp. 87–108; Lawrence A. Cremin, *American Education: The Colonial Experience, 1607–1783* (New York: Harper & Row, 1970), pp. 124–125.

13. Cremin, *American Education,* pp. 135–136; Morgan, *Puritan Family,* pp. 143–145. Even the large land holdings of the first generation apparently strengthened patriarchal authority, for fathers could maintain considerable control over their sons by delaying the transmission of promised property (see Philip J. Greven, *Four Generations: Population, Land, and Family in Colonial Andover, Massachusetts* [Ithaca, N. Y.: Cornell University Press, 1970]).

14. One study on England concludes that manuals directed themselves to fathers as much as to mothers until the eighteenth century (see Abigail J. Stewart, David G. Winter, and A. David Jones, "Coding Categories for the Study of Childrearing from Historical Sources," *Journal of Interdisciplinary History* 5 [Spring 1975]: 701; on America, see Chapter 3.

15. John Robinson, *The Works of John Robinson Pastor of the Pilgrim Fathers,* ed. Robert Ashton (Boston: Doctrinal Tract and Book Society, 1851) 1: 242–245; as quoted in Philip J. Greven, *Child-Rearing Concepts, 1628–1861* (Itasca, Ill.: Peacock Publishers, 1973).

16. For aristocrats see Stone, *Crisis of Aristocracy,* p. 592; and Hunt, *Parents and Children,* pp. 100–109. Even among the less affluent, it evidently was fairly common practice for mothers to employ wet nurses (see Olwen Hufton, "Women and the Family Economy in Eighteenth-Century France," *French Historical Studies* 9 [Spring 1976]: 9–22; Shorter, *Making of the Modern Family,* pp. 175–183; and Julia Cherry Spruill, *Women's Life and Work in the Southern Colonies* [Chapel Hill: University of North Carolina Press, 1938], pp. 55–57).

17. Peter Laslett, "Size and Structure of the Household in England over Three Centuries," *Population Studies* 23 (1969): 216–217; Micheline Baulant, "La Famille en miettes: Sur un aspect de la demographie du XVIIIe siècle, " *Annales,*

Economies, Sociétés, Civilisations 27 (Juillet-Octobre 1972): 959–968. In New England there were more stable two-parent families because of a lower mortality rate (see Philip J. Greven, "Family Structure in Andover," *William and Mary Quarterly,* 3ᵈ ser. 23 [1966]: 239; and Peter Laslett, "Introduction," *Household and Family in Past Time,* ed. Peter Laslett and Richard Wall [Cambridge: Cambridge University Press, 1972], pp. 80–82).

18. Peter Laslett (*The World We Have Lost* [New York: Charles Scribner's Sons, 1965], pp. 90–92; and "Size and Structure," p. 219) offers evidence that about 6 percent of the households in preindustrial England contained three generations (also see Lutz Berkner, "The Stem Family and the Developmental Cycle of the Peasant Household," *American Historical Review* 77 [April 1972]: 389–418, and "Recent Research on the History of the Family in Western Europe," *Journal of Marriage and the Family* 35 [August 1973]: 395–405).

19. Edmund S. Morgan, *Virginians at Home* (Williamsburg, Va.: Colonial Williamsburg, 1952), pp. 23–25, and *Puritan Family,* pp. 38, 75–78; John Demos, *A Little Commonwealth* (New York: Oxford University Press, 1970), pp. 71–75; and Laslett, "Introduction," p. 82.

20. Various works by Laslett underscore the point that most preindustrial families were nuclear in structure (see his *World We Have Lost,* "Size and Structure," and "Introduction").

21. Matthew Griffith, *Bethel: Or a Forme for Families* (London, 1633), as quoted in Margaret George, "From 'Goodwife' to 'Mistress': The Transformation of the Female in Bourgeois Culture," *Science and Society* 37 (Summer 1973): 165.

22. Clark, *Working Life of Women,* pp. 178–183; Davis, *Society and Culture,* pp. 71–72.

23. Paul Delany, *British Autobiography in the Seventeenth Century* (New York: Columbia University Press, 1969), p. 166.

24. Clark, *Working Life of Women,* pp. 195, 265–284.

25. Edmund S. Morgan, *American Slavery, American Freedom: The Ordeal of Colonial Virginia* (New York: Norton, 1975), pp. 111, 163–70, 235; Herbert Moller, "Sex Composition and Correlated Cultural Patterns in Colonial America," *William and Mary Quarterly,* 3d ser., 2 (1945): 116–117. On how the marriage market ceased to be so favorable to women by the eighteenth century, see Alexander Keysar, "Widowhood in Eighteenth-Century Massachusetts: A Problem in the History of the Family," *Perspectives in American History* 8 (1974): 83–119.

26. Mary P. Ryan, *Womanhood in America: From Colonial Times to the Present* (New York: New Viewpoints, 1975), pp. 21–41; Mary Sumner Benson, *Women in Eighteenth-Century America* (New York: Columbia University Press, 1935), pp. 235–241; Richard Morris, *Studies in the History of America Law* (New York: Columbia University Press, 1930), pp. 126–127, 236–239; Spruill, *Women's Life and Work;* Elizabeth Anthony Dexter, *Colonial Women of Affairs* (New York: Houghton Mifflin Company, 1924). Most women's work, however, was situated in the home as it was in Europe (see Mary Beth Norton, "Eighteenth-Century American Women in Peace and War: The Case of the Loyalists," *William and Mary Quarterly,* 3d ser. [July 1976]: 386–409).

27. Catherine M. Scholten, "'On the Importance of the Obstetrick Art': Changing Customs of Childbirth in America, 1760 to 1825," *William and Mary Quarterly*, 3d ser. 34 (July 1977): 426–445); and Jane B. Donegan, "Man-Midwifery and the Delicacy of the Sexes," in *"Remember the Ladies,"* ed. Carol V. R. George (Syracuse, N. Y.: Syracuse University Press, 1975), pp. 90–109.

28. Wright, *Middle-Class Culture,* pp. 465–501; and Margaret George, "From 'Goodwife' to 'Mistress.'"

29. See esp. Ivy Pinchbeck, *Women Workers and the Industrial Revolution,* rev. ed. (London: Fank Cass, 1969), pp. 33–37, 129–156, 202–239, 310–316, and passim; see Nancy F. Cott, *The Bonds of Womanhood: "Woman's Sphere" in New England, 1780–1835* (New Haven, Conn.: Yale University Press, 1977), pp. 39–40, 43–45. On working-class mothers, see Michael Anderson, *Family Structure in Ninteenth Century Lancashire* (Cambridge: Cambridge University Press, 1971), pp. 171. There is no comparable study of American working-class family structure in the nineteenth century, a study that would need to consider ethnic variations among immigrant groups. For articles on a somewhat later period that also draw attention to the low proportion of industrially employed mothers, see Virginia Yans McLaughlin, "Patterns of Work and Family Organization: Buffalo's Italians," *Journal of Interdisciplinary History* 2 (Autumn 1971): 299–314; and Daniel J. Walkowitz, "Working-Class Women in the Gilded Age: Factory, Community and Family Life among Coboes, New York, Cotton Workers," *Journal of Social History* 5 (Summer 1972): 464–490.

30. On the ideology of romantic love, see Ian Watt, *The Rise of the Novel* (Berkeley: University of California Press, 1957), pp. 135–173. The link between sexual repression and genteel belief in feminine frailty is perhaps best revealed in nineteenth-century attitudes toward puberty (see Elaine and English Showalter, "Victorian Women and Menstruation," *Victorian Studies* 14 [September 1970]: 83–89; and Caroll Smith-Rosenberg, "Puberty to Menopause: The Cycle of Femininity in Nineteenth-Century America," in *Clio's Consciousness Raised: New Perspectives in the History of Women,* ed. Mary Hartman and Lois W. Banner [New York: Harper & Row, 1974], pp. 23–27). For the relationship between this nineteenth-century feminine ideal and widespread female hysteria, see Carroll Smith-Rosenberg, "The Hysterical Woman: Sex Roles and Role Conflict, in Nineteenth-Century America," *Social Research* 39 (Winter 1972): 652–678.

31. Steven Marcus, *The Other Victorians* (New York: Basic Books, 1966), pp. 1–33; and Ben Barker-Benfield, "The Spermatic Economy: A Nineteenth Century View of Sexuality," in *The American Family in Socio-Historical Perspective,* ed. Michael Gordon (New York: St. Martin's Press, 1973), pp. 336–372.

32. Ibid. Also see Peter T. Cominos, "Late-Victorian Sexual Respectability and the Social System," *International Review of Social History* 8 (1963): 27–31.

33. Daniel Scott Smith, "Family Limitation, Sexual Control, and Domestic Feminism in Victorian America," in Hartman and Banner, *Clio's Consciousness Raised,* pp. 119–136.

34. Marcus, *Other Victorians,* pp. 147–148. For the marriage market, see H. J. Habakkuk, "Marriage Settlements," and J. Hajnal, "European Marriage Patterns in Perspective," in *Population in History,* ed. D. V. Glass and D. E. C.

Eversley (Chicago: Aldine Publishing Co., 1965), pp. 127–128. For evidence of a similar situation developing in the American marriage market as the population of women rose, see Keyssar, "Widowhood." There is clear evidence of a transatlantic increase in nonmarital sex in the late eighteenth century, although historians differ in interpreting it (on America see Daniel Scott Smith and Michael S. Flindus, "Premarital Pregancy in America, 1640–1971: An Overview and Interpretaion," *Journal of Interdisciplinary History* 2 [Autumn 1971]: 237–272; on Europe, Shorter, *Making of the Modern Family*, pp. 79–108; for a brief but penetrating critque of Shorter, see Joan W. Scott and Louise A. Tilly, "Women's Work in Nineteenth-Century Europe," *Comparative Studies in Society and History* 17 [1975]: 55–56, n. 71).

35. Marcus, *Other Victorians*.

36. For America, see Cedric B. Cowing, "Sex and Preaching in the Great Awakening;" *American Quarterly* 20 (Fall 1968): 625; Nancy F. Cott, "Young Women in the Second Great Awakening in New England," *Feminist Studies* 3 (Fall 1975): 15–29; Cott, *Bonds*, pp. 126–159; Barbara Welter, "The Feminization of American Religion: 1800–1860," in Hartman and Banner, *Clio's Consciousness Raised*, pp. 137–157; Keith Melder, "Ladies Bountiful: Organized Women's Benevolence in Early Nineteenth Century America," *New York History* 48 (July 1967): 231–254. For women's participation in the English Methodist revivals and Evangelical movement, see R. F. Wearmouth, *Methodism and the Common People of the Eighteenth Century* (London: Epworth Press, 1945), pp. 223–228; and Ford K. Brown, *Fathers of the Victorians* (Cambridge: Cambridge University Press, 1961).

37. For a similar interpretation see Welter, "Feminization of American Religion," pp. 140–142.

38. The genre of sentimental fiction stemming from Richardson's *Pamela* carried this message (see Watt, *Rise of the Novel*). For this rise in female moral authority, also see Herman R. Lantz, Margaret Britton, Raymond Schmitt, and Eloise C. Snyder, "Pre–Industrial Patterns in the Colonial Family in America: A Content Analysis of Colonial Magazines," *American Sociological Review* 33 (June 1968): 413–426; and Cott, *Bonds*, pp. 69–70, 120–121, 146–148. In her analysis of this emerging separate woman's sphere, Cott cogently identifies both oppressive and reinforcing features.

39. Melder, "Ladies Bountiful"; Charles T. Foster, *An Errand of Mercy* (Chapel Hill: University of North Carolina Press, 1960), pp. 95–97, 228; Cott, *Bonds*, pp. 135–137; Welter, "Feminization of American Religion"; and Carroll Smith-Rosenberg, "Beauty, the Beast and the Militant Woman: A Case Study in Sex Roles and the Social Stress in Jacksonian America," *American Quarterly* 23 (October 1971): 562–584.

40. On women and sentimental literature see esp. Watt, *Rise of Novel*, 35–39, passim; Barbara Welter, "The Cult of True Womanhood: 1820–1860," *American Quarterly* 28 (Summer 1966): 151–174; Ann Douglas, *The Feminization of American Culture* (New York: Alfred A. Knopf, 1977).

41. See, for example, William L. O'Neill, *Everyone Was Brave* (Chicago: Quadrangle Books. 1969), pp. 34–44; Jill Conway. "Women Reformers and American Culture, 1870–1930," *Journal of Social History* (Winter 1971–72):

164–177; Linda Gordon, "Voluntary Motherhood: The Beginnings of Feminist Birth Control Ideas in the United States," in Hartman and Banner, *Clio's Consciousness Raised,* pp. 54–71; J. A. and Olive Banks, *Feminism and Family Planning in Victorian England* (Liverpool: Liverpool University Press, 1964). Daniel Scott Smith's concept of "domestic feminism" highlights this newfound female authority in the home (see his "Family Limitation" in Hartman and Banner, *Clio's Consciousness Raised*).

42. Servants were still often employed by those who could afford it but were evidently less common among the urban and rural middle class than previously (see Pinchbeck, *Women Workers,* pp. 37–40; Roger Smith, "Early Victorian Household Structure: A Case Study of Nottinghamshire," *International Review of Social History* 15 [1970]: 81–82; and Cott, *Bonds,* pp. 48–58). In addition to these structural changes, a common piece of child–rearing advice was not to entrust children to servants.

43. Anderson, *Family Structure,* pp. 44, 46–47, 71, 142; W. A. Armstrong, "A Note on the Household Structure of Mid–Nineteenth–Century York in Comparative Perspective," in Laslett and Wall, *Household and Family,* pp. 205–214; and Smith, p. 82. Even in nonindustrial Salem, Massachusetts, in 1800 kinship ties appear to have been stronger among the artisan class than among the merchant class (see Bernard Farber, *Guardians of Virtue: Salem Families in 1800* [New York: Basic Books, 1972]).

44. Neil J. Smelser, *Social Change in the Industrial Revolution* (Chicago: University of Chicago Press, 1959), pp. 180–312 and passim; Anderson, *Family Structure,* pp. 114–117. Smelser and Anderson both refer to "children" without regard to sex, but I imagine that these were mainly boys. While, in spinning, some preparatory processes still occupied a few females, this work seems to have gone on in a separate location (see Pinchbeck, *Women Workers,* pp. 152–153).

45. See Anne L. Kuhn, The *Mother's Role in Childhood Education* (New Haven, Conn.: Yale University Press, 1947) pp. 35, passim. On the shift in the literature, also see Chapter 3. The major writers of this didactic literature included the Reverends J. S. C. Abbott, Harvey Newcombe, Hubbard Winslow, and religious middle–class women such as Almira Phelps, Lydia Maria Child, and Catharine Beecher (see Kathryn Kish Sklar, *Catharine Beecher: A Study in American Domesticity* [New Haven, Conn.: Yale University Press, 1973]; Robert Sunley, "Early Nineteenth–Century American Literature on Childrearing," *Childhood in Contemporary Cultures,* ed. Margaret Mead and Martha Wolfenstein [Chicago: University of Chicago Press, 1955], pp. 150–167; and Kuhn, *Mother's Role*). On maternal associations, see Cott, *Bonds,* pp. 149–151.

3. AMERICAN FEMININE IDEALS IN TRANSITION:
THE RISE OF THE MORAL MOTHER, 1785–1815

1. See especially Anne L. Kuhn, *The Mother's Role in Childhood Education* (New Haven, Conn.: Yale University Press, 1947); Barbara Welter, "The Cult of True Womanhood: 1820–1860," *American Quarterly* 18 (Summer 1966): 151–74; Kathryn Kish Sklar, *Catharine Beecher* (New Haven, Conn.: Yale University

Press, 1973); Ann Douglas, *The Feminization of American Culture* (New York: Knopf, 1977).

2. Elizabeth Anthony Dexter, *Colonial Women of Affairs* (New York: Houghton Mifflin, 1924); Julia Cherry Spruil, *Women's Life and Work in the Southern Colonies* (Chapel Hill: University of North Carolina Press, 1938); Mary Sumner Benson, *Women in Eighteenth-Century America* (New York: Columbia University Press, 1935); Edmund S. Morgan, *The Puritan Family*, rev. ed. (New York: Harper and Row, 1966); John Demos, *A Little Commonwealth* (New York: Oxford University Press, 1970); Mary P. Ryan, *Womanhood In America* (New York: New Viewpoints, 1975), pp. 211–235; Laurel Thatcher Ulrich, "Vertuous Women Found: New England Ministerial Literature, 1668–1735," *American Quarterly* 28 (Spring 1976): 20–40; Margaret W. Masson, "The Typology of the Female as a Model for the Regenerate: Puritan Preaching, 1690–1730," *Signs* 2 (Winter 1976): 304–315.

For examples of the more recent trend see Linda K. Kerber, "Daughters of Columbia: Educating Women for the Republic, 1787–1805," in *The Hofstadter Aegis: A Memorial*, ed. Stanley Elkins and Eric McKitrick (New York: Knopf, 1974), pp. 36–59; Linda K. Kerber, "The Republican Mother: Women and the Enlightenment—An American Perspective," *American Quarterly* 28 (Summer 1976): 187–205; Nancy F. Cott, *The Bonds of Womanhood* (New Haven, Conn.: Yale University Press, 1977), pp. 46–47, 58–62, 85–92, and *passim*.

3. This portrait of the Puritan "help-meet" ideal is drawn from Morgan, Ryan, Ulrich, and from my own reading of numerous Puritan published sermons and treatises on women and family life.

4. A few examples are Benjamin Franklin, *Reflections on Courtship and Marriage* (Philadelphia: B. Franklin, 1746); John Witherspoon, "Letters on Marriage," in *A Series of Letters on Courtship and Marriage* (Springfield, Mass.: F. Stebbins, 1798); "On the Choice of a Wife," *The Columbian Magazine and the Universal Asylum* 8 (March 1792): 176–179.

5. This genteel ideal has received far less scholarly treatment than the help-meet, although it has been observed by Ryan and Benson. Also see Robert Middlekauff, *Ancients and Axioms* (New Haven, Conn.: Yale University Press, 1963), pp. 106–108, 167–168. This sketch draws primarily from my own reading of the eighteenth-century sources.

6. John Oliver, *A Present for Teeming Women* (Boston: Benjamin Harris, 1694); Cotton Mather, *Elizabeth on Her Holy Retirement* (Boston: B. Green, 1710). Also see Catherine M. Scholten, "'On the Importance of the Obstetrick Art: Changing Customs of Childbirth in America, 1760 to 1825," *William and Mary Quarterly* 34 (July 1977): 426–445.

7. Benjamin Colman, *Some of the Honours that Religion Does unto the Fruitful Mothers in Israel* (Boston: B. Green, 1715).

8. The evidence on wet-nursing in western Europe is summarized in Edward Shorter, *The Making of the Modern Family* (New York: Basic Books, 1975), pp. 175–177. For some scattered evidence on American wetnursing, see Joseph E. Illick, "Child-Rearing in Seventeenth-Century England and America," in *The History of Childhood*, ed. Lloyd de Mause (New York: Harper and Row, 1974),

p. 325; Carl Bridenbaugh, *Cities in Revolt* (New York: Oxford University Press, 1955), p. 149; Spruill, *Women's Life and Work*, pp. 55–57.

9. A few examples of numerous admonitions against wetnursing are Robert Cleaver, *A Godlie Forme of Householde Government* (London: Felix Kingston, 1598), pp. 235–239; William Gouge, *Of Domesticall Duties* (London: John Haviland, 1622), pp. 507–517; Cotton Mather, *Ornaments for the Daughters of Zion* (Cambridge, Mass.: Samuel Phillips, 1692), p. 93; Benajmin Wadsworth, *The Well-Ordered Family* (Boston: B. Green, 1712), p. 46; Sophia Hume, *An Exhortation to the Inhaibtants of South-Carolina* (Philadelphia: William Bradford, 1748?), pp. 119–124. Cleaver and Gouge very briefly mention psychological effects.

10. Many contemporary historians, primarily of Europe, have come to this dubious conclusion. Their case is based on at least two faulty assumptions: The first is that caring mothers should have known that wetnursing was medically dangerous, and the second is that a lack of written attention to maternal affection means that it did not exist. See especially David Hunt, *Parents and Children in History* (New York: Harper and Row, 1970); Lloyd de Mause "The Evolution of Childhood," *History of Childhood Quarterly* 1 (1974): 503–575; and Shorter, *The Making of the Modern Family*.

11. Cleaver, *A Godlie Forme*, pp. 60, 297; John Taylor, *The Value of a Child* (Philadelphia: B. Franklin and D. Hall, 1753), p. 7; Mather, *Ornaments*, p. 95; Cotton Mather, *Help for Distressed Parents* (Boston: John Allen, 1795), pp. 8–9; Philip Doddridge, *Sermons on the Religious Education of Children*, 4th ed. (Boston: Kneeland, 1763).

12. Cotton Mather, *Maternal Consolations* (Boston: T. Fleet, 1714), pp. 18, 21. Another unusual funeral sermon by a mourning son that praises maternal tenderness is Thomas Foxcroft, *A Sermon Preach'd at Cambridge, After the Funeral of Mrs. Elizabeth Foxcroft* (Boston: B. Green, 1721).

13. See especially Phillipe Ariès, *Centuries of Childhood*, trans. Robert Baldick (New York: Vintage Books, 1962).

14. This genre included numerous works. The best summary is Morgan, *Puritan Family*, pp. 65–108. Other historians have noted the relatively undifferentiated parental roles prescribed in Puritan literature. See Ryan, *Womanhood in America*, p. 60; Ulrich, "Vertuous Women Found," p. 39; Masson, "Typology of Female," pp. 306–307.

15. For a few of many examples, see Mather, *Ornaments*, pp. 88–89; Mather, *Maternal*, pp. 11–15; Foxcroft, *A Sermon;* and Benjamin Colman, *The Honour and Happiness of the Vertuous Woman* (Boston: B. Green, 1716).

16. See, for example, Gouge, *Of Domesticall Duties*, pp. 546–547; Increase Mather, *Call from Heaven to the Present and Succeeding Generations* (Boston: John Foster, 1679), p. 23; Taylor, *The Value of a Child*, p. 3.

17. Cotton Mather, *Help*, pp. 8–9. Also see Cleaver, *A Godlie Forme*, pp. 60–61; Gouge, *Of Domesticall Duties*, pp. 259–60; John Robinson, "Of Children and their education," in *New Essayes or Observations Divine and Morall* (n.p., 1628), p. 306.

18. See, for example, Richard Mather, *A Farwell Exhortation to the Church and People of Dorchester in New-England* (Cambridge, Mass.: S. Green, 1657),

p. 11; Cotton Mather, *Cares about the Nurseries* (Boston: n.p., 1702), pp. 4–8; Benjamin Bass, *Parents and Children Advised and Exhorted to their Duty* (Newport: James Franklin, 1730).

19. The now obscure edition of *The Mother's Catechism* — possibly not by Willison but by Richard Baxter — was printed in Boston in 1729. Puritan works written explicitly for fathers are numerous. A few examples are Deodat Lawson, *The Duty & Property of a Religious Householder* (Boston: B. Green, 1693); Cotton Mather, *A Family-Sacrifice* (Boston: B. Green and J. Allen, 1703); Joseph Buckminister, *Heads of Families, to Resolve for their Households, No Less than for Themselves, that They Will Serve the Lord* (Boston: S. Kneeland, 1759).

20. Richard Baxter, *A Christian Directory* (London: Robert White, 1673), p. 548; Richard Mather, *A Farewel Exhortation*, p. 13; Cotton Mather, *Cares*, pp. 44–45.

21. Gouge, *Of Domesticall Duties*, pp. 486–87. Also see Foxcroft, *A Sermon*, pp. 8, 18.

22. Morgan, *Puritan Family*, pp. 75–79, and Demos, *Little Commonwealth*, pp. 70–75.

23. Morgan, *Puritan Family*, pp. 117–118. For servants' responsibilities to children, see Cotton Mather, *Corderius Americanus* (Boston: J. Allen, 1708), pp. 12–13.

24. On women in the colonial economy, see especially Dexter, *Colonial Women*. She, however, exaggerates the extent and autonomy of women engaged in nondomestic work. See Mary Beth Norton, "Eighteenth-Century American Women in Peace and War: The Case of the Loyalists," *William and Mary Quarterly*, 3d ser., 33 (July 1976): 386–409.

25. Gusti Wiesenfeld Frankel, "Between Parent and Child in Colonial New England: Analysis of the Religious Child-Oriented Literature and Selected Children's Works" (unpublished doctoral thesis, University of Minnesota, 1977). I am indebted to Gusti Wisenfeld Frankel of the Hebrew University for conversation and tips on other aspects of this paper as well.

26. Hugh Smith, *Letters to Married Women, on Nursing and the Management of Children* (Philadelphia: Mathew Carey, 1792), p. 121; Elizabeth Griffiths, "Letters to Ladies — Married and Single. With Useful Advice," *New York Weekly Magazine I* (September 1795), p. 92; Clark Brown, *The Importance of the Early and Proper Education of Children* (Newbedford: John Spooner, 1795), p. 17; Enos Hitchcock, *A Discourse on Education* (Providence: Bennett Wheeler, 1785), p. 6. This evolving perspective on child psychology owed much to the long-term influence of such philosophers as Locke and Rousseau, although much of their work did not circulate widely in eighteenth-century America. See David Lundberg and Henry F. May, "The Enlightened Reader in America: 1700 to 1813," *American Quarterly* 28 (Summer 1976): 262–271 and appendix.

27. Cleaver, *A Godlie Forme*, p. 237, is the only example I know of a work read in America using the "humour" theory. Others explicitly dismissed it. See Nicholas Culpeper, *A Directory for Midwives* (London: George Sawbridge, 1675), pp. 152–160, and Hume, *An Exhortation*, p. 120.

28. Enos Hitchcock, *Memoirs of the Bloomsgrove Family* (Boston: Thomas and Andrews, 1790) 1: 79.

29. Mary Watkins, *Maternal Solicitude, or, Lady's Manual, &c.* (New York: H. C. Southwick, 1809), pp. 9–10.

30. Henry Home (Lord Karnes), *Sketches of the History of Man* (Edinburgh: W. Strahan and T. Cadell, 1778), p. 92; Smith, *Letters to Married Women*, p. 51.

31. Smith, *Letters to Married Women*, p. 51; William Buchan, *Domestic Medicine* (Boston: Joseph Bumstead, 1793), pp. 3, 23–35; *The Maternal Physician* (New York: Isaac Riley, 1811; rpt. ed., New York: Arno Press, 1972), p. 14

32. "The Advantage of Maternal Nurture," *The Weekly Visitor, or, Ladies' Miscellany* 2 (May 1804): 260–261. Also see Richard Polwhele, "On the Domestic Character of Women," *The New York Magazine, or, Literary Repository* 7 (November 1796): 600–602; Henry Home, *Loose Hints upon Education* (Edinburgh: John Bell, 1782), p. 44; Watkins, *Maternal Solicitude, pp.* 8–9.

33. Smith, *Letters to Married Women*, p. 60.

34. This paragraph is drawn from numerous pieces of medical literature printed (or reprinted) in America. Salient examples include: Dr. Willich, "Method of Treating that Excruciating Complaint Incident to Married Ladies, — Sore Nipples," *The Weekly Visitor, or, Ladies Miscellany* 2 (March 1804): 196; George Wallis, *The Art of Preventing Disease, and Restoring Health* (New York: Samuel Campbell, 1794), pp. 114–128; Michael Underwood, *A Treatise on the Diseases of Children with General Directions for the Management of Infants from the Birth* (Philadelphia: T. Dobson, 1793), pp. 327–404; William Cadogan, *An Essay upon Nursing and the Management of Children* (Boston: Cox and Berry, 1772), pp. 10–49; Alexander Hamilton, *Management of Female Complaints, and of Children in Early Infancy* (Philadelphia: A. Bartram, 1806), pp. 225–242; William Buchan, *Advice to Mothers* (Philadelphia: J. Bloren, 1804); Buchan, *Domestic*; Smith, *Letters to Married Women;* Samuel Kennedy Jennings, *Married Lady's Companion, or Poor Man's Friend* (Richmond, Va.: T. Nicholson, 1804); Watkins, *Maternal Solicitude*, pp. 7–18; anon., *Maternal Physician*, pp. 5–28, 93–135. The last three are American. Many of these prescriptions were also in Locke's *Some Thoughts Concerning Education* and were taken up in other, nonmedical books such as Richardson's *Pamela* and Enos Hitchcock's *Memoirs*.

35. Cadogan, *An Essay upon Nursing*, pp. 3–5; Underwood, *A Treatise on Diseases*, pp. 1–2, 335–337; Buchan, *Domestic*, pp. 4–5.

36. Anon., *Maternal Physician*, p. 7.

37. Buchan, *Advice*, p. 294.

38. George Strebeck, *A Sermon on the Character of the Virtuous Woman* (New York: n.p. 1800), p. 23; John Burton, *Lectures on Female Education and Manners* (Elizabethtown, N. J.: S. Koliock, 1799), p. 54; Griffiths, "Letters to Ladies," pp. 91–92, 99–100; Thomas Barnard, *A Sermon Preached before the Salem Female Charitable Society* (Salem: William Carlton, 1803), p. 13; Hitchcock, *Memoirs*, 1: 47–48.

39. Jesse Appleton, *A Discourse Delivered before the Members of the Portsmouth Female Asylum* (Portsmouth: S. Whidden, 1806), p. 15.

40. Aside from the medical literature noted above, see, for example, anon., *Advice to the Fair Sex* (Philadelphia: Robert Cochran, 1803), pp. 121–133; Jane West, *Letters to a Young Lady* (Troy, N. Y.: O. Penniman & Co., 1806), pp.

406–441; [Judith Sargeant Murray], "On the Domestic Education of Children," *The Massachusetts Magazine* 2 (June 1790): 275–277.

41. Anon., *The Mother's Gift* (Worcester: Isaiah Thomas, 1787).

42. Elizabeth Heime, *Maternal Instruction, or Family Conversations* (New York: James Oram, 1804).

43. Anon., *Early Christian Instructions in the Form of a Dialogue between a Mother and Child* (Philadelphia: James P. Parke, 1807); Priscilla Wakefield, *Domestic Recreation* (Philadelphia: Jacob Johnson, 1803); [Mary Jane Kilner], *Familiar Dialogues for the Instruction and Amusement of Children of Four and Five* (Boston: Hall and Hiller,1804). On mothers in Quaker literature, see J. William Frost, *The Quaker Family in Colonial America* (New York: St. Martin's Press, 1973), p. 85.

44. After one American edition in 1729, it went into 14 new editions between 1783 and 1811.

45. See, for example, Helme, *Maternal Instruction;* Wakefield, *Domestic Recreation;* Kilner, *Familiar Dialogues;* Griffiths, "Letters to Ladies"; anon., *The Mother's Remarks on a Set of Cuts for Children* (Philadelphia: Jacob Johnson, 1803).

46. John Cosens Ogden, *The Female Guide* (Concord: George Hough, 1793), p. 8.

47. Burton, *Lectures on Female Education,* p. 55.

48. Jennings, *Married Ladies,* pp. 123–125; anon., *The Parent's Friend* (Philadelphia: Jane Aitken, 1803), pp. xi–xiii.

49. Cott, *Bonds of Womanhood,* pp. 48–50. On changes in class composition see Lawrence W. Towner, "'A Fondness for Freedom': Servant Protest in Puritan Society," *William and Mary Quarterly,* 3rd ser., 19 (April 1962): 213–215.

50. On parental role differentiation due to fathers leaving home to work, see Cott, *Bonds of Womanhood,* esp. p. 46. This phenomenon has received more extended analysis in its relation to the Industrial Revolution, which in America occurred only later. See especially Neil J. Smelser, *Social Change in the Industrial Revolution* (Chicago: University of Chicago Press, 1959), pp. 180–312

51. On home manufacturing in America, see Cott, *Bonds of Womanhood,* pp. 19–62. For England, see Alice Clark, *Working Life of Women in the Seventeenth Century* (London: Frank Cass, 1919); Ivy Pinchbeck, *Women Workers and the Industrial Revolution,* rev. ed. (London: Frank Cass, 1969).

52. Ian Watt makes this argument in *The Rise of the Novel* (Berkeley: University of California Press, 1957), pp. 43–45. Ann Douglas, in *Feminization,* also makes this case for a later period in America. On literacy, see Kenneth A. Lockridge, *Literacy in Colonial New England* (New York: Norton, 1974), pp. 38–42. Note especially the Boston figures.

53. See, for example, Smith, *Letters to Married Women,* p. 129; Buchan, *Advice,* p. 4; Jennings, *Married Lady's Companion,* p. 5; *Maternal Physician,* p. 278.

54. Cott, *Bonds of Womanhood,* pp, 85–86, 147–148; Douglas, *Feminization, passim.*

55. William Lyman, *A Virtuous Woman the Bond of Domestic Union* (New London: S. Green, 1802), p. 22.

56. Barnard, *A Sermon*, p. 14.

57. Mary Wollstonecraft, *A Vindication of the Rights of Woman* (London, 1792; rpt. ed., New York: Norton, 1967), p. 280.

58. New England clergymen now frequently stressed such female virtues. For a more complete discussion and listing of such clerical writings, see Cott, *Bonds of Womanhood,* pp. 126–159, and her bibliography. In addition, numerous secular comparative histories and biographies of women began to appear that emphasized these qualities.

59. Examples are numerous. A few are: "Scheme for Encreasing the Power of the Fair Sex," *The Baltimore Weekly Magazine* 1 (April 1801): 241–242; *The Female Advocate* (New Haven, Conn.: Thomas Green and Son, 1801), p. 14; "On the Influence of Women," *The Literary Magazine and* American *Register* 5 (June 1806): 403–408; Thomas Branagan, *The Excellency of the Female Character Vindicated* (New York: Samuel Wood, 1807), pp. 61–62, 111–112.

60. See, for example, Samuel Worcester, *Female Love to Christ* (Salem: Pool and Palfray, 1809), p. 14; Daniel Dana, *A Discourse Delivered May 22, 1804, before the Members of the Female Charitable Society of Newburyport* (Newburyport: Edmund M. Blunt, 1804), pp. 15–19; Timothy Woodbridge, *A Sermon, Preached April 20th, 1813, in Compliance with a Request of the Gloucester Female Society* (Boston: Samuel T. Armstrong, 1813), pp. 18–19; Daniel Chaplin, *A Discourse Delivered before the Charitable Female Society in Groton* (Andover: Flagg and Gould, 1814), pp. 8–10.

61. See, for example, anon., *The Mother's Gift;* Griffiths, "Letters to Ladies"; [Murray], "On Domestic Education," pp. 275–77; Worcester, *Female Love,* p. 7.

62. "A Mother's Address," *The Weekly Visitor, or, Ladies Miscellany* 2 (August 1804): 344; "Sweet Infant," *The Lady's Weekly Miscellany* 8 (November 1808): 63; "The Mother to Her Child," *The Lady's Weekly Miscellany* 7 (May 1808): 64.

63. Anon., *Family-Religion Revived* (New Haven, Conn.: James Parker, 1775), p. 96. Also Smith, *Letters to Married Women,* p. 123.

64. Examples of sentimentalized paternal fondness are: Mason Locke Weems, *Hymen's Recruiting Sergeant* (Philadelphia: R. Cochran, 1802); "On the Happiness of Domestic Life," *The American Museum* I (February 1787): 156–158; for examples of tyrannical fathers, see "Honour Eclipsed by Love," *The Boston Magazine* 2 (August 1785): 293–295; M. Imbert, "The Power of Love and Filial Duty," *The New-York Magazine; or, Literary Repository* 2 (August 1791): 468–475; "On Parental Authority," *The Ladies Magazine* I (October 1792): 237–241.

65. Anon., *Sketches of the History, Disposition, Accomplishments, Employments, Customs and Importance of the Fair Sex* (Philadelphia: Samuel Samson, 1797), pp. 103–104.

66. Judith Sargeant Murray, *The Gleaner* (Boston: I. Thomas and E. T. Andrews, 1798) 3: 223–224; [Murray), "On Domestic Education"; anon., "Maternal Affection: Extract from the Beauties of Wollstoncraft [sic]," *The Lady's Weekly Miscellany* 7 (April 1808): 14–15; William Boyd, *Woman: A*

Poem (Boston: John W. Folsom, 1796), p. 9; 77 *The Female Character Vindicated* (Leominster: Charles Prentiss, 1796), p. 10; anon., *Female Advocate,* pp. 33–34.

67. See Kerber, "Daughters of Columbia," and "Republican Mother." Contrary to Kerber's impression, however, still only a small minority of those advocating improved female education stressed the responsibilities of mothers. Prospects of improvement in the quality of women's companionship, personal fulfillment, and even intellectual contributions to society were still more often invoked.

68. A few outstanding examples are: Wollstonecraft, *Vindication,* pp. 32–33, 280; Murray, *Gleaner* 2: 6–7, 3: 188–224; *Female Advocate,* pp. 33–34; "Oration upon Female Education," in *The American Preceptor,* ed. Caleb Bingham (Boston: Manning and Loring, 1813), pp. 47–51; "Plan for the Emancipation of the Fair Sex," *Lady's Magazine and Musical Repository* 3 (January 1802): 43–44; "Present Mode of Female Education Considered," *The Lady's Weekly Miscellany* 7 (June 1808): 43–44; "On the Supposed Superiority of the Masculine Understanding," *The Columbian Magazine and the Universal Asylum* (July 1791): 11.

69. Benjamin Rush, "Thoughts upon Female Education," in *Essays on Education in the Early Republic,* ed. Frederick Rudolph (Cambridge, Mass.: Harvard University Press, 1965), pp. 25–40. Also see Noah Webster, "On the Education of Youth," A *Collection of Essays and Fugitiv Writings* (Boston: 1. Thomas and E. T. Andrews, 1790), pp. 27–30; Hitchcock, *Memoirs,* 2: 23–94, 289–300. Hitchcock drew from Rousseau in his stress on female domesticity, but, like other Americans in this period, thought more highly of female intellect.

70. Hannah More, *Strictures on the Modern System of Female Education* (London: R. Cadell and W. Davies, 1799) 1: 97–98; 2: 2.

71. Hannah More. "Essays for Young Ladies," in *The Lady's Pocket Library* (Philadelphia: Mathew Carey, 1792), p. 67.

72. Henry F. May, *The Enlightenment in America* (New York: Oxford University Press, 1976), pp. 153–304, *passim.*

73. Douglas, *Feminization, passim.* She, however, wrongly associates such views with northeastern liberal (later Unitarian) Protestants alone. Most of the religious figures cited in this chapter were decidedly evangelical (either English Low Church Anglicans or American "moderate" revivalist Calvinists in the Congregational or Presbyterian churches). Significantly, some of the next-generation Victorian "liberals" featured in Douglas' book, such as the Beecher siblings, came from strong evangelical backgrounds.

74. See especially Timothy Dwight, as "Morpheus," *New-England Palladium,* March 15, 1802. As cited in Kerber, "Daughters of Columbia," p. 52.

75. See especially Nancy Chodorow, *The Reproduction of Mothering* (Berkeley: University of California Press, 1978). Many essays by Talcott Parsons have also drawn this connection. Fred Weinstein and Gerald M. Platt's *The Wish to Be Free* (Berkeley: University of California Press, 1969) is a historical work largely organized in these terms, but it focuses on male personality.

76. Cott, *Bonds of Womanhood,* pp. 160–196.

4. WOMEN AND THE LAW OF COURTSHIP
IN EIGHTEENTH-CENTURY AMERICA

1. Briefly, during the Interregnum, English civil marriage law moved in a direction similar to that of the colonies. For the most part, however, jurisdiction over marriage fell to ecclesiastical courts, with mixed results. On England, see John Addy, *Sin and Society in the Seventeenth Century* (London: Routledge, 1989); Lawrence Stone, *The Family, Sex, and Marriage in England, 1500–1800* (London: Weidenfeld and Nicolson, 1977); Martin Ingram, *Church Courts, Sex and Marriage in England, 1570–1640* (Cambridge: Cambridge University Press, 1987); Susan Staves, *Married Women's Separate Property in England, 1660–1833* (Cambridge, Mass., Harvard University Press, 1990); John R. Gillis, *For Better, For Worse: British Marriages 1600 to the Present* (New York: Oxford University Press, 1985).

2. For another perspective on this development, see Carol Shammas, "Anglo-American Household Government in Comparative Perspective," *William and Mary Quarterly* 52 (1995): 104–144.

3. These laws are summarized in George Elliott Howard, *A History of Matrimonial Institutions: Chiefly in England and the United States* (Chicago: University of Chicago Press: Callaghan, 1904) 2: 144, 162–163. See also Mary Beth Norton, *Founding Mothers and Fathers: Gendered Power and the Forming of American Society* (New York: Knopf, 1996), pp. 62–67.

4. See Howard, *History of Matrimonial Institutions*, 2: 268.

5. On New Jersey, see Howard, *History of Matrimonial Institutions*, 2: 310–311; on Pennsylvania, Staughton George et al., comps., *Charter to Wm Penn and the Laws of the Province of Pennsylvania Passed Between the Years 1682 and 1700: Preceded by the Duke of York's Laws in Force from the Year 1676 to the Year 1682* (Harrisburg: Lane S. Hart, 1879), pp. 37, 101, 151, 171, 229; James T. Mitchell and Henry Flanders, eds., *The Statutes at Large of Pennsylvania from 1682 to 1801*, vol. 2: 1700– 1712 (Philadelphia: Clarence M. Busch, 1896), p. 21.

6. Hening, *Statutes*, 1:156–157 for 1646, 181 for 1661–1662; 3: 149–151 for 1696.

7. Stone, *Family, Sex, and Marriage*, pp. 35–36; Lawrence Stone, *Road to Divorce: A History of the Making and Breaking of Marriage in England* (New York: Oxford University Press, 1995), pp. 115–120; Paul Langford, *A Polite and Commercial People: England 1727–1783* (Oxford: Clarendon, 1989), p. 114; Stephen Parker, *Informal Marriage, Cohabitation, and the Law, 1750–1989* (London: MacMillan Press, 1990), pp. 29–43. While the aristocracy represented in the House of Lords had a longstanding interest in reform, the House of Commons was finally pushed to concur by the growing notoriety of easy irregular marriages conducted by unscrupulous clergymen working out of the London Fleet Prison for debtors.

8. David Pulsifer, ed., *Records of the Colony of New Plymouth in New England: Laws 1623–1682* (orig. ed. Boston, 1861; rpt. New York, 1968), p. 29; "Act of 1647," *The Charter and General Laws of the Colony and Province of*

Massachusetts Bay (Boston, 1814), p. 151; [Colony of Connecticut], *The Book of General Laws* (Cambridge: Samuel Green, 1673), p. 46.

9. Howard, *History of Matrimonial Institutions,* 2: 164, citing New Haven Colonial Records, 2: 600); Edward E. Atwater, *History of the Colony of New Haven* (Meriden, Conn., 1902), p. 362.

10. "Abduction." 1558 (4 & 5 Ph. and Mar. cap 8) in *Statutes at Large, King Henry the Eighth to the End of the Reign of King Charles the Second* 2 (London, 1758), paragraph 4.

11. This clause was reiterated in 1705 and 1748; Hening, *Statutes* 3: 149–151 for 1696, 443–444 for 1705; 6: 83 for 1748.

12. For examples of cases brought to court under this statute in Middlesex County, Massachusetts, see Upham v. Wilson, June 1658, as indexed in David Pulsifer, transcription of order books, Middlesex County Court Archives, 4 vols (hereafter cited as Pulsifer, Middlesex) 1: 156; Green v. Johnson, April 1, 1662, Pulsifer, Middlesex, 1: 249; Monsall v. Fosket and Tirrell, June 16, 1663, Pulsifer, Middlesex, 1: 286; Dexter v. Pinson, August 6, 1661, Pulsifer, Middlesex, 1: file 642.

13. On the 1603 Canon law, which gave the age limit of twenty-one, see [Church of England], *Constitutions and Canons Ecclesiastical: Treated upon by the Bishop of London, . . . and agreed upon with the King's Majesty's license in their synod begun at London . . . 1603* (London: Samuel Mearne and Robert Pawlet, 1678), p. 28.

14. Hening, *Statutes* 1: 156–157, 181 (1632) and 3: 441–442 (1705). Virginia laws of 1696 and 1789 also specify additional punishment in cases where the wife is under sixteen.

15. Howard, *History of Matrimonial Institutions,* 2: 312–313.

16. Pennsylvania in 1730 specified age twenty-one with some qualification. See James Dunlop, comp., *The General Laws of Pennsylvania, from the Year 1700 to 1849* (Philadelphia, 1849), pp. 82–83; Massachusetts in 1786 gave age eighteen for females, twenty-one for males: *The Perpetual Laws of the Commonwealth of Massachusetts: From the Establishment of its Constitution in the Year 1780 to the End of the Year 1800* (Boston, 1780–1788) 1: 321.

17. Holly Brewer, *By Birth or Consent: Children, Law, and Revolution in England and America, 1550–1820* (Chapel Hill: University of North Carolina Press, 2002). Even though Blackstone and other documents refer to "age of consent" (also "age of discretion"), there is apparently no evidence that one particular age, in years, was specified by law.

18. Plymouth laws of 1636 and 1658 cited by Howard, *History of Matrimonial Institutions,* 2: 144; *Acts and Resolves of the Province of Massachusetts Bay (1692–1714)* (Boston, 1869) 1: 61, 210; *The Code of 1650: Being a Compilation of the Earliest Laws . . . of Connecticut* (Hartford, 1830), pp. 67–68.

19. Dunlop, *General Laws,* p. 82.

20. *Acts and Laws of Connecticut* (New London, 1784), p. 136.

21. J. R. Bartlett, ed., *Records of the Colony of Rhode Island and Providence Plantations* (orig. ed. 1856–1865, rpt. New York, 1968) 1: 187.

22. Howard, *History of Matrimonial Institutions,* 2: 287–292.

23. Howard, *History of Matrimonial Institutions,* 2: 229–30. Finally, much

later and still more briefly, North Carolina enacted a similar statute in 1766 aimed especially against evangelical Baptists and Presbyterians who refused to pay required fees to the Church of England. See John E. Semonche, "Common Law Marriage in North Carolina: A Study in Legal History," *The American Journal of Legal History* 9 (Oct 1965): 340.

24. In *For Better, For Worse,* John Gillis emphasizes the large-scale disregard of the Hardwicke Act. Also see A. Newman, "An Evaluation of Bastardy Recordings in an East Kent Parish," in Peter Lasett, Karla Oosterveen, and Richard M. Smith, eds., *Bastardy and Its Comparative History* (Cambridge: Harvard University Press, 1980), p. 51.

25. Bartlett, ed., *Records of Rhode Island and Providence,* 11: 104, 105.

26. Ibid., 361. Also see Robert V. Wells, "Illegitimacy and Bridal Pregnancy in Colonial America" in Lasett et al., *Bastardy and Its Comparative History,* p. 350.

27. Hening, *Statutes* 3: 149–151 for 1696.

28. Howard, *History of Matrimonial Institutions,* 2: 269–270, 274–277, 277–278, 287–292.

29. Parker, *Informal Marriage,* pp. 71–74.

30. For example: Nathaniel B. Shurtleff and David Pulsifer, eds., *Records of the Colony of New Plymouth in New England (1639–1692),* 12 vols. (orig. ed. Boston, 1855–1861; rpt. New York, 1968) 3: 46, 47, 52; 5: 263; Bartlett, *Records of Rhode Island and Providence,* 11: 103–104.

31. Howard, *History of Matrimonial Institutions* 2: 211, citing Winthrop, *History* 2: 51–52.

32. For Plymouth cases of 1648, 1652, 1660, see Shurtleff and Pulsifer, *Records of New Plymouth,* 2: 136; 3: 5, 206; Howard, *History of Matrimonial Institutions,* 2: 163. The same case also cited by John Abbot Goodwin, *The Pilgrim Republic; An Historical Review of the Colony of New Plymouth* (Boston: Houghton Mifflin, 1920), p. 598. Also see Roger Thompson, *Sex in Middlesex: Popular Mores in a Massachusetts County, 1649–1699* (Boston: University of Massachusetts Press, 1986), pp. 35, 61.

33. Howard, *History,* 2: 163; Goodwin, *Pilgrim Republic,* p. 597; Shurtleff and Pulsifer, *Records of New Plymouth* 2:110.

34. *The Code of 1650 . . . of Connecticut,* p. 114.

35. Thompson, *Sex in Middlesex,* especially pp. 64–70. Also see Norton, *Founding Mothers and Father,* pp. 67–71, to the effect that these young couples were in essence conforming to traditional English law and viewed themselves as married upon having intercourse. Her interpretation, however, leaves no room for sex that occurred without the advance promise of marriage, and the subsequent pressure to marry upon pregnancy.

36. Bartlett, *Records of Rhode Island and Providence,* 11: 105.

37. For example, Cornelia Dayton, *Women Before the Bar;* Flaherty, *Privacy in New England,* pp. 189–218; Wells, "Illegitimacy"; Hendrick Hartog, "The Public Law of a County Court," *American Journal of Legal History* 20 (1976): 299–308; Norton, *Founding Mothers,* pp. 66–72.

38. Robert Geoffrey Quaife, *Wanton Wenches and Wayward Wives: Peasants and Illicit Sex in Seventeenth-Century England* (New Brunswick, N. J.: Rut-

gers University Press, 1979) most forcefully makes this case; also see Gillis, *For Better or Worse*, pp. 52, 110–111. Martin Ingram argues that ecclesiastical laws against fornication were more tightly enforced in the first half of the seventeenth century than earlier. However, as he makes clear, church courts were limited to punishments of excommunication, admonition, and penance, and they concentrated on cases of notorious sinners. See Ingram, *Church Courts*, pp. 219–291.

39. For the contrast between fornication in New England and bastardy in the Chesapeake region, see Norton, *Founding Mothers*, pp. 69, 335–339.

40. For the 1648 Code in Massachusetts, see Max Farrand, *The Laws and Liberties of Massachusetts* (Cambridge: Harvard University Press, 1929), p. 23; on Connecticut, see Wells, "Illegitimacy," p. 355; On New York, Howard, *Matrimonial Institutions*, 2: 296.

41. On Middlesex County, Massachusetts, in the 1650s see Thompson, *Sex in Middlesex*, pp. 22, 61–64, 206 n. 24. A 1660 case in Plymouth is documented in Shurtleff and Pulsifer, *Records of Plymouth*, 3: 206. On Connecticut until 1715 see Wells, "Illegitimacy," p. 355–358. On Maryland, Raphael Semmes, *Crime and Punishment in Early Maryland* (orig. ed. 1938; rpt. Montclair, N. J.: Patterson Smith, 1970), p. 188.

42. New England historians, in particular, keen to eradicate the stereotype of repressed Puritans, have stressed the extent of premarital sexuality and the lack of parental control. See especially David H. Flaherty, *Privacy in Colonial New England* (Charlottesville: University of Virginia, 1967), pp. 76–84; and Thompson, *Sex in Middlesex*, pp. 19–70.

43. Daniel Scott Smith and Michael Hindus, "Premarital Pregnancy in America, 1640–1971," *Journal of Interdisciplinary History* 2 (1971): 237–272.

44. Howard, *History of Matrimonial Institutions*, 2: 287–292. The most colorful and protracted case of illegal marriage in the early Dutch colony, that of Johan Van Beeck and Maria Verleth, is also detailed in Berthold Fernow, ed., *The Records of New Amsterdam from 1653 to 1674*, 7 vols. (New York: Knickerbocker Press, 1987), 1: 155, 159–160, 164–165, 173; 2: 36.

45. For a 1685 case in Pennsylvania, Samuel W. Pennypacker, *Pennsylvania Colonial Cases: The Administration of Law in Pennsylvania prior to A. D. 1700 . . .* (Philadelphia, 1892), p. 72; for a 1699 case in New Jersey, see *From The Burlington Court Book: A Record of Quaker Jurisprudence in West New Jersey 1680–1709*, H. Clay Reed and George Miller, eds. (orig. pub. 1944; rpt. Millwood, N. Y., 1975), pp. 95, 223, 226.

46. Dunlop, *General Laws of Pennsylvania*, pp. 82–83.

47. Chester County Quarter Session Records, Aug. 31, 1756.

48. For examples, see Susie Ames, ed., *County Court Records of Accomock-Northhampton, Virginia, 1632–1640* (Washington: American Historical Association, 1954), pp. 20, 128–129, 151; Ames, ed., *County Court Records of Accomock-Northhampton, Virginia, 1640–45* (Charlottesville: University Press of Virginia, 1973): pp. 117, 120, 236, 287, 291.

49. *Maryland Archives*, 10: 174, 494, 515–516, 549–551.

50. E.g., Lorena Walsh, "Death Do Us Part," in Tate, ed., *Chesapeake in the Seventeenth Century*, pp. 130–131; Norton, *Founding Mothers*, p. 69, 335–339.

51. Walsh, "Death," p. 133.

52. Hening, *Statutes* 3: 441–442; also see Neil Larry Shumsky, "Parents, Children, and the Selection of Mates in Colonial Virginia," *Eighteenth-Century Life* 2 (1975–1976): 83–88.

53. John E. Semonche, "Common Law Marriage in North Carolina: A Study in Legal History," *The American Journal of Legal History* 9 (Oct 1965): 327–329.

54. Walsh, "Death," p. 130 n. 9.

55. Charles Woodmason, *The Carolina Backcountry on the Eve of the Revolution,* ed. J. Hooker (Chapel Hill: University of North Carolina Press, 1953), pp. 15, 81.

56. From Byrd, "History of the Dividing Line," as quoted in Semonche, p. 332; for South Carolina examples, see Gutman, *Black Family,* p. 339 and note 14 p. 607.

57. Connecticut, where laws requiring parental consent were updated into the nineteenth century, seems to have resisted changes more than other places. See, for example, *Acts and Laws of Connecticut* (New London: Timothy Green, 1784), p.136; *The Public Statute Laws of the State of Connecticut* (Hartford, 1808), p. 478; *Laws of the State of Connecticut. as Revised and Enacted by the General Assembly in May 1821* (Hartford, 1821), p. 317.

58. Semonche, "Common Law Marriage in North Carolina," 322; citing Cheseldine's Lessee v. Brewer, 1 Harris and McHenry (My.) 152 (1739).

59. [Josiah Quincy, Jr.,] *Reports of Cases Argued and Adjudged in the Superior Court of Judicature of the Province of Massachusetts Bay between 1761 and 1772* (Boston, 1865), quote on p. 123; also pp. 119–156, 162–163.

60. [A. Holmes,] "A Brief View of the State of Religious Liberty in the Colony of New York," read before the Reverend General Convention of the Delegates from the Consociated Churches of Connecticut and the Synod of New York and Philadelphia, September 1, 1773. Printed from the papers of Ezra Stiles, in *Massachusetts Collection* 2: p. 152. Howard attributes this to the Rev. John Rodgers. See Howard, *History of Matrimonial Institutions,* 2: 306–308.

61. Jefferson worked on this reform, known as bill 86, together with Wythe and Pendleton. Madison introduced it to the legislature. Jefferson, *Papers* 2: 557.

62. Hening, *Statutes* 13: 7–8.

63. On the post-revolutionary judicial rulings see Howard, *Matrimonial Institutions,* III: 175–178.

64. This was later tightened up again in 1730, probably because of the rising numbers of indentured servants and the wish to prohibit marriages lacking the consent of masters.

65. Howard, *Matrimonial Institutions,* 2: 151 n. 3.

66. *Burlington Court Book,* p. 229.

67. Woodmason, *Carolina Backcountry;* Rev. Henry Addison of Maryland in 1786 in Walsh, "Death," p. 130 n. 9.

68. Wells, "Illegitimacy," p. 352; Also, William E. Nelson, *Americanization,* pp. 110–111, 251–253; Dayton, *Women Before Bar.*

69. Massachusetts law eliminated this sanction in 1668, although there is evidence as late as the 1680s of courts enjoining marriage; see Thompson, *Sex in*

Middlesex, pp. 61–64, 206 n. 24. In Connecticut the requirement of forced marriage was dropped in 1715. See Wells, "Illegitimacy," p. 358 citing Connecticut Laws, 1715, p. 7.

70. A third common-law action, "criminal conversation," enabled husbands to sue their wife's lover. This action, however, appears to have come to American courts only in the late eighteenth century. Hendrik Hartog, *Man and Wife in America: A History* (Cambridge: Harvard University Press, 2000), pp. 137–142; Susan Staves, "Money for Honor: Damages for Criminal Conversation," *Studies in Eighteenth-Century Culture* 11 (1982): 279–297; Ingram, *Church Courts;* Stone, *Road to Divorce,* pp. 231–300.

71. An exception is the useful, if highly uneven, three-volume 1904 study by George Elliot Howard, *A History of Matrimonial Institutions.* Cf. the brief treatment in Michael Grossberg, *Governing the Hearth: Law and the Family in the Nineteenth Century* (Chapel Hill: University of North Carolina Press, 1985), p. 35.

72. For the history of this law in early modern England see Stone, *Road to Divorce,* pp. 80–95; Susan Staves, "British Seduced Maidens," *Eighteenth-Century Studies* 14 (1980–1981): 126–129. W. S. Holdsworth, *A History of English Law* (London: Methuen, 1925) 8: 428–429. For a precedent-setting seventeenth-century English case, "Norton and Jason. Michaelmas 1653" in *The English Reports King's Bench Division* (London, 1908) 82: 809–810.

73. M. B. W. Sinclair, who, like other scholars studying seduction, concentrates on the nineteenth and twentieth centuries, has the mistaken impression that early American courts were more strict about such evidentiary requirements than the English. This conclusion stems from viewing late-eighteenth- and early-nineteenth-century cases as "early." See Sinclair, "Seduction and the Myth of the Ideal Woman," pp. 41, 45–46.

74. The English requirement of written proof of the promise is also underlined by a pre-Blackstone legal manual for women: *A Treatise of Feme Coverts: Or the Lady's Law* (orig. ed. 1732; rpt. Hackensack, N. J.: Rothman, 1974), p. 30.

75. Linfield v. Whitticus, April 2, 1661, David Pulsifer, transcription of order books, Middlesex County Court Archives, 4 vols., 1: 226–227.

76. Ball v. Bacon, March–April, 1671), Pulsifer, Middlesex County Court Archives, 3: folio 55. Also see Robert Proctor v. Thomas Marrable, April 8, 1680, Pulsifer, Middlesex County Court Archives, 3:309.

77. Pulsifer, Middlesex County Court Archives, 3: folio 125, April 1686. See also Thompson, *Sex in Middlesex,* pp. 61–64.

78. Samuel W. Pennypacker, *Pennsylvania Colonial Cases: The Administration of Law in Pennsylvania Prior to A. D. 1700 . . . in the cases decided and in the court proceedings* (Philadelphia: Rees Welsh, 1892), pp.79–84, 108, 112–114.

79. William H. Browne, ed., *Archives of Maryland: Judicial and Testamentary Business of the Provincial Court 1649/50–1657,* 72 vols. (Baltimore, 1891) 10: 499–500, 531–533. Also discussed in Howard, *History of Matrimonial Institutions,* 2: 245–247.

80. Browne, *Archives of Maryland,* 10:500.

81. Ibid., 10:532.

82. Ibid., 10: 532.

83. Lea VanderVelde's study of nineteenth-century seduction cases especially stresses their affinity to rape. VanderVelde, "The Legal Ways of Seduction," *Stanford Law Review* 48 (April 1996): 817–901.

84. In England the action of breach of promise became popular only in the late eighteenth century — especially after the Hardwicke Act deprived the Church of the leverage to compel marriages on the grounds of pre-contract. See Staves, "British Seduced," p. 127; Stone, *Road,* pp. 86–89. Seduction suits seem to have been used by the wealthy from the seventeenth century on, but their English "heydey," as Stone puts it, was 1790–1844. Staves, "British," p. 130; Stone, *Road,* pp. 81–84. Hendrik Hartog, in *Man and Wife,* underscores the rise of civil law in the colonial period (especially as compared to equity law), but his study of marriage does not deal with courtship actions and his discussion of "criminal conversation" cases, while similar to seduction, focuses on the nineteenth century.

85. VanderVelde, "Legal Ways of Seduction"; Sinclair, "Seduction and the Myth"; Grossberg, *Governing,* pp. 34–51. Such studies at most briefly mention colonial precedents. Grossberg's citations of seventeenth- and eighteenth-century precedents are English, not colonial, cases (*Governing,* p. 320 n. 3).

86. Examination of Margaret Flin, August 1731, Quarter Session Indictments, Chester County Archives. For a similar case involving both bastardy and breach of promise, see "Examination of Hannah Gother," October 23, 1733, Quarter Session Indictments, Chester County Archives.

87. Holding v. Bright, August 25, 1730, Inferior Court of Common Pleas, Middlesex Folio Collection, folio 37A, traces the case from 1729 to 1731. Upon appeal on January 26, 1731, Holding used still more extreme language, claiming that her "name and Person is wounded with an Ireparable & grevious wound."

88. Depositions of James Bernard and John Holland taken in July 1731, ibid.

89. A later, similarly inconclusive suit for breach of promise in Connecticut also proceeded to court without written evidence. Polly Lamphear v. Joshua Woodburn, 1791, Preston Town Papers, Folder S, Document 112, Connecticut Court Records, Hartford. I am indebted to Anne Lombard and Nancy Steenberg for this reference.

90. Frederick County Legislative Petitions, May 29, 1784 (Frederick County Court Archives, Virginia). Note that it's unclear whether Brown was prevented from testifying because she was his wife or because she was underage. It is also unknown if the father successfully prosecuted on grounds other than rape (for example, abduction).

91. Hening, *Statutes* 13: 7–8; Samuel Shepard, *The Statutes at Large of Virginia (1792–1806),* 3 vols. (rpt. New Jersey, 1970) 1: 134–135.

92. "Coryell v. Colbaugh" in Richard Coxe, *Reports of Cases . . . Supreme Court . . . New Jersey I* (Jersey City: Frederick o. Linn, 1886), as discussed further below.

93. See Norman Fiering, *Moral Philosophy at Seventeenth-Century Harvard* (Chapel Hill: University of North Carolina Press, 1981); and Fiering, *Jonathan*

Edwards's Moral Thought in its British Context (Chapel Hill: University of North Carolina Press, 1981). Also see Chapters 5 and 7.

94. The influence of both religion and sentimental fiction are discussed further in Chapters 3 and 6.

95. Here I differ sharply with Lea VanderVelde, "Legal Ways of Seduction," who views the courts as consistently unsympathetic to women. My view is more consistent with Norma Basch, *Framing American Divorce: From the Revolutionary Generation to the Victorians* (Berkeley: University of California Press, 1999); Hartog, *Man and Wife;* and Grossberg, *Governing* — all of which describe nineteenth-century judges as often compensating for the "weakness" of the female sex in their decisions. My point is that this gendered moral framework arose earlier.

96. Zephaniah Swift, *A System of the Laws of the State of Connecticut in Six Books* (Windham: Byrne, 1795) 1: 188.

97. Ibid., 1:189.

98. "Coryell v. Colbaugh" in Richard Coxe, *Reports of Cases . . . Supreme Court . . . New Jersey* (Jersey City: Frederick O. Linn, 1886), 1: 91ff.

99. Ibid., p. 91.

100. "Boynton v. Kellogg" in Dudley Tyng, *Reports of Cases . . . Supreme Judicial Court . . . Massachusetts* (Boston, 1865), 3: 188–191.

101. William E. Nelson, *Americanization of the Common Law: The Impact of Legal Change on Massachusetts Society, 1760–1830* (Athens: University of Georgia Press, 1994), pp. 110–111; Hendrik Hartog, "The Public Law of a County Court; Judicial Government in Eighteenth Century Massachusetts," *American Journal of Legal History* 20 (1976): 282–329; David Flaherty, "Law and the Enforcement of Morals in Early America," *Perspectives in American History* 5(1971). Compare to M. B. W. Sinclair, in "Seduction and the Myth of the Ideal Woman," who, concentrating on a later period, reverses the order, arguing for a shift *away from* property concerns to broader moral ones after the turn of the nineteenth century.

102. Wells, "Illegitimacy," p. 355; Flaherty, *Privacy;* John D'Emilio and Estelle B. Freedman, *Intimate Matters: A History of Sexuality in America,* (New York: Harper and Row, 1988), p. 49; Mary Beth Norton, "Evolution of White Women's Experience," *American Historical Review* 89 (June 84), p. 611–612; Wai Chee Dimock, "Criminal Law, Female Virtue, and the Rise of Liberalism," *Yale Journal of Law and the Humanities* 4 (Summer 1992): 209–247. Dimock argues that the regulation of morality shifted from criminal law to the novel in the early nineteenth century.

103. Dayton, *Women Before the Bar: Gender, Law, and Society in Connecticut, 1639–1789* (Chapel Hill: University of North Carolina Press, 1995).

104. Hartog, "Public Law of County Court," pp. 303, 308. Although Dayton does not make the distinction between women and their fathers, she notes that after 1740 paternity actions were increasingly "filed under the female complainant's surname and not under *Rex.*" See *Women before Bar,* p. 221 n. 128.

105. Dayton, *Women before Bar,* pp.182–183.

106. Ulrich, *The Life of Martha Ballard,* p. 153. Like Hendrick Hartog, Ulrich sees fornication and bastardy/paternity cases as often coming together.

Dayton suggests that New Haven was perhaps unique in allowing these two types of cases to be pursued separately. *Women Before Bar,* p. 217.

107. Chester County, Quarter Sessions Dockets. This generalization is based on a comparison of 1751–1760, 1781–1790, and 1811–1820 conducted by Holly Brewer.

108. Holly Brewer, "Children's Labor and Children's Citizenship: The Decrease of Poor-Apprenticeship and the Increase of Parental Custody in the New Republic," Paper Presented at the North American Labor History Conference, Wayne State University, October 1993.

109. In their recent studies of nineteenth-century marriage, Hendrik Hartog and Nancy F. Cott have taken a similar position on the "public" nature of "private" life. Hartog, *Man and Wife;* Nancy F. Cott, *Public Vows: A History of Marriage and the Nation* (Cambridge: Harvard University Press, 2000). They both, however, pick up their stories only after the eighteenth-century transition I am describing here, and, in focusing upon marriage rather than courtship, deal with a more clearly state-regulated institution.

110. See, for example, Johnson v. Caulkins, Supreme Court of Judicature of New York, 1 Johns. Cas.116 (July 1799); and Gaskill v. Dixon, Supreme Court of North Carolina, Newbern, 2 Hayw. 350 (July 1805). The latter case is especially interesting because, while it affirmed the *principle* that a woman's impurity could void a marriage contract, the jury did not believe the testimony against this particular female plaintiff.

111. For further elaboration of this theme, see Ruth H. Bloch, "Changing Conceptions of Sexuality and Romance in Eighteenth-Century America," *The William and Mary Quarterly,* 3d. ser., 60 (forthcoming, January 2003).

5. WOMEN, LOVE, AND VIRTUE
IN THE THOUGHT OF EDWARDS AND FRANKLIN

I would like to thank Joyce Appleby, Patricia Bonomi, Daniel Walker Howe, and Thomas Shafer for their helpful readings of an earlier draft of this paper.

1. The many works on the Puritan family and women from which this paragraph is drawn include: Edmund S. Morgan, *The Puritan Family: Religion and Domestic Relations in Seventeenth-Century New England,* rev. ed. (New York: Harper and Row, 1966); Laurel Thatcher Ulrich, *Good Wives: Image and Reality in the Lives of Women in Northern New England, 1650–1750* (New York: Oxford University Press, 1980); Carol F. Karlsen, *The Devil in the Shape of a Woman: Witchcraft in Colonial New England* (New York: Norton, 1987); Margaret Masson, "The Typology of the Female as a Model for the Regenerate," *Signs: Journal of Women in Culture and Society* 2 (1976); Gerald F. Moran, "'Sisters' in Christ: Women and the Church in Seventeenth-Century New England," in *Women in American Religion,* ed. Janet Wilson James (Philadelphia: University of Pennsylvania Press, 1980), pp. 47–65.

2. The less extensive literature on this transitional period includes Nancy F. Cott, *The Bonds of Womanhood: Woman's 'Sphere' in New England, 1780–1835* (New Haven, Conn.: Yale University Press,1978); Linda Kerber, *Women of*

the Republic: Intellect and Ideology in Revolutionary America (Chapel Hill: University of North Carolina Press, 1980); Mary Beth Norton, *Liberty's Daughters: The Revolutionary Experience of American Women, 1750–1800* (Boston: Little, Brown, 1980); and Chapter 7. On Scottish moral philosophy, Norman Fiering, *Jonathan Edwards's Moral Thought and Its British Context* (Chapel Hill, N. C.: University of North Carolina Press, 1981); Daniel Walker Howe, "Why the Scottish Enlightenment was Useful to the Framers of the American Constitution," *Comparative Studies in Society and History,* 31 (July 1989): 572–587; and John Dwyer, *Virtuous Discourse: Sensibility and Community in Late Eighteenth-Century Scotland* (Edinburgh: J. Donald, 1987).

3. See especially Elisabeth D. Dodds, *Marriage to a Difficult Man: The 'Uncommon Union' of Jonathan and Sarah Edwards* (Philadelphia: Westminster Press, 1971); Claude-Anne Lopez, *Mon Cher Papa: Franklin and the Ladies of Paris* (New Haven, Conn.: Yale University Press, 1966); Claude-Anne Lopez and Eugenia W. Herbert, *The Private Franklin: The Man and His Family* (New York: Norton, 1975).

4. *The Works of Jonathan Edwards* (New Haven, Conn.: Yale University Press, 1957–), 2: 107–108

5. *The Works of President Edwards,* ed. Sereno Dwight, 10 vols. (New York: G. C. H. Carvill, 1830), 9: 511.

6. See also Fiering, *Edwards's Moral Thought,* pp. 150–199.

7. "Miscellanies," no. 189, as quoted in *Works of Jonathan Edwards,* 8: 617–618, n. 3. Thomas Shafer alerted me to this passage and pointed out that Edwards probably wrote it in the spring or early summer of 1725, about the time of his engagement.

8. "Miscellanies," no. 530, in *The Philosophy of Jonathan Edwards from His Private Notebooks,* ed. Harvey G. Townsend (Eugene: University of Oregon, 1955), pp. 203–204.

9. *Works of Jonathan Edwards,* 8: 258.

10. Ibid.

11. Ibid., 4: 469–470.

12. "Great Care Necessary, Lest We Live in Some Way of Sin," (1734), *Works of President Edwards,* 4:522.

13. *Works of Jonathan Edwards,* 4: 470. Fiering notes that Edwards turned his full attention to exposing the deceptions of self-love only in *True Virtue* (though there are earlier foreshadowings in "Miscellanies" nos. 473 and 534 of the earlier 1730s). See Fiering, *Edwards's Moral Thought,* p. 174.

14. *Works of Jonathan Edwards,* 8: 555.

15. Ibid., pp. 558–559.

16. Ibid., p. 546. See also pp. 545, 571. This argument is presaged in *Works of Jonathan Edwards,* 2: 257.

17. *Works of Jonathan Edwards,* 8: 605.

18. Fiering, *Edwards's Moral Thought,* pp. 174, 197.

19. Patricia J. Tracy, *Jonathan Edwards, Pastor: Religion and Society in Eighteenth-Century Northampton* (New York: Hill and Wang, 1979), pp. 56, 218–219 n. 38.

20. "The Justice of God in the Damnation of Sinners" (1735), *Works of*

President Edwards, 4: 233–234. For a long quotation from this sermon see Tracy, *Jonathan Edwards,* pp. 81–82. See also *Works of Jonathan Edwards,* 4: 146.

21. "Joseph's Great Temptation and Gracious Deliverance," *The Works of President Edwards,* 4: 595–596.

22. *Works of Jonathan Edwards,* 4: 468.

23. Ibid., 149.

24. Tracy, *Jonathan Edwards,* 160–164; Thomas H. Johnson, "Jonathan Edwards and the 'Young Folks' Bible," *New England Quarterly* 5 (1932): 437–514.

25. Tracy, *Jonathan Edwards,* pp. 164–166; Kathryn Kish Sklar, "Culture Versus Economics: A Case of Fornication in Northampton in the 1740s," *University of Michigan Papers in Women's Studies,* Special Issue, May 1978, pp. 35–56.

26. Sklar, "Culture," p. 45, as quoted from Jonathan Edwards Papers, Folder n.d. 2, item 15, Andover Newton Theological School, Newton Center, Mass.

27. Sereno E. Dwight, *The Life of President Edwards* (New York: G. C. H., 1830), pp. 114–115.

28. Ibid., p. 578.

29. *Works of Jonathan Edwards,* 4: 158. On earlier feminine religious imagery, see Moran, "'Sisters' in Christ," and Masson, "The Typology of the Female."

30. Dwight, *Life of President Edwards,* p. 172.

31. Ibid., pp. 171–172. For a similar interpretation, see Julie Ellison, "The Sociology of 'Holy Indifference': Sarah Edwards' Narrative," *American Literature* 56 (1984): 479–495.

32. Dwight, *Life of President Edwards,* p. 183.

33. *Works of Jonathan Edwards,* 4: 334–335.

34. Patricia Bonomi, "Comment," unpublished paper, National Conference on Jonathan Edwards and Benjamin Franklin, Yale University, February 24, 1990.

35. Fiering, *Edwards's Moral Thought,* p. 174.

36. Dwight, *Life of President Edwards,* pp. 60–61, 65, 132–133, *Works of Jonathan Edwards,* 4: 194–195, 332.

37. *Works of Jonathan Edwards,* 2: 100.

38. Ibid., 7: 500.

39. Ibid., 8: 603–5.

40. *The Papers of Benjamin Franklin* (New Haven, Conn.: Yale University Press, 1959–), 3: 5.

41. Ibid., p. 8; also 2: 9.

42. Ibid., 15: 184; *The Works of Benjamin Franklin,* ed. John Bigelow, 10 vols. (New York: Knickerbocker Press, 1904), 10: 81; *Autobiography and Other Writings,* ed. Kenneth Silverman (New York: Penguin Books, 1986), p. 207.

43. *Papers of Benjamin Franklin,* 5: 471; see also 2: 396.

44. Ibid., 3: 62; see also 2: 5 and *Autobiography,* ed. Silverman, p. 88.

45. *Papers of Benjamin Franklin,* 7: 216; see also 3: 479–480.

46. Ibid., 4: 227–243.

47. Ibid., 9: 175.

48. Ibid., 3: 120–125.

49. On how Franklin's definition of happiness reduces to the instrumental satisfaction of natural, physical wants, see Herbert Schneider, *The Puritan Mind* (New York: H. Holt, 1930), p. 251; Flower and Murphey, *History of Philosophy,* 1: 110–111.

50. *Papers of Benjamin Franklin*, 6: 324; also 5: 471.

51. Benjamin Franklin, *Dr. Benj. Franklin and the Ladies* (Mt. Vernon, N. Y.: Peter Pauper Press, 1939), pp. 17–18.

52. *The Autobiography of Benjamin Franklin*, ed. Leonard Labaree et al. (New Haven: Yale University Press, 1964), pp. 91–92.

53. Ibid., pp. 74–75.

54. *Papers of Benjamin Franklin*, 15: 185.

55. Ibid., 2: 353–354.

56. These relationships are described vividly in Lopez, *Mon Cher Papa.*

57. Ibid., pp. 261–262.

58. *Autobiography,* ed. Labaree, p. 76.

59. "To Miss Alexander," Passy, June 24, 1782, in *Dr. Benj Franklin and the Ladies,* p. 32.

60. *Autobiography,* ed. Labaree, p. 88.

61. Ibid., pp. 88–89.

62. *Papers of Benjamin Franklin*, 6: 425, and 14: 193–194.

63. Ibid., 18: 91.

64. *Papers of Benjamin Franklin*, 7: 167–168, and 10: 100–101.

65. See, for example, *Papers of Benjamin Franklin*, 1: 21–23, 240–243.

66. Ibid., pp. 237–240. Also see Gary E. Baker, "He That Would Thrive Must Ask His Wife: Franklin's Anthony Afterwit Letter," *Pennsylvania Magazine of History and Biography,* 109 (January 1985): 27–41.

67. *Papers of Benjamin Franklin*, 1: 315. See also pp. 100 and 239; and *The Private Correspondence of Benjamin Franklin,* 2 vols. (London, 1817), 1: 42.

68. *Papers of Benjamin Franklin*, 1: 311. See also 2: 137, 169, 191, 371.

69. For example, ibid., 1: 39–40, 243–248, 316 and 2: 139, 223, 235, 369, 400.

70. Ibid., 1: 37–38; 2: 166–167, 251, 399; 3: 65.

71. Examples are the pseudonyms Silence Dogood, ibid., 1: 8–46; Cecilia Single, pp. 20–43; and Martha Careful and Caelia Shortface, pp. 112–113.

72. *Papers of Benjamin Franklin*, 1: 18–21.

73. Ibid., p. 356.

74. Ibid., 2: 22–23.

75. Whereas I counted twenty-two short pieces on women and marriage in the almanac from 1733 through 1738 (3.6 an issue), there were only ten in 1739–1744 (1.6 per issue), twelve in 1745–1750 (2 per issue), and two in 1751–1758 (less than 0.5 per issue).

76. For example, *Papers of Benjamin Franklin*, 2: 294; 3: 62; 5: 471.

77. Ibid., 3: 60.

78. Ibid., pp. 65, 66.

79. Ibid., pp. 103, 342.

80. Ibid., pp. 30–31.

81. Ibid., 8: 92.

82. Letter to Mme Brillon, Nov. 29, 1780; as quoted in Lopez, *Mon Cher Papa*, p. 82.

83. Lopez, *Mon Cher Papa*, p. 222.

84. *Autobiography,* ed. Labaree, p. 103–105.

85. Ibid., p. 106.

6. RELIGION, LITERARY SENTIMENTALISM, AND POPULAR REVOLUTIONARY IDEOLOGY

I wish to thank Robert Abzug, Joyce Appleby, and especially Daniel Howe for their helpful readings of earlier drafts of this essay.

1. For example, J. G. A. Pocock, *The Machiavellian Moment: Florentine Political Thought and the Atlantic Republican Tradition* (Princeton, N. J.: Princeton University Press, 1975); Bernard Bailyn, *The Ideological Origins of the American Revolution* (Cambridge, Mass.: Harvard University Press, 1967); Gordon S. Wood, *The Creation of the American Republic, 1776–1787* (Chapel Hill: University of North Carolina Press, 1969); Lance Banning, *The Jeffersonian Persuasion: Evolution of a Party Ideology* (Ithaca, N. Y.: Cornell University Press, 1978); Drew R. McCoy, *The Elusive Republic: Political Economy in Jeffersonian America* (Chapel Hill: University of North Carolina Press, 1980).

2. See, for example, Joyce Appleby, *Capitalism and a New Social Order: The Republican Vision of the 1790s* (New York: New York University Press, 1984); Isaac Kramnick, "Republican Revisionism Revisited," *American Historical Review* 87 (1982): 629–664.

3. John Phillip Reid, *Constitutional History of the American Revolution: The Authority of Rights* (Madison: University of Wisconsin Press, 1987).

4. The main lines of this debate can be followed in Pocock, *The Machiavellian Moment;* Appleby, *Capitalism and a New Social Order;* James T. Kloppenberg, "The Virtues of Liberalism: Christianity, Republicanism, and Ethics in Early American Political Discourse," *Journal of American History* 74 (June 1987). In challenging the "republican synthesis," Joyce Appleby has not only pointed to the importance of a different set of values but questioned the usefulness of attributing any one dominant cultural understanding to the Revolutionary period. See especially, Joyce Appleby, "Republicanism and Ideology," *American Quarterly* 37 (Fall 1985).

5. Ruth H. Bloch, "The Social and Political Base of Millennial Literature in Late Eighteenth-Century America," *American Quarterly* 40 (Fall 1988): especially pp. 385–386. Also see Robert B. Winans, "The Growth of a Novel-Reading Public in Late Eighteenth-Century America," *Early American Literature* 9 (1975): 267–275; David Lundberg and Henry F. May, "The Enlightened Reader in America," *American Quarterly* 28 (Summer 1976): 262–271.

6. David Paul Nord, "A Republican Literature: A Study of Magazine Reading and Readers in Late Eighteenth-Century New York," *American Quarterly* 40 (March 1988): 42–64.

7. Perry Miller, "From the Covenant to the Revival," in *Nature's Nation* (Cambridge, Mass.: Harvard University Press, 1967). Also see Alan Heimert, *Religion and the American Mind* (Cambridge: Harvard University Press, 1966).

8. Bernard Bailyn, *Ideological Origins,* pp. 6–7, 32–33; Bailyn, "Religion and Revolution: Three Biographical Studies" *Perspectives in American History* 4 (1970): 85–169.

9. See especially: Nathan O. Hatch, *The Sacred Cause of Liberty: Republican Thought and the Millennium in Revolutionary New England* (New Haven, Conn.: Yale University Press, 1977); Ruth H. Bloch, *Visionary Republic: Millennial Themes in American Thought, 1756–1800* (New York: Cambridge University Press, 1985); Harry S. Stout, *The New England Soul: Preaching and Religious Culture in Colonial New England* (New York: Oxford University Press, 1986); David S. Lovejoy, *Religious Enthusiasm in the New World: Heresy to Revolution* (Cambridge, Mass.: Harvard University Press, 1985); Patricia U. Bonomi, *Under the Cope of Heaven* (New York: Oxford University Press, 1987).

10. Alfred F. Young, "English Plebian Culture and Eighteenth-Centruy American Radicalism," in *The Origins of Anglo-American Radicalism,* ed. Margaret Jacob and James Jacob (London: George Allen and Ulwin, 1984), pp. 195–197. It is clear from Young's reliance on evidence from leading clergymen and other prominant figures that this tradition was not, however, as "plebian" as he otherwise suggests.

11. Young, "Plebian Culture and American Radicalism"; Peter Shaw, *American Patriots and the Rituals of Revolution* (Cambridge, Mass.: Harvard University Press, 1981).

12. Stout, *New England Soul.*

13. See, for example, Bonomi, *Under the Cope of Heaven;* Stout, *New England Soul;* Bloch, *Visionary Republic.*

14. There has been a fruitful historical debate about the connection between the Great Awakening and the Revolution. My own view is that the connection was subtle and indirect, but significant nonetheless. For opposing views, see Heimert, *Religion and the American Mind;* Lovejoy, *Religious Enthusiasm;* Jon Butler, "Enthusiasm Described and Decried: The Great Awakening as an Interpretive Fiction," *Journal of American History* 69 (September 1982): 305–325.

15. On these developments see especially Edwin G. Burrows and Michael Wallace, "The American Revolution: The Ideology and Psychology of National Liberation," *Perspectives in American History* 6 (1972): 190–214; Linda K. Kerber, *Women of the Republic: Intellect and Ideology in Revolutionary America* (Chapel Hill: University of North Carolina Press, 1980); Mary Beth Norton, *Liberty's Daughters: The Revolutionary Experience of American Women, 1750–1800* (Boston: Little Brown, 1980); Jay Fliegelman, *Prodigals and Pilgrims* (New York: Cambridge University Press, 1982); Jan Lewis, "The Republican Wife," *William and Mary Quarterly,* 3d. ser., 44 (October 1987): 689–721; and Chapter 7.

16. Cathy N. Davidson, *Revolution and the Word: The Rise of the Novel in America* (New York: Oxford University Press, 1986), pp. vii, 55–79.

17. Winans, "Growth of a Novel-Reading Public"; David D. Hall, "The Uses of Literacy in New England, 1600–1850," *Printing and Society in Early Amer-*

ica, ed. William L. Joyce, David D. Hall, Richard D. Brown, and John B. Hench (Worcester: American Antiquarian Society, 1983), pp. 1–47. Hall and Davidson disagree about whether this marked a shift from an "intensive" to an "extensive" reading style. See Davidson, *Revolution,* pp. 72–73.

18. Herbert Ross Brown, *The Sentimental Novel in America, 1789–1860* (Durham, N. C.: Duke University Press, 1940): Davidson, *Revolution.*

19. Fliegelman, *Prodigals and Pilgrims;* Jan Lewis, "Republican Wife;" Davidson, *Revolution.*

20. A few of the many examples include: anon., *Fidelty Rewarded: Or the History of Polly Granville* (Boston, 1796); Samuel Relf, *Infidelity, or the Victims of Sentiment* (Philadelphia, 1797); "Arria, Forced Marriage," *American Museum* (Sept. 1789); "Maternal Affection," *Boston Magazine* (January 1784); "Honour Eclipsed by Love," *Boston Magazine* (August 1785).

21. Martha Read, *Monima; Or, The Beggar Girl* (New York, 1802), p. 255.

22. John Bennet, *Letters to a Young Lady, on a Variety of Useful and Interesting Subjects,* 2 vols. (New York, 1796) 2: 94. Also see *The Lady's Pocket Library* (Philadelphia: Mathew Carey, 1792), pp. 10–18; John Cosens Ogden, *The Female Guide* (Concord: George Hough, 1793), pp. 39–41; Thomas Gisborne, *An Enquiry into the Duties of the Female Sex* (Philadelphia: James Humphreys, 1798); John Burton, *Lectures on Female Education and Manners* (Elizabethtown, 1799); Benjamin Silliman, *Letters of Shahcoolen, a Hindu Philosopher* (Boston: Russell and Cutler, 1802), pp. 49–62; Thomas Branagan, *The Excellency of the Female Character Vindicated* (New York, 1807).

23. John Bennet, *Strictures on Female Education; Chiefly as it Relates to the Culture of the Heart* (Philadelphia, 1793).

24. Terrence Martin, *The Instructed Vision: Scottish Common Sense Philosophy and the Origins of American Fiction* (Bloomington, Ind.: Indiana University Press, 1961); Davidson, *Revolution,* pp. 13, 41–50, 53–54.

25. David Reynolds has drawn this connection in a different way. See his "From Doctrine to Narrative: The Rise of Pulpit Story-Telling in America," *American Quarterly* 32 (Winter 1980): 479–498.

26. Thomas H. Johnson, "Jonathan Edwards' Background of Reading" *Publications of the Colonial Society of Massachusetts* 28 (1931): 193–222; Thomas H. Johnson, "Jonathan Edwards and the 'Young Folks' Bible' " *New England Quarterly* 5 (1932): 37–54; Terrence Erdt, *Jonathan Edwards: Art and the Sense of the Heart* (Amherst: University of Massachusetts Press, 1980), pp. 78–79; Sereno E. Dwight, *The Life of President Edwards* (New York: Carvill, 1830), p. 601. Erdt notes that Dwight wrongly reports that Edwards read Richardson's *Sir Charles Grandison* already before leaving Northampton; the novel Edwards's son was referring to might well have been *Pamela,* which appeared earlier and which Edwards definitely owned by the mid-1750s. See Ola Elizabeth Winslow, *Jonathan Edwards, 1703–1758* (New York: Macmillan, 1940), p. 287.

27. *The Diary of Ebenezer Parkman,* ed. Francis G. Walett (Worcester: American Antiquarian Society, 1974), pp. 138–139.

28. Samuel Miller, *Brief Retrospect of the Eighteenth Century* (New York: T. & J. Swords, 1803), pp. 158–167.

29. Ibid., p.173.

30. Hitchcock, *Memoirs of the Bloomsgrove Family* (Boston, 1790) 2: 82.

31. Hester Chapone, *Letters on the Improvement of the Mind* (Boston, 1783), pp. 205–206. Fordyce's *Sermons to Young Women* and Blair's *Lectures on Rhetoric* and *Belles Lettres*, both of which took this position, each went into several editions in late-eighteenth-century America. On the Scottish clergy's openness to a type of sentimental fiction, see John Dwyer, *Virtuous Discourse: Sensibility and Community in Late Eighteenth-Century Scotland* (Edinburgh: John Donald Publishers, 1987), pp.141–167.

32. See, for example: Joseph Buckminister, *Heads of Families, to resolve for their Households, no less than for themselves, that they will serve the Lord* (Boston, 1759); John Witherspoon, "Reflections on the Married State" Pennsylvania Magazine 1 (1775): 408–413, 543–548, 2 (1776): 109–114, 319–323; Timothy Dwight, "Reflexions on Second Marriages of Men," American Museum 6 (Dec. 1789): 437–439; Benjamin Bell, The Character of a Virtuous Woman, Delineated (Windsor, Vt., 1794); Amos Chase, *On Female Excellence: Or, a Discourse in which Good Character in Women is Described* (Litchfield, Conn., 1792); John Cosens Ogden, *The Female Guide* (Concord, 1793); George Strebeck, *A Sermon on the Character of the Virtuous Woman* (New York, 1800); Eli Forbes, *A Family Book* (Salem, 1801).

33. For example: Joseph Lathrop, "Female Honour," *The American Museum* 8 (Dec. 1790): 280–282; Thomas Barnard, *A Sermon Preached before the Salem Female Charitable Society, July 6th, 1803* (Salem, 1803), p. 17; Daniel Chaplin, *A Discourse delivered before the Charitable Female Society in Groton Oct. 19, 1814* (Andover, 1814), pp. 8–10; Samuel Worcester, *Female Love to Christ* (Salem, 1809), pp. 8–10.

34. For an account of later Unitarian thought that elaborates upon such a connection between religion, literature, and sentimentalism, see Daniel Walker Howe, *The Unitarian Conscience: Harvard Moral Philosophy, 1805–1861* (Middletown, Conn.: Wesleyan University Press, 1988), pp. 174–204.

35. Shaw, *Patriots and Revolution*.

36. Bloch, *Visionary Republic*, esp. 53–74.

37. John Allen, *An Oration Upon the Beauties of Liberty* (Boston, 1773).

38. Bloch, *Visionary Republic*, esp. 75–93. Also see Stout, *New England Soul;* Nathan O. Hatch, *The Sacred Cause of Liberty* (New Haven, Conn.: Yale University Press, 197).

39. Thomas Paine, *Common Sense*, ed. Isaac Kramnick (New York: Penguin, 1976), pp. 83–84, 107.

40. Jonathan Mayhew, *The Snare Broken* (Boston: Draper, Gill, and Fleet, 1776), p. 36.

41. Burrows and Wallace, "The American Revolution."

42. For an analysis of this transition, see Fliegelman, *Progidals*.

43. Isaac, *Transformation*.

44. David Avery, *The Lord Is to Be Praised for the Triumphs of His Power* (Norwich, 1778).

45. Patricia Bonomi, *Under the Cope of Heaven: Religion, Society, and Politics in Colonial America* (New York: Oxford University Press, 1987), p. 158.

46. For example: Richard Bushman, *From Puritan to Yankee* (Cambridge,

Mass.: Harvard University Press, 1967); Rhys Isaac, "Radicalised Religion and Changing Lifestyles" in *Origins of Anglo-American Radicalism,* ed. Jacob and Jacob.

47. This duality is explored in Davidson, *Revolution.*

48. Ian Watt, *The Rise of the Novel* (Berkeley: University of California Press, 1957); also see Terry Eagleton, *The Rape of Clarissa* (Oxford: Basil Blackwell, 1982).

49. See, for example, "Directory of Love," *Royal American Magazine* (April and May 1774); "Honour Eclipsed by Love," *Boston Magazine* (August 1785); "Reflections on Parental Care and Filial Duty," *Christian Scholar's and Farmer's Magazine* (February 1790); "Reflections on Marriage Unions," *New York Magazine* (Oct. 1790); "Parental Authority," *The Ladies Magazine* (Oct. 1792). Also see Jay Fliegelman, *Prodigals and Pilgrims.*

50. This position is powerfully argued for the case of Scotland in Dwyer, *Virtuous Discourse.* Many of the Scottish texts he discusses were popular in America as well.

51. This duality is explored in Davidson, *Revolution and the Word.*

52. A brilliant analysis of this novel, which argues that Eliza's inability to achieve the republican synthesis of independence, virtue, and happiness embodied developing tensions within American ideology, is Carroll Smith-Rosenberg, "Domesticating 'Virtue:' Coquettes and Revolutionaries in Young America," unpub. ms. delivered at the Meeting of the Organization of American Historians, April 1987.

53. Jan Lewis, "Republican Wife."

54. The prototype is, again, found in the work of Samuel Richardson, in this case *Pamela.* Also see, for example: "Conjugal Prudence," *New York Magazine* (March 1791); "Regrets on the Loss of Domestic Happiness," *New York Magazine* (March 1793). Nonfictional magazine essays frequently delivered the same message. See, for example, "Panegyrick on the Fair Sex," *Boston Magazine* (Feb. 1785); "Advantages of Society of Virtuous Women," *Boston Magazine* (Aug. 1785); "Female Influence," *New York Magazine* (April 1795).

55. Hugh Smith, *Letters to Married Women* (Philadelphia, 1792), p.123; *The Lady's Pocket Library,* pp. 10–12; James Fordyce, *Sermons to Young Women* (Boston: Thomas Hall, 1796), pp. 17–23; Gisborne, *Enquiry into Duties of Female Sex,* pp. 8–9; Chaplin, *Discourse Delivered before the Charitable Female Society,* pp. 8–10; John Gregory, *A Father's Legacy to His Daughters* (Boston, 1779).

56. This is a central point of Fliegelman, *Prodigals.* The novels are Samuel Richardson, *Pamela,* (first American ed. 1744), vol. 2; Susanna Rowson, *Charlotte Temple,* orig. ed. 1794, ed. Cathy Davidson (New York: Oxford University Press, 1986).

57. Isaac, "Radicalised Religion."

58. "On Love," *New York Magazine* (June 1791), p. 311.

59. I explore these themes in Chapter 7.

60. Alexis de Tocqueville, *Democracy in America,* 2 vols. (NewYork: Vintage, 1945).

61. Other recent works taking a similarly synthetic position, although con-

fining themselves to an internal analysis of political ideology, are Kloppenberg, "Virtues of Liberalism," and Bernard Bailyn, *The Ideological Origins of the American Revolution*, rev. ed. (Cambridge, Mass.: Harvard University Press, 1992).

7. THE GENDERED MEANINGS OF VIRTUE IN REVOLUTIONARY AMERICA

Earlier versions of this paper were presented to the 1985–1986 Gender Seminar at the Institute for Advanced Study in Princeton and to the Faculty Research Seminar on Women at the University of California, Los Angeles. Many members of these seminars provided useful criticisms. I am especially grateful to the anonymous readers for *Signs* and to Joyce Appleby, Daniel Walker Howe, Jan Lewis, Phyllis Mack, Debora Silverman, and Kathryn Kish Sklar for their helpful suggestions.

1. Morton W. Bloomfield, *The Seven Deadly Sins* (East Lansing: Michigan State University Press, 1952), pp. 64, 137.

2. For a useful review of this literature, see Robert Shalhope, "Republicanism and Early American Historiography," *William and Mary Quarterly* 39 (1982): 334–356. The classical republican idea of virtue has also been invoked outside the historical discipline. See, e.g., Sheldon Wolin, *Politics and Vision: Continuity and Innovation in Western Political Thought* (Boston: Little, Brown, 1960); Robert N. Bellah, *The Broken Covenant: American Civil Religion in a Time of Trial* (New York: Seabury Press, 1975); Alasdair MacIntyre, *After Virtue: A Study in Moral Theory* (Notre Dame, Ind.: University of Notre Dame Press, 1981).

3. See esp. Linda K. Kerber, *Women of the Republic: Intellect and Ideology in Revolutionary America* (Chapel Hill: University of North Carolina Press, 1980); Mary Beth Norton, *Liberty's Daughters: The Revolutionary Experience of American Women 1750–1800* (Boston: Little, Brown, 1980); Joan Hoff-Wilson, "The Illusion of Change: Women and the American Revolution," in *The American Revolution: Explorations in the History of American Radicalism*, ed. Alfred F. Young (Dekalb: Northern Illinois University Press, 1976), pp. 383–445.

4. A few studies that partly address this question and helped to stimulate this article are: Kerber, *Women of the Republic*, pp. 269–288, and "The Republican Ideology of the Revolutionary Generation," *American Quarterly* 37 (1985): 474–495; Paula Baker, "The Domestication of Politics: Women and American Political Society, 1780–1920," *American Historical Review* 89 (1984): 620–647; Jan Lewis, "The Republican Wife," *William and Mary Quarterly*, 3d ser., vol. 44 (October 1987); J. G. A. Pocock, "Modes of Political and Historical Time in Early Eighteenth Century England," in his *Virtue, Commerce and History* (New York: Cambridge University Press, 1985), pp. 98–100; Hanna Fenichel Pitkin, *Fortune Is a Woman* (Berkeley: University of California Press, 1984).

5. Joan W. Scott calls for this in her "Gender: A Useful Category of Analysis," *American Historical Review* 91 (December 1986): 1053–1075.

6. See esp. J. G. A. Pocock, *The Machiavellian Moment: Florentine Political*

Thought and the Atlantic Republican Tradition (Princeton, N. J.: Princeton University Press, 1975), and *Virtue, Commerce, and History;* Bernard Bailyn, *The Ideological Origins of the American Revolution* (Cambridge, Mass.: Harvard University Press, 1967); Caroline Robbins, *The Eighteeenth-Century English Commonwealthmen* (Cambridge, Mass: Harvard University Press, 1959); Gordon S. Wood, *The Creation of the American Republic, 1776–1787* (Chapel Hill: University of North Carolina Press, 1969); Lance Banning, *The Jeffersonian Persuasion: Evolution of a Party Ideology* (Ithaca, N. Y.: Cornell University Press, 1978); Drew R. McCoy, *The Elusive Republic: Political Economy in Jeffersonian America* (Chapel Hill: University of North Carolina Press, 1980).

7. For example, from the perspective of liberalism, Joyce Appleby, *Capitalism and a New Social Order: The Republic Vision of the 1790s* (New York: New York University Press, 1984); from the perspective of American Protestantism, Ruth H. Bloch, *Visionary Republic: Millennial Themes in American Thought* (New York: Cambridge University Press, 1985).

8. The key text is James Harrington, *Oceana,* ed. S. B. Liljegren (Heidelberg: Carl Winters Universitätsbuchlung, 1924).

9. Gordon Schochet, *Patriarchalism in Political Thought* (Oxford: Basil Blackwell, 1975). The patriarchal familial imagery within New England Puritan writings about political leadership is well known. For a recent explication, see Melvin Yazawa, *From Colonies to Commonwealth: Familial Ideology and the Beginnings of the American Republic* (Baltimore: Johns Hopkins University Press, 1985).

10. John Winthrop, as quoted in Thomas Hutchinson, ed., *A Collection of Original Papers Relative to the History of the Colony of Massachusetts Bay* (Boston: Thomas & John Fleet, 1769), reprinted in Joyce O. Appleby, ed., *Materialism and Morality in the American Past: Themes and Sources* (Reading, Mass.: Addison-Wesley, 1974), pp. 34, 38. For the Aristotelian notion of virtue, see Norman Fiering, *Moral Philosophy at Seventeenth-Century Harvard* (Chapel Hill: University of North Carolina Press, 1981), p. 72. The abundant literature documenting the negative cultural evaluation of female reason is summarized briefly in Chapter 2.

11. These cases are described in more detail in Laurel Thatcher Ulrich, *Good Wives* (New York: Oxford University Press, 1982), pp. 184–201; Nancy Woloch, *Women and the American Experience* (New York: Alfred A. Knopf, 1984), pp. 1–15.

12. For examples of the specialized debate over the various classical meanings of these terms, see MacIntyre, *After Virtue,* pp. 114–153; Arthur Madigan, "Plato, Aristotle and Professor MacIntyre," and A. A. Long, "Greek Ethics after MacIntyre and the Stoic Community of Reason," both in *Ancient Philosophy* 3 (1983):171–183, 184–197. That *virtù* was a fundamentally male quality, associated with courage and involvement in civic life, is a common theme. For the purposes of this essay, what is important is that these elements were revived by Machiavelli and other Renaissance republicans and then transmitted to America.

13. Pocock, *The Machiavellian Moment,* p. 92. The traditional idea of virtue as glory is also explicated in Albert O. Hirschman, *The Passions and the Inter-*

ests: Political Arguments for Capitalism before Its Triumph (Princeton, N. J.: Princeton University Press, 1977), 7–66.

14. Pitkin, *Fortune Is a Woman*, p. 25.

15. Ibid.; Pocock, "Modes of Political and Historical Time," pp. 98–100. Quentin Skinner has taken issue with Pitkin's exclusive emphasis on the negative feminine symbolism in Machiavelli, pointing out that he used feminine Italian nouns (including *virtù* itself) to describe the abstract goals and ideals of the republic. Yet Pitkin herself questions the value of this kind of narrow linguistic analysis (*Fortune Is a Woman*, p. 131), and even Skinner agrees that Machiavelli's words to describe "the active and shaping features of public life" are masculine "Ms. Machiavellis," *New York Review of Books* [March 14, 1985], pp. 29–30).

16. Isaac Story, *The Love of Our Country Recommended and Enforced* (Boston: John Boyle, 1774), pp. 13–16. The association of virtue with military courage during the *"rage militaire"* of 1775 is described in Charles Royster, *A Revolutionary People at War* (Chapel Hill: University of North Carolina Press, 1979), pp. 25–53.

17. Joseph Warren, *An Oration Delivered March Sixth 1775* (Boston: Edes & Gill, 1775), p. 21.

18. John Witherspoon, *The Dominion of Providence over the Passions of Men* (Philadelphia: Aitken, 1776), p. 60.

19. Phillips Payson, *A Sermon Preached before the Honourable Council . . . of the State of Massachusetts Bay* (Boston: John Gill, 1778), 32.

20. John Hurt, *The Love of Our Country* (Philadelphia: Styner & Cist, 1777), 17. Also, see Richard Henry Lee as quoted in Pauline Maier, *The Old Revolutionaries: Political Lives in the Age of Samuel Adams* (New York: Vintage Trade Books, 1980), p. 198.

21. Peter Thacher, *Oration Delivered March 5, 1776*, as quoted in Wood, *Creation of the Republic*, p. 100. Morally deficient American as well as British men were frequently depicted as feminine. See, e.g., John Witherspoon, *Dominion of Providence*, p. 57; [Royall Tyler], *The Contrast* (Philadelphia: Prichard & Hall, 1790); Kerber, *Women of the Republic*, p. 31; Wood, *Creation of the Republic*, p. 110, Within the classical republican tradition, such rhetoric goes back to Machiavelli and beyond (see Pitkin, *Fortune Is a Woman*, pp. 109–110).

22. Such rare if dramatic examples of female heroism are recounted in Sally Smith Booth, *The Women of '76* (New York: Hastings House, 1973), pp. 173–174, 266–270.

23. For a full account and analysis of these activities, see Norton, *Liberty's Daughters*.

24. Kerber, *Women of the Republic*, p. 106. For more examples of the maternal imagery, see Royster, *Revolutionary People*, pp. 30, 90; Story, *Love of Our Country*, p. 16–17. For examples of women physically abused by the enemy, see Jay Fliegelman, *Prodigals and Pilgrims* (New York: Cambridge University Press, 1982), pp. 117, 137–144. A similar religious image was that of America as the woman in the wilderness of the book of Revelation, pursued by minions of Satan: see, e.g., William Foster, *True Fortitude Delineated* (Philadelphia: John Dunlap, 1776), 17; [Wheeler Case], *Poems, Occasioned by Several Circumstances and*

Occurrencies (New Haven, Conn.: Thomas & Green, 1778), p. 21. This theme of women as innocent, passively virtuous victims of male vice, tyranny, and lust was an extension of the themes of popular fiction into political discourse. Jan Lewis explores this association in "The Republican Wife." For the opposite image, of Great Britain as a bad mother, see Edwin G. Burrows and Michael Wallace, "The American Revolution: The Ideology and Psychology of National Liberation," *Perspectives in American History* 6 (1972): 190–214. This theme also had its analogues in fiction about bad mothers (see Fliegelman, *Prodigals and Pilgrims,* pp. 51–52, 118). For examples of the biblical scarlet whore image, see Henry Cumings, *A Sermon Preached in Billerica on the 3rd of November, 1775* (Worcester, Mass.: L. Thomas, 1775), p. 12; Enoch Huntington, *A Sermon, Delivered at Middletown, July 20th,* A.D. *1775* (Hartford, Conn.: Ebenezer Watson, 1775), p. 21. The rebellious implications of unmasking ignoble political origins are explored in Judith N. Shklar, "Subversive Genealogies," in *Myth, Symbol, and Culture,* ed. Clifford Geertz (New York: W. W. Norton, 1971), pp. 129–153.

25. Kerber, *Women of the Republic,* pp. 265–288.

26. See Chapter 3.

27. As quoted in Kerber, *Women of the Republic,* p. 229. Also see Benjamin Rush, "Thoughts upon Female Education" (originally published in 1787), in *Essays on Education in the Early Republic,* ed. Frederick Rudolph (Cambridge, Mass.: Harvard University Press, 1965), pp. 25–40; "Oration upon Female Education, Pronounced . . . in Boston, September, 1791," in *The American Preceptor,* ed. Caleb Bingham, 44th ed. (Boston: Manning & Loring, 1813), pp. 47–51.

28. William Lyman, *A Virtuous Woman the Bond of Domestic Union* (New London, Conn.: S. Green, 1802), p. 22.

29. In this period there was still far more literature on courtship, marriage, and the social utility of female education than on motherhood per se. In her 1987 article "The Republican Wife," Jan Lewis argues that the image of the "republican wife" was more prevalent than that of the "republican mother."

30. For example, Rush, "Thoughts upon Female Education"; Jane West, *Letters to a Young Lady* (Troy, N. Y.: O. Penniman, 1806), p. 27; "Scheme for Encreasing the Power of the Fair Sex," *Baltimore Weekly Magazine* 1 (April 1801): 241–242; *Advice to the Fair Sex; in a Series of Letters on Various Subjects: Chiefly Describing the Graceful Virtues* (Philadelphia: Robert Cochran, 1803), pp. 3–4; Samuel Kennedy Jennings, *The Married Lady's Companion, or Poor Man's Friend* (Richmond, Va.: T. Nicholson, 1804), p. 5.

31. "Female Influence," *New York Magazine* (May 1795), pp. 299–305.

32. Thomas Branagan, *The Excellency of the Female Character Vindicated* (New York: Samuel Wood, 1807), p. xii.

33. "Panegyrick on Marriage," *Columbia Magazine and Universal Advertiser* (October 1786), p. 74; "On Love," *New York Magazine* (June 1791), p. 311.

34. See, e.g., Robert Middlekauff, *The Mathers: Three Generations of Puritan Intellectuals* (New York: Oxford University Press, 1971); Norman Pettit, *The Heart Prepared: Grace and Conversion in Puritan Spiritual Life* (New Haven, Conn.: Yale University Press, 1966); Charles Hambrick-Stowe, *The Prac-*

tice of Piety (Chapel Hill: University of North Carolina Press, 1982); Charles Lloyd Cohen, *God's Caress: The Psychology of Puritan Religious Experience* (New York: Oxford University Press, 1986).

35. Norman Fiering, *Moral Philosophy at Seventeenth-Century Harvard,* and *Jonathan Edwards's Moral Thought in Its British Context* (Chapel Hill: University of North Carolina Press, 1981).

36. Jonathan Edwards, "The Nature of True Virtue," in *Jonathan Edwards,* ed. Clarence H. Faust and Thomas H. Johnson, rev. ed. (New York: Hill & Wang, 1962), p. 351

37. Ibid., p. 365.

38. Story, *The Love of Our Country,* pp. 7, 10. This religious use of the word "virtue" in revolutionary literature is discussed in Bloch, *Visionary Republic,* esp. p. 109; Royster, *Revolutionary People,* pp. 17–25.

39. Cotton Mather, *Ornaments for the Daughters of Zion* (Cambridge: Samuel Phillips, 1692), p. 45. Also see Cotton Mather, *Elizabeth on Her Holy Retirement* (Boston: B. Green, 1710).

40. For a few examples of this literature, see Benjamin Colman, *The Honour and Happiness of the Vertuous Woman* (Boston: B. Green, 1716); Chauncy Whittelsey, *A Discourse . . . Mary Clapp* (New Haven, Conn.: Thomas & Samuel Green, 1769); Deborah Prince, *Dying Exercises of Mrs. Deborah Prince; and Devout Meditations of Mrs. Sarah Gill* (Newburyport, Mass.: John Mycall, 1789); George Strebeck, *A Sermon on the Character of the Virtuous Woman* (New York: n.p., 1800); Samuel Worcester, *Female Love to Christ* (Salem, Mass.: Pool & Palfray, 1809).

41. Despite one perfunctory remark to a female friend on how the education of the sexes should be largely the same, at least "in their younger years," Locke explicitly focused *Some Thoughts Concerning Education* — including key passages on virtue — on the upbringing of "young Gentlemen." "When women do appear, as mothers, they tend (by their excessive 'Fondness') to be an obstacle to good education." *(The Educational Writings* of John *Locke,* ed. James L. Axtell [London: Cambridge University Press, 1968], pp. 117, 117n.3, 123, 125, 166–167, 170, 344–346).

42. On differences among Scottish moral philosophers, see Daniel W. Howe, "European Sources of Political Ideas in Jeffersonian America," *Reviews in American History* 10 (1982): 28–44.

43. As quoted in Fliegelman, *Prodigals and Pilgrims,* p. 24.

44. Fliegelman (*Prodigals and Pilgrims,* pp. 23–26) points to this underlying similarity, in contrast to the sharp separation drawn between Locke and the Scots by Garry Wills in his *Inventing America: Jefferson's* Declaration of *Independence (Garden* City, N. Y.: Doubleday, 1978), and *Explaining America: The Federalist (Garden* City, N. Y.: Doubleday, 1981).

45. See Chapter 3.

46. Fiering, *Moral Philosophy* at *Seventeenth-Century Harvard* and *Jonathan Edwards's Moral Thought in Its British Context.*

47. Hirschman, *Passions and the Interests.*

48. Fiering, *Moral Philosophy at Seventeenth-Century Harvard,* pp. 147 206, 239–294, and *Jonathan Edwards's Moral Thought in Its British Context,* p. 106.

49. Fiering, *Moral Philosophy at Seventeenth-Century Harvard* and *Jonathan Edwards's Moral Thought in Its British Context.*

50. "On Woman," *Pennsylvania Magazine* (November 1775), p. 527; Thomas Branagan, *Excellency of the Female Character,* pp. 111–112.

51. Marchioness de Lambert, "Reflections on Female Virtues," *Royal American Magazine* (June 1774), p. 220; "Qualifications Required in a Wife," *American Museum* (December 1788), p. 578; [Noah Webster], "Address to Ladies," *American Museum* (March 1788), p. 244; "On Sensibility," *Pennsylvania Magazine* (April 1774), p. 176.

52. "Comparison of the Sexes," *American Museum* (January 1789), p. 59. This piece was reprinted at least twice, in the *Christian Scholar's and Farmer's Magazine* (April and May 1789), pp. 85–87; and in *Lady's Magazine* (August 1792), 111–113.

53. For example, John Gregory, *A Father's Legacy to His Daughters* (Boston: J. Douglass M'Dougall,1779), p. 35; John Bennet, *Letters to a Young Lady* (New York: John Buel, 1796), p. 68.

54. Enos Hitchcock, *Memoirs of the Bloomsgrove Family* (Boston: Thomas & Andrews, 1790), pp. 47–48.

55. For example, [William Kenrick], *The Whole Duty of Woman . . . Sixth Ed.* (Boston: Hall, 1790), p. 46; Gregory, *A Father's Legacy,* pp. 12, 16, 18, 22, 41; "A Letter," *Lady's Magazine* (November 1782), p. 281; Branagan, *Excellency of the Female Character.*

56. "Reflections on Chastity," *Royal American Magazine* (February 1775), p. 61. For the popularity of the forgiving-wife plot, see Lewis, "The Republican Wife."

57. Lewis, "The Republican Wife"; see also Chapter 3.

58. For example: Rush, "Thoughts upon Female Education"; Thomas Dawes, "Resolves Respecting the Education of Poor Female Children," *American Museum* 6 (September 1789): 213; John Bennet, *Strictures on Female Education* (Philadelphia: W. Spotswood & H. P. Rice, 1793).

59. For the argument that this female-nature/male-culture dichotomy is universal, see esp. Sherry Ortner, "Is Female to Male as Nature Is to Culture?" in *Women, Culture, and Society,* ed. Michelle Rosaldo and Louise Lamphere (Stanford, Calif: Stanford University Press, 1974), pp. 67–88. For another work on the eighteenth century that qualifies this perspective, see L. J. Jordanova, "Natural Facts: A Historical Perspective on Science and Sexuality," in *Nature, Culture, and Gender,* ed. C. MacCormack and M. Strathern (New York: Cambridge University Press, 1980).

60. [Tyler], *The Contrast,* pp. 48–49, 55.

61. For example, Wood, *Creation of the American Republic;* most recently, Yazawa, *Colonies to Commonwealth.*

62. Thomas Paine, *Common Sense,* ed. Isaac Kramnick (New York: Viking Penguin, Inc., 1976), 68.

63. For example, [James Madison], "Federalist Paper Number 57," in *The Federalist Papers,* ed. Clinton Rossiter (New York: New American Library, 1961), p. 350. On virtue in the *Federalist Papers,* see Wood, *Creation of the American Republic,* 610; and Wills, *Explaining America.* The distinction

between these meanings of virtue is clarified in Daniel W. Howe, "The Political Psychology of *The Federalist*," *William and Mary Quarterly*, 3d ser., vol. 4 (1987).

64. Howe, "The Political Psychology of *The Federalist*."

65. Lance Banning, *The Jeffersonian Persuasion: Evolution of a Party* (Ithaca, N. Y.: Cornell University Press, 1978); Drew R. McCoy, *The Elusive Republic: Political Economy in Jeffersonian America* (Chapel Hill: University of North Carolina Press, 1980); Sean Wilentz, *Chants Democratic: New York City and the Rise of the American Working Class* (New York: Oxford University Press, 1984); Dorothy Ross, "The Liberal Tradition Revisited and the Republican Tradition Addressed," in *New Directions in American Intellectual History*, ed. John Higham and Paul K. Conkin (Baltimore: Johns Hopkins University Press, 1979); and a special issue on republicanism, ed. Joyce Appleby, *American Quarterly*, vol. 37 (Fall 1985).

66. Compare MacIntyre, *After Virtue*.

67. In France, however, prior to the ascendance of the conservative images of Marianne and Liberty in the late 1790s, a militant version of Marianne competed with that of the male radical symbol Hercules (see Lynn Hunt, *Politics, Culture, and Class in the French Revolution* [Berkeley and Los Angeles: University of California Press, 1984], pp. 87–119).

68. *Providence Gazette*, December 29, 1787, as quoted in Wood, *Creation of the American Republic*, p. 610.

69. Hirschman, *Passions and the Interests*; Appleby, *Capitalism and a New Social Order*; Howe, "The Political Psychology of *The Federalist*"; Michael Zuckerman, "A Different Thermidor: The Revolution beyond the American Revolution" (paper presented to the Philadelphia Center for Early American Studies, May 1986).

70. Lester Cohen, "Explaining the Revolution: Ideology and Ethics in Mercy Otis Warren's Historical Theory," *William and Mary Quarterly*, 3d ser., 37 (1980): 200–218, and "Mercy Otis Warren: The Politics of Language and the Aesthetics of Self," *American Quarterly* 35 (1983): 481–498; Kerber, "The Republican Ideology of the Revolutionary Generation," p. 483.

71. Pocock has pointed similarly to a shift from virtue to manners, although he misses the gender symbolism involved in this change and associates it only with elite English culture (Pocock, *Virtue, Commerce, and History*, pp. 49, 50).

72. This historical overview is especially indebted to the interpretation in Nancy F. Cott, *The Bonds of Womanhood: Woman's Sphere in New England, 1780–1835* (New Haven, Conn.: Yale University Press, 1977).

73. Daniel Scott Smith, "Family Limitation, Sexual Control, and Domestic Feminism in Victorian America," *Feminist Studies* 1 (Winter–Spring 1973): 40–57; Carl Degler, *At Odds: Women and the Family in America from the Revolution to the Present* (New York: Oxford University Press, 1980), pp. 144–278.

74. Katherine Kish Sklar, *Catherine Beecher. A Study in American Domesticity* (New Haven, Conn: Yale University Press, 1973); Keith Melder, "Woman's High Calling: The Teaching Profession in America, 1830–1860," *American Studies* 13 (Fall 1972): 19–32; Nancy Hoffman, *Women's 'True' Profession* (Old Westbury, N. Y.: Feminist Press, 1981); Anne Firor Scott, "What, Then, Is This

American: This New Woman?" *Journal of American History* 65 (December 1978): 679–703.

75. Keith Melder, *The Beginnings of Sisterhood: The American Women's Rights Movement, 1800–1850* (New York: Schocken Books, 1977); Barbara Leslie Epstein, *The Power of Domesticity: Women, Evangelism, and Temperance in Nineteenth-Century America* (Middletown, Conn.: Wesleyan University Press, 1981); Mary P. Ryan, "The Power of Women's Networks: A Case Study of Female Moral Reform in Antebellum America," *Feminist Studies* 5 (Spring 1979): 66–86; Ann Douglas, *The Feminization of American Culture* (New York: Alfred A. Knopf, 1977); Susan P. Conrad, *Perish the Thought: Intellectual Women in Romantic America, 1830–1860* (New York: Oxford University Press, 1976).

76. As quoted in Fliegelman, *Prodigals and Pilgrims,* p. 89.

77. This sexual symmetry is stressed in Gerda Lerner, "The Lady and the Mill Girl: Changes in the Status of Women in the Age of Jackson, 1800–1840," in *A Heritage of Her Own,* ed. Nancy F. Cott and Elizabeth H. Pleck (New York: Simon and Schuster, 1979), pp. 182–196.

78. Christine Stansell, *City of Women: Sex and Change in New York, 1789–1860* (New York: Alfred A.Knopf, 1986), pp. 19–37.

8. GENDER AND THE PUBLIC/PRIVATE DICHOTOMY IN AMERICAN REVOLUTIONARY THOUGHT

1. Linda Kerber, *Women of the Republic* (Chapel Hill: University of North Carolina Press, 1980); Jan Lewis, "The Republican Wife," *William and Mary Quarterly,* 3rd ser., 44 (October 1987); Rosemary Zagarri, "Morals, Manners, and the Republican Mother," *American Quarterly* 44 (June 1992): 192–215.

2. Kerber and Lewis differ over whether images of mothers or those of wives were the more important.

3. See Chapter 3.

4. In France, a very different revolutionary case, there was an explicit demand by women for political rights.

5. See also Chapter 7.

6. A useful summary is contained in J. G. A. Pocock, "The Mobility of Property," in *Virtue, Commerce, and History* (New York: Cambridge University Press, 1985), pp. 103–105. Also see Leo Strauss, *Natural Right and History* (Chicago: University of Chicago Press, 1953).

7. Most clear in their conceptualization of conversion and in the organization of church polity. Holly Brewer, "Understanding Intent," unpublished paper delivered in Phildaphia at MacNeill Center, 1999.

8. From Winthrop's 1645 speech on civil liberty in *The Puritans: A Sourcebook,* ed. Perry Miller and Thomas Johnson, rev. ed. (New York: Harper and Row, 1963) 1: 207. For an elaboration of this theme within Puritanism (which Norton, however, misleadingly calls "Hobbesian"), see Mary Beth Norton, *Founding Mothers and Fathers* (New York: Knopf, 1996)

9. This was true not only of Puritans but also of strict adherents to the

Church of England, for whom the public/private distinction was bridged by the king and the church.

10. James Tully, *A Discourse on Property: John Locke and His Adversaries* (New York and Cambridge, Eng.: Cambridge University Press, 1980); Duncan Forbes, *Hume's Philosophical Politics* (New York: Cambridge University Press, 1975). Both Tully and Forbes insist on the importance of natural law tradition. J. G. A. Pocock denies the importance of Locke and argues that the "new economic forces" were defined in opposition to civic rather than juristic conceptions of property. (Pocock, "Mobility of Property," in *Virtue, Commerce, and History*, p. 105). Joyce Appleby (*Economic Thought and Ideology in Seventeenth-Century England* [Princeton, N. J.: Princeton University Press, 1978]) concentrates on lesser-known figures of the late seventeenth century and offers another type of interpretation based more on economic change.

11. Moreover men's right of sexual access precludes women having even the property of their own persons. As Carole Pateman has argued in *The Sexual Contract* (Stanford, Calif.: Stanford University Press, 1988), the social arrangements between the sexes preceded the Lockean social contract, which assumed men's sexual access to women. See also Ruth Perry, *The Celebrated Mary Astell: An Early English Feminist* (Chicago: University of Chicago Press, 1986).

12. John Locke, *Essay Concerning . . . Civil Government: Second Treatise of Government* C. B. Macpherson, ed. (Indianapolis, Ind.: Hackett, 1980), p. 7.

13. As quoted in Perry, *Mary Axtell*, p. 447

14. For example, the mother of George III and aristocratic ladies generally. On such newspaper depictions, see Susan Dion, "Women in the *Boston Gazette,* 1755–1775," *Historical Journal of Massachusetts* 14 (June 1986): 87–102.

15. This 1781 quote is cited in Mary Beth Norton, *Liberty's Daughters* (Boston: Little Brown, 1980), p. 225.

16. For an overview of these ideas see Gladys Bryson, *Man and Society: The Scottish Inquiry of the Eighteenth Century* (Princeton, N. J.: Princeton University Press, 1945), p. 149.

17. Adams, *Diary and Autobiography,* in *The Adams Papers* (Cambridge: Harvard University Press, 1961) 4: 123.

18. For an argument for the compatibility of Smith's economic and moral theories see D. D. Raphel's "Introduction" to Adam Smith, *The Theory of Moral Sentiments,* ed. D. D. Rafael and A. L. Macfie (Oxford: Clarendon, 1976), pp. 20–22.

19. See Ruth H. Bloch, "Changing Conceptions of Sexuality and Romance in Eighteenth-Century America, *William and Mary Quarterly* 3d. ser., 60 (forthcoming, January 2003). Albert Hirschman, *The Passions and the Interests* (Princeton, N. J.: Princeton University Press, 1977), pp. 60–63; J. G. A. Pocock, "Cambridge Paradigms and Scotch Philosophers," in Istvan Hont and Michael Ignatieff, eds. *Wealth and Virtue: The Shaping of Political Economy in the Scottish Enlightenment* (Cambridge, Eng: Cambridge University Press, 1983), p. 241.

20. Francis Hutcheson, *A System of Moral Philosophy in Three Books* (London, 1755) 2: 187.

21. David Hume, *Treatise of Human Nature* (London: Thomas and Joseph Allman, 1817) 2:191.

22. Rosemarie Zagarri, "Morals, Manners, and the Republican Mother," *The American Quarterly* 44 (June 1992): 192–215; Pocock, "Mobility of Property," p. 117.

23. Nancy Armstrong, *Desire and Domestic Fiction* (New York: Oxford University Press, 1987); On the self, see Charles Taylor, *Sources of the Self: The Making of Modern Identity* (Cambridge, Mass.: Harvard University Press, 1989); Colin Campbell, *The Romantic Ethic and the Spirit of Modern Consumerism* (Oxford: Basil Blackwell, 1987), especially pp. 58–76.

24. Here I differ from the tendency of scholars to emphasize either the anarchic sexual impulses of romantic love or, to the contrary, its passionlessness. See, for example, Norma Basch, *Framing American Divorce* (Berkeley: University of California Press, 1999), pp. 179–180; Nancy F. Cott, "Passionlessness: An Interpretation of Victorian Sexual Ideology," *Signs* 4 (Winter 1978): 219–236. Jan Lewis, in "The Republican Wife," *William and Mary Quarterly* 3rd series 44 (1987), portrays love as ideally controlled by reason. This hierarchy of reason over emotion was, however, no longer the way love was typically conceived, although this had been more true of the Puritans. On changes in so-called "faculty psychology," see Norman Fiering, *Moral Philosophy at Seventeenth-Century Harvard* (Chapel Hill: University of North Carolina Press, 1981) and Daniel W. Howe, "The Political Psychology of *The Federalist*," *William and Mary Quarterly* 3rd ser., 44 (1987). On the Miltonic ideal of romantic love based on reason; see Jay Fliegelman, *Prodigals and Pilgrims: The American Revolution Against Patriarchal Authority* (New York: Cambridge University Press, 1982), pp. 127–128.

25. Hume, "Of the Passions," in *Treatise of Human Nature,* 2: 81.

26. Hume, "Of Polygamy," in *Essays and Treatises on Several Subjects* (Edinburgh: Bell and Bradfute, 1817), p. 186.

27. Henry Home [Lord Kames], "Progress of the Female Sex," *Sketches of the History of Man,* 3rd ed. (Dublin, 1779) 1: 310.

28. John Dwyer, *Virtuous Discourse: Sensibility and Community in Eighteenth-Century England,* (Edinburgh, 1987), p. 153, citing Henry MacKenzie's *Man of Feeling* of 1771. For an American novel making such a distinction between false and sincere love, see William Hill Brown, *The Power of Sympathy* (Boston: New Frontiers Press, 1961), pp. 26, 33, 58.

29. Hume, *Essays and Treatises,* p. 124.

30. Quoted in Norton, *Liberty's Daughters,* p. 245.

31. Lewis, "Republican Wife."

32. Garry Wills, *Inventing America: Jefferson's Declaration of Independence* (Garden City, N. Y.: Doubleday, 1978); Jay Fliegelman, *Declaring Independence: Jefferson, Natural Language and the Culture of Performance* (Stanford, Calif.: Stanford University Press, 1993).

33. The best example is the heart-head parable in "Thomas Jefferson to Maria Cosway," Paris, October 12, 1786, as reprinted in Fawn Brodie, *Thomas Jefferson: An Intimate History,* Appendix 2, pp. 654–667, from *The Papers of Thomas Jefferson,* ed. Julian P. Boyd (Princeton, N. J.: Princeton University Press, 1950) 10: 443–453.

34. This argument is developed in Chapters 5 and 7.

35. Nancy F. Cott, *The Bonds of Womanhood: "Woman's Sphere" in New England, 1780–1835* (New Haven, Conn.: Yale University Press, 1977).

36. Few novels devote much attention to domestic life per se, although the implied message of most is that domestic bliss is the fulfillment of courtship. For two notable sentimental works that do dwell on the pleasures of married life, see Samuel Richardson, *Pamela, or Virtue Rewarded,* (orig. ed., 1744), especially volume 2, and Enos Hitchcock, *The Memoirs of the Bloomsgrove Family* (Boston, 1790).

37. Brown, *Power of Sympathy,* p. 67.

38. Ibid, p. 68.

39. As cited in Martha Tomhave Blauvelt, ed., "Women, Words, and Men: Excerpts from the Diary of Mary Guion," in *Journal of Women's History* 2 (Fall 1990): 180–181

40. Ibid., p. 183. Other evidence of this dissemination can be found in the conflict between the marital ideals of the older generation and those of the young. See, e.g., the letters of George Washington and Benjamin Franklin counseling young relatives against excessive reliance on romantic love. Washington's letter to his stepdaughter is quoted in James Flexner, *George Washington and the New Nation, 1783–1793* (Boston: Little Brown, 1970) pp. 39–40; Franklin's, letter, dated April 12, 1779, is in *The Papers of Benjamin Franklin*, ed. Leonard W. Labaree et al. (New Haven, Conn.: Yale University Press, 1959), 29: 283–284, 318–319. For more on Franklin, see Chapter 5.

41. For example, Lawrence Stone, *The Family, Sex and Marriage in England, 1500–1800* (New York: Harper and Row, 1979). A more extensive consideration of this issue may be found in Bloch, "Changing Conceptions of Sexuality and Romance."

42. Nancy Armstrong, *Desire and Domestic Fiction;* Colin Campbell, *The Romantic Ethic.*

Index

Compositor:	BookMatters
Text:	10/13 Sabon
Display:	Sabon
Printer and Binder:	Sheridan Books, Inc.